WELCOME TO...
THE MACINTOSH:

FROM MYSTERY
TO MASTERY

John Rethorst

MIS:
PRESS

A Subsidiary of
Henry Holt and Co., Inc.

First Edition—1993

ISBN 1–55828–264–5

Printed in the United States of America.

10 9 8 7 6 5 4 3 2 1

MIS:Press books are available at special discounts for bulk purchases for sales promotions, premiums, fund-raising, or educational use. Special editions or book excerpts can also be created to specification.

For details contact: Special Sales Director
                         MIS:Press
                         a subsidiary of Henry Holt and Company, Inc.
                         115 West 18th Street
                         New York, New York 10011

*To Anna, who came to love the Macintosh
through this book. I hope that everyone will do the same.*

FOREWORD

I wrote this book with two purposes in mind: to provide a complete reference for independent study of Macintosh system and application software, and to support directed study in a college environment.

Beyond these uses, a third purpose is implicit and, finally, more important: The book and its course *Computers and Education* are products of extensive development over several years at Cornell. The original vision for the course, uniquely viable in the Department of Education, sought to teach computers not so that facility with the tool was the only end result; rather, that the student might also cultivate a broader understanding of where tools and information fit and how they work, in culture and in human endeavor.

Tom Hughes, who taught the course before me, contributed exceptional competence and energy towards the precursor to this book. It has been my task to preserve the quality he established, and extend where possible the conceptual and philosophical emphasis that makes this curriculum uniquely valuable. Dan Smellow and Anne Chetham-Strode, teaching assistants, provided copious and consistently valuable insight into how best to explain and illustrate concepts that the beginner finds incomprehensible, and that the practiced user feels ought to be obvious to everyone.

I owe many a great deal of appreciation. In the end, though, I feel as Schönberg must have when he began his Theory of Harmony with "I have learned this book from my students." They have helped me write this one too.

John Rethorst

CONTENTS

Introduction

Yet another book on achieving basic competence on the Macintosh? No—this one's quite a bit different.

The question of how to teach something never was easy and, when the subject is personal computers, it becomes difficult in manifold ways. It's a somewhat technical environment, yes, but for what most people want it's far less complicated than most beginners could imagine.

The Macintosh environment is profoundly untechnical. It's almost playful at times, and strongly spurs creativity. In a wonderful way, it invites the user to explore.

All of this starts to happen, though, after a big hurdle has been breached— *computer anxiety*. People of every age, educational background, vocation and purpose share this when they first sit down in front of a computer. You might feel that you simply have no talent for the thing, that it's too complicated, that you're just a few short steps from disaster.

If so, this book is for you.

I learned how to teach what's in this book when I came to Cornell for a Ph.D. in Education, bringing with me twelve years of computer experience. I joined the teaching staff of the University's course whose task was to take 200 people a semester who knew nothing about computers, and get them up and running on the Macintosh in seven weeks.

The hardest part of it (aside from convincing them that they could do it) was showing the why as well as the how—critical for any real understanding, and being able to go further on your own. Teaching which buttons to push is decidedly easier. Which button to push is—well, there's almost nothing to it. Explaining the concepts behind the keystrokes is a tougher job, though, requiring that the teacher have a critical appreciation of the computer and the ideas behind it, seen through a beginner's eyes.

After the first year I was put in charge of the course, and immediately began to develop this material. I was convinced that, given a positive educational environment, anyone could start off on the Macintosh and progress, step by step, so that they couldn't help but learn it well, and have a lot of fun at the same time.

That's the key to the focus of this whole book—fun. Reviewers of what you're about to read have called it "warm, inviting, and trustworthy." But make no mistake about its serious intent. You'll do better at absolutely anything you want to do if you have a Macintosh to help. And if you take this book a step at a time, you'll enjoy it, and be much more advanced than most personal computer users when you finish.

So get set for a good time.

CHAPTER 1

GETTING STARTED

In this chapter, you'll learn how to:

- use icons and windows

- work with menus and scroll bars

- get help from the Mac's Balloon Help feature

- work with a floppy disk

- copy a file from one disk to another

- make and use folders

- find any file in your Mac

Welcome to what will be a wonderful learning experience for you as a computer user! These easy, step-by-step tutorials show you everything you'll need to know about using the Macintosh.

We say 'using' rather than 'programming', because there's quite a difference. The latter is technical and difficult. But using a Macintosh computer with programs that are already written is easy and convenient. Take your time and don't skip any steps. After each chapter, a little more practice is all that you'll need to be a competent user of that kind of program.

First, though, let's take a short look at the why as well as the how of what we'll be doing here.

STARTING SOMETHING NEW

We live in what's often been termed the "Age of Information," a phrase with special meaning in almost any environment—corporate, educational, or civic.

How are we going to approach and prepare for this age? Let's begin with an overview of the ideas of information and learning, and how these contribute to the whole person and to growth. What do we mean, when we say we want information about something? What counts? Futurists discuss information theory, game theory, and such esoteric concepts, but we mostly find ourselves looking for greater quantities of information, as though that alone will help us.

Yet it is not the amount, but the quality and relevance of what we know, that solves problems. The task of this book is, in large part, to address both that and the process, not the product: how to get and work with information, make it work for us, and pass it along to others.

It was not so long ago that most of the world survived by bartering things— products and services—and what anyone knew played a supporting role. A revolution, in which the computer played a vital part, has taken place within the last decade, and decisions now are based not so much on whether you can obtain resources but on how to manage them: decisions that require a quality of information beyond what we used to expect and what we thought possible.

Managing information is critical and primary, and the computer has become one of the most important tools we have in commerce and government—and in how we educate.

Think for a moment of the aphorism, "The power of the printed word." It certainly has a great deal of power, but how much power was required to achieve it? The incunabula of the Middle Ages had enormous beauty, but each book required a good part of a year to produce, and could be read only by limited numbers of people. Transporting a volume of information took a horse and cart, and at least two people to support the effort and guard such a precious article.

More recently, the typewriter and printing press, and universal literacy, have changed how information is transmitted. However, the path they describe is still in only one direction: print a book or article and distribute it. You could copy part of my work or react to it, but the interaction between those who develop information, and the target audience, is largely a monologue.

It's quite a step up from the fourteenth century, but a much larger change has occurred in the last few years. I can send text to you via electronic mail, and you won't need to retype anything I wrote, but can make corrections to the original text and send it to me or others for their response. The printed word has taken on the quality of conversation to a degree it did not have before, and the change benefits us both enormously. Ideas move faster today.

The same is true with numbers or other organizations of data. The telephone book is like any other printed work: even with a great quantity of information available, it is fixed. We can retrieve information from it, but may have to shuffle lots of pages, take a fair amount of time, and be willing to correct numbers of mistakes.

What if you could manipulate the data in the phone book in a matter of seconds—for example, to find the telephone numbers of everyone who lived on your street, to call them to organize a neighborhood meeting? You could do that in about ten seconds, with a computer program we'll learn in this book.

The meaning of what you know comes from two places: first, input of imagination and theory; second, the factual side. They're equal in importance, and we need both to make information make sense.

Managing and using information, as opposed to just having it, is a tool of empowerment. You can ask a computer to make decisions by formulating 'what-if' questions: where to invest if interest rates go up or down by a specified amount, for instance. By having the computer do the repetitive and quantitative work, we can free ourselves for choices that require intelligence and understanding.

That last paragraph contains one of the most important words in any description of what a computer does for us: 'free.' If you find yourself retyping a whole page of a college paper or business report because you left out a line, or getting artistic with the white-out to make the third correction on a page look presentable, you are hardly free. You're spending time with mechanics instead of letting the machine do the mechanics, while you spend time with ideas.

Getting used to the value of your time and efforts is an important part of an introduction to using information. As we go along, your learning experience will be greatly enhanced if you let machines do what they can do for you—both in the concrete terms of careers and in the process of life-long learning enhanced by the freedom to deal with ideas.

The American philosopher and educator John Dewey thought that education was simply growth that, properly conceived, should never stop. The power of information can be instrumental to that goal. And we'll be looking here not only at the specifics. Those are important but, even more, we'll want to take a step back from the details now and then to see what we're doing as we do it, and thereby grasp a much greater tool: learning how to learn.

As the educational researcher David Kolb points out, each of us has a learning style that works best for us. Learning styles are combinations of experimentation and observation, concrete experience and abstract reasoning, and each of us has a different best combination.

It's a mistake to think that we have to learn about computers in only this or that way or style. For some, going right through each step in each chapter is the best means to do it. For others, stopping to understand the concept behind each step works better. Don't feel you're not learning as well because you're not moving as fast as someone else.

In accordance with this, the different chapters of this manual explore different ways of learning how programs and ideas fit together, keeping in mind that the purpose of this machine is really to help you think better.

THE MACINTOSH ENVIRONMENT

A tool is an extension of its user. A wrench allows you to do things with your hand you couldn't otherwise do. A computer is the same thing, but is an extension of your mind rather than hand.

When we use a wrench on a lawnmower, we can say that we have an interface with the tool and the object. We understand how we're using the tool to manipulate the object. On the Macintosh, our first tool is the screen, which shows us pictures representing ideas. We call these *icons*—pictures with meanings. One icon may represent a *program*—a set of instructions to the Macintosh to make a drawing, or write a letter, for example. Another icon might represent a *file* or a *document*—the drawing or letter itself.

Figure 1.1   *Icons such as these form a large part of the Mac's user interface—the conversation between computer and user. This visual operating system—also called a graphical user interface, is far easier to use than some other systems that require you to type codes that were difficult to understand and remember.*

This interface is, simply enough, how we talk with the computer. We give it certain information, and it gives us information in return. We talk to it with the keyboard and mouse: Letters and numbers go in by the keyboard, as with a type-writer, and the mouse is something we use to point to an object on the screen. As you move your mouse, an arrow moves in like fashion on the screen.

Figure 1.2   *The arrow moves on the screen as you move your mouse. You use the arrow to tell the computer what you want it to do.*

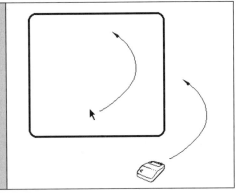

When we want to choose, or select something we see, we press the button on top of the mouse, or click on what we see on the screen.

Point and *click* are not simplistic synonyms for technical terms; they're words that Macintosh programmers use to describe the process of pointing to something on the screen and selecting it.

Figure 1.3	*To select the Composer icon, move your mouse, and see how the arrow follows your movement. When the tip of the arrow is over the icon, press the button on top of the mouse or, in other words, click on the icon.*	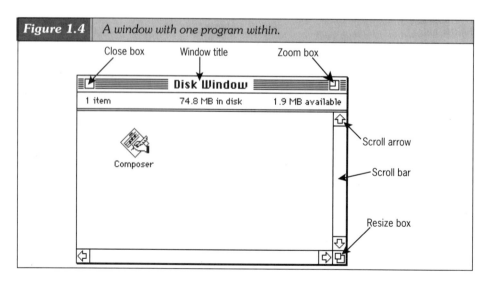

What you're doing is called *input*. The other half of the conversation is output—what the computer tells you. It does this with the screen and printer and those are, more or less, the same thing. It prints what you see on the screen.

The next part of the Macintosh interface is *windows*. Just like an icon for a program, such as Composer, a window is a graphic representation of a part of the environment you're working in. Just as you can look in a window of a house to see what's inside, you can look in a window on the Macintosh screen to see what's on a disk.

A typical Macintosh window looks something like Figure 1.4. "Something like" because your computer might be set up a little differently; for now, those differences aren't important.

Figure 1.4 | *A window with one program within.*

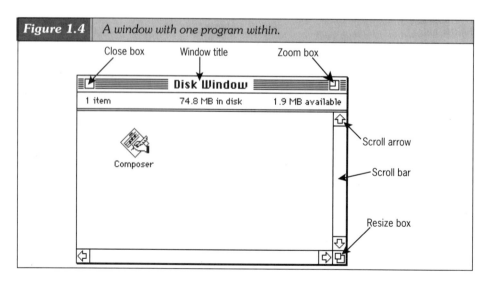

This is just a way of looking at what's on a disk you might have inserted into your computer. There seem like a lot of parts at first, but note two important points:

- Operation is highly intuitive. You'll know how to work a window five minutes from now.

- Nearly every Macintosh program uses the same kind of window. Learn one program, and you've learned an important part of all of them.

Let's look at a typical window:

The *zoom box* and *resize box* control the size of the window. You may want a window to be as big as your screen, to work with everything available. Or, you may want to make it much smaller, so you can open another window and look at both at once.

The *scroll bars* and *scroll arrows* let you move around the window, if it's too small to see all the icons.

Figure 1.5 *A window at full size, with all icons visible. The scroll bars are inactive—white or gray.*

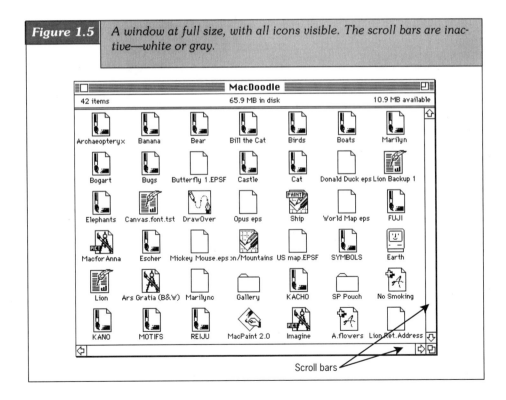

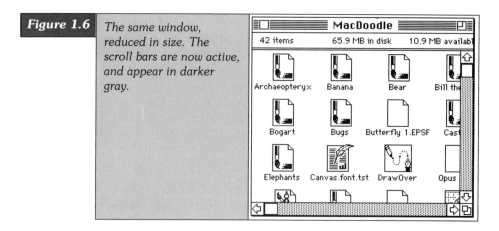

Figure 1.6 *The same window, reduced in size. The scroll bars are now active, and appear in darker gray.*

NOTE Figures 1.5 and 1.6 are two views of one window. You can click in the zoom box, at the top right of the window, to change from one size to the other. The scroll bars of the smaller window are dark, or active; this means that we can use them to move, or *scroll*, around to look at all the icons.

Speaking of icons: so far, we've looked at icons for programs. Other icons represent files—say letters or drawings—or they can represent *folders*. A folder on your screen does just what a manila folder does: it's a way to organize things. You can put programs and documents into folders.

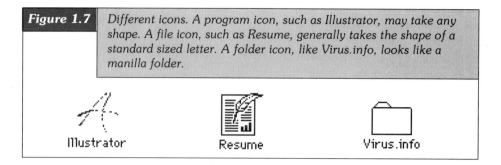

Figure 1.7 *Different icons. A program icon, such as Illustrator, may take any shape. A file icon, such as Resume, generally takes the shape of a standard sized letter. A folder icon, like Virus.info, looks like a manilla folder.*

You can move windows around, as well as resize them. You can put folders inside other folders—all in the interest of setting up your computer environment for the way you want to work.

Now let's look at the rest of what you see on a Macintosh screen.

The first thing you'll notice is the *menu bar*, across the top of your screen. The menu bar has listings of commands that you work with: to open a program or a file, make a copy of a file, or print.

As well, there are icons outside of the window. These usually represent disks that you've inserted into the computer, or are built in to the computer.

All of the icons, taken together, and the menu bar, are called the *desktop*. As with all of the terms we're using, the computer term is a representation of things we already know. A desktop is simply the place where you work. On it, you can see icons for disks and programs, and other tools we'll look at. Here's an example of a desktop:

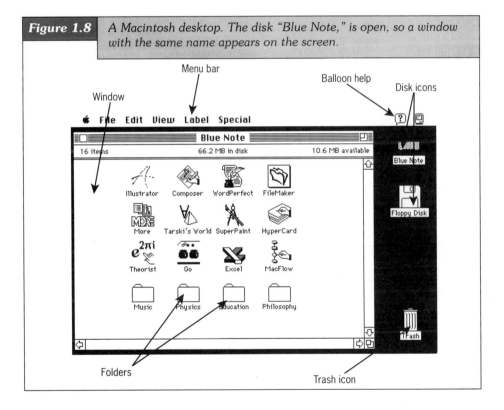

Figure 1.8 | *A Macintosh desktop. The disk "Blue Note," is open, so a window with the same name appears on the screen.*

You access the menu bar with the mouse: by clicking and holding the mouse button down on any menu; you'll see a list of commands.

For example, if you clicked your mouse on the File menu, you'd see this:

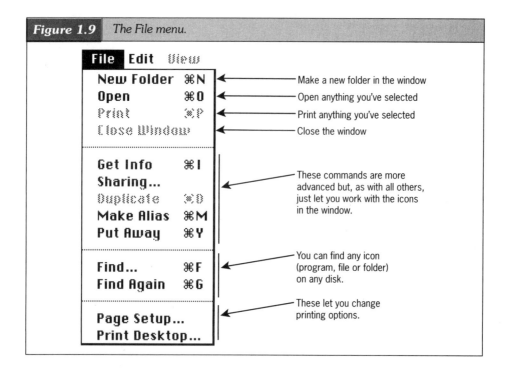

Figure 1.9   The File menu.

Outside of the window, there are separate icons for disks, and one for the trash—logically enough, when we want to throw something away.

The "Blue Note" window shows the contents of the disk of the same name, visible at the top right of the desktop. The window contains several icons. Note the difference between program and folder icons.

We're learning a lot of terms here—desktop, folder, window. But note that each term, and the picture it represents, is designed to be something you're already familiar with.

This is becoming generally true for personal computers: they're made to work the way you think, instead of the other way around.

An especially nice feature as we go is *Balloon Help*: if you want some help on any menu or tool, go to the Balloon menu, towards the right of the menu bar, and choose **Show Balloons**. Then move your mouse over any part of the screen, and wait for a second. You'll see a short explanation, in the form of a cartoon-like dialog box, for any feature you point to with your mouse.

Let's work with the things we've seen.

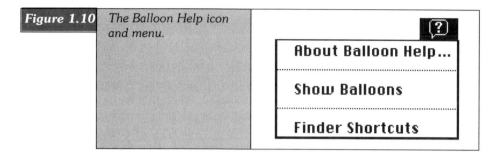

Figure 1.10 *The Balloon Help icon and menu.*

About Balloon Help...

Show Balloons

Finder Shortcuts

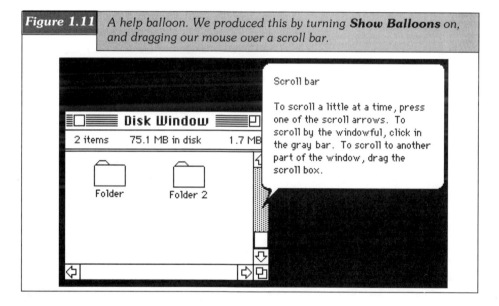

Figure 1.11 *A help balloon. We produced this by turning **Show Balloons** on, and dragging our mouse over a scroll bar.*

HANDS-ON

1 **Mouse and Cursor.** Move your mouse around and see how the arrow cursor moves correspondingly on the screen.

2 **Selecting.** Point to a folder (put the tip of the arrow on any folder icon) and click the button on top of the mouse—press it once lightly, and release it. The folder you chose should change its appearance: it used to be dark on light, and is now light on dark. We say it's *selected* and, in the Mac world, what we usually do is select something and then perform an action on it.

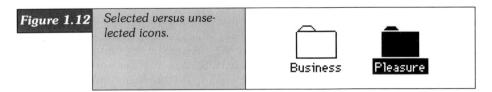

Figure 1.12 *Selected versus unse-lected icons.*

3 **Dragging**. Click on an icon, hold the mouse button down, and move the mouse in any direction. Whatever you selected moves with the cursor.

4 **Moving Windows**. Click and hold in the *title bar*, and move the whole window around. Click in the zoom box to change the size of the window.

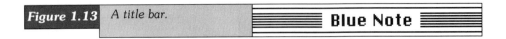

Figure 1.13 *A title bar.*

Click in it again to restore the previous size. Press the mouse button and hold it down in the resize box at the bottom right of the window. Move your cursor down and to the right to increase the size, up and to the left to decrease it.

5 **Closing Windows.** Click in the close box, at the top left of the window. Oops. The window closed, and where it was, we see a closed folder of the same name. No worry—we can get that window back.

Figure 1.14 *The close box.*

Just click on the folder to select it, and choose **Open** from the File menu.

6 **The menu bar**. Remember that this is at the top of your screen, above any windows. There's a small picture at the top left of an apple with a bite taken out of it, and then the words *File, Edit, View, Label,* and *Special*.

7 **Menus**. Move your mouse so the cursor is over the File menu, and then click and hold the mouse button. See how the menu 'drops' to show the various commands available.

Move the cursor down the menu and see how most items in turn change from dark on light to the reverse, to show each is selected.

Release the menu, go back to your window, and:

8 Click on a folder, to select it.

9 Click on the File menu, and select the **Open** command. Your folder should open.

10 **Scrolling**. If the window is too small, not all of the icons may be visible. Note in Figure 1.15 that you can see only part of some icons at the bottom of the window. If you don't want to change the size of a window, you can scroll around the window.

This is hard to visualize at first, but think of the screen within the window as a piece of paper and, through the window, you can see part of it. Scrolling is moving the paper behind the window.

You can scroll both vertically and horizontally—as long as there's part of the window that isn't visible. The window in Figure 1.15 is sized so that we can't see all of the contents of the folder—part of some icons are cut off at the bottom. We need to scroll the window to see all of those icons.

11 **How to scroll**. We do that with scroll bars, found at the right side and at the bottom of the window. At either end of a scroll bar is an arrow.

If there's anywhere to scroll, the bar itself will be dark gray, and there'll be a scroll box somewhere in the bar. Click on the bottom arrow in the vertical scroll bar until those mysterious icons are fully in view.

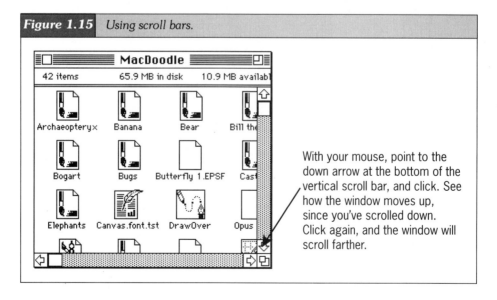

Figure 1.15 *Using scroll bars.*

With your mouse, point to the down arrow at the bottom of the vertical scroll bar, and click. See how the window moves up, since you've scrolled down. Click again, and the window will scroll farther.

DISK BASICS

Now that we have the idea of windows and menus, let's look at a disk, specifically floppy disks. These small disks are called floppies because the actual material inside the protective jacket is pliable. Most floppies measure 3.5 inches on a side.

That size was chosen so that they would fit into a shirt pocket or a business envelope. The actual disk is a sheet of plastic with a coating on both sides like that on cassette tape. Other disks are larger devices called hard disks, often built into the computer, which can hold many times more data (that is, programs and files).

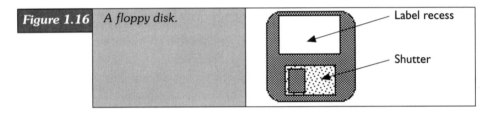

Figure 1.16 *A floppy disk.*

Label recess

Shutter

The computer accesses a floppy disk through the *shutter*, the metal part of the disk. Let the computer open the shutter—we don't need to, and doing so risks letting dirt, or a fingerprint, get onto the disk surface. Aside from coffee, the greatest natural enemy of a floppy disk is your fingerprint.

A prime rule of computing: be good to your disks, and they might be good to you.

When you're starting out with computers, losing work seems like a main concern. It's actually not an easy thing to do, if you keep a few simple rules in mind. Among them is to take good care of floppies.
WARNING   The blank disk costs a dollar or so, and can hold weeks of work. The value you add to a blank floppy argues strongly for taking care of it, as well as making backup copies. What you're really caring for is your data.

WORKING WITH A DISK

1 **Labeling a disk.** First, write your name on the adhesive label that came with your disk. It's best to do this before putting the label on the disk because otherwise, the pressure of your pen on the protective cover might cause it to touch the disk surface, rendering that part of it less reliable.

| Tip #1 | How to Take Care of Floppy Disks. |

- Keep them in a protective case. If they're loose in a desk or briefcase, they're easily damaged.

- Don't expose them to temperature extremes, such as you might find in a car trunk or dashboard.

- Magnetic fields, such as near telephones or on the left side of a compact Macintosh, can erase data.

- Walk floppies around airport X-ray machines. The X-rays don't do the damage; the magnetic field around the motor moving the belt does.

2 Put the label on the disk, in the recessed area on the top—that is, the side without the turntable showing. (Depending on the size of the label, part of it may fit over the top of the disk onto the back, but the whole label should fit entirely within the recessed area).

If you put the label on the wrong side, over the turntable the computer uses to turn the disk, it will be even less reliable.

3 **Inserting a disk**. We always put the disk in the Mac with the shutter forward and label side up. Insert the disk and push it in the drive slot—the computer catches it and pulls it in when you have it in most of the way.

4 **Formatting**. You will see a box with a question (called a *dialog box*) like Figure 1.17. It tells us that since this new disk has never been used, the computer doesn't recognize it, and so it needs to format it to hold data—like putting grooves in a record (remember records?) to hold music.

| Figure 1.17 | The formatting dialog box. |

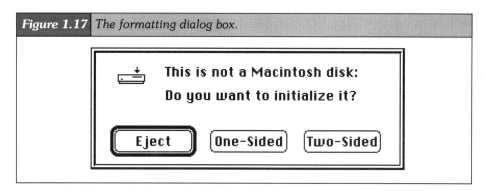

We're going to format this disk as *two-sided*, which most are these days. Older disks were *one-sided*.

⑤ Click your mouse on the Two-Sided button.

WARNING

The Macintosh cautions you that this will erase anything already on this disk. This is valuable information if you're erasing a disk that already has data on it. But this is a new disk, so you're OK.

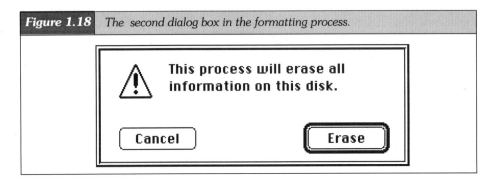

Figure 1.18 | *The second dialog box in the formatting process.*

⑥ Click on **Erase**. The Mac then asks you to name your disk.

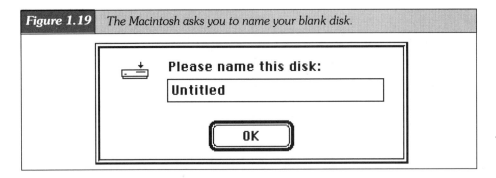

Figure 1.19 | *The Macintosh asks you to name your blank disk.*

⑦ Type your name, and click on **OK**. If you mistype, just backspace past the error and retype. You can change the disk name at any time—you'll see how a little later.

The computer takes a minute to format the disk. After the noise in the disk drive stops, look on the desktop on the screen, toward the top right. There should be a new icon representing a disk, with your name below the icon. This disk icon should be selected. If it isn't:

8 Click on it to select it.

9 Choose **Open** from the File menu.

Or, as a shortcut, you can *double-click* on the disk icon: click on it twice, quickly.

SHORTCUT

You'll see a window for your disk. In Figure 1.20, we formatted a floppy and named it "My Floppy." We then opened its window.

Its window is largely on top of the hard disk window, and is next to the window for MacDoodle, a folder on this computer's hard disk.

Looking at these three windows, note that MacDoodle looks different from the others. It's the only one to have thin horizontal lines along the top, on either side of the title. It's also the only one to have visible scroll bars, although the other windows have rectangles set aside for them.

MacDoodle is the *active* window on the screen. At any time, there can only be one active window, and that window is always in front of any others.

To make another window active, just click on it.

Tip #2	*Manipulating Windows on the Desktop.*

- To make a window active and bring it to the front, click in any visible part of it.

- To move the active window on the screen, click and hold its title bar. You may then drag and position it where you want it.

- Any icons that appear gray on the desktop have open windows.

- Windows will reopen in the same position they were in when they were last closed.

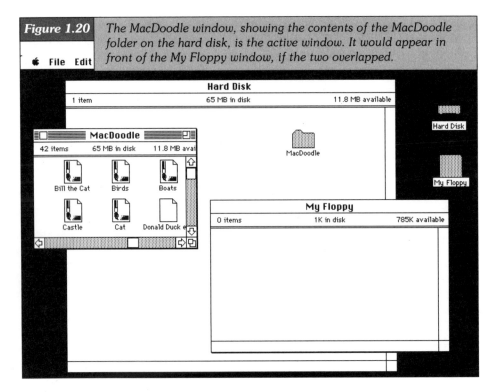

Figure 1.20

🍎 File Edit

The MacDoodle window, showing the contents of the MacDoodle folder on the hard disk, is the active window. It would appear in front of the My Floppy window, if the two overlapped.

With different disks and folders, all with windows, in your computer, you can do necessary things like compare what's on one disk with what's on another, by checking out their windows.

As well, you can copy a file from one disk to another, by dragging its icon from a window of one disk, or a folder on that disk, to the window of another disk.

COPYING FILES

Copying a file, as shown in Figure 1.21, is as easy as dragging an icon from one window to another.

1 Choose a window on your computer that has files in it that you can copy to your floppy disk.

Before copying any file, whether a document or a program, make sure you have permission to do it. Most programs are copyrighted, and you cannot legally make a copy unless you have bought a license to use the program.

N O T E

2 Move windows around, by dragging their title bars, so that both the file you want to copy, and the disk window you want to copy it to, are visible.

3 Click and hold on the file icon, and drag it into the receiving window, as shown in Figure 1.21.

Your Mac tells you it's copying and, after a moment, you'll see an icon for the file appear in the receiving window.

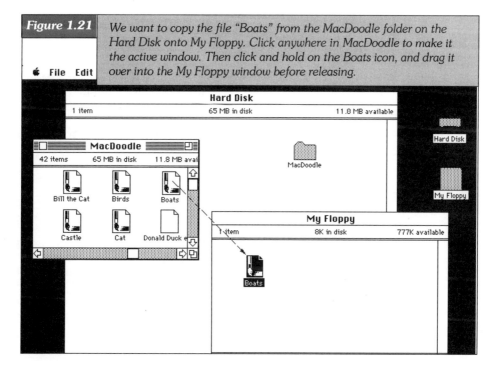

Figure 1.21 *We want to copy the file "Boats" from the MacDoodle folder on the Hard Disk onto My Floppy. Click anywhere in MacDoodle to make it the active window. Then click and hold on the Boats icon, and drag it over into the My Floppy window before releasing.*

ORGANIZING YOUR DESKTOP

A primary use of folders is to keep things organized. If you copy several files, perhaps of different types, onto My Floppy, you may want to make some folders on that disk, and put files in them.

[1] Click in your floppy disk window to make it active.

[2] Choose **New** from the File menu.

You now have another icon in your floppy's window, named Untitled Folder.

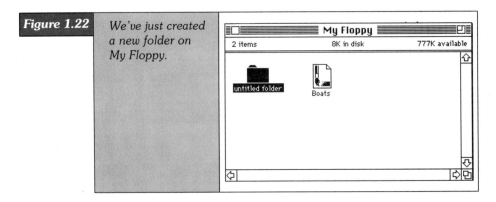

Figure 1.22 *We've just created a new folder on My Floppy.*

To name it, type anything you want. Try "New Files," for example. Shorter names are advantageous.

[3] Click on your file icon, and drag it over on top of your folder icon. When both icons are selected, release the mouse button.

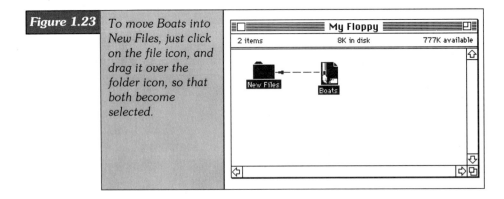

Figure 1.23 *To move Boats into New Files, just click on the file icon, and drag it over the folder icon, so that both become selected.*

The Boats icon disappears. Not to worry—you haven't lost it. It's in the New Files folder.

[4] Double-click on the **New Files** folder, to open its window, and confirm that your file is actually there.

NOTE When we dragged Boats from the hard disk onto My Floppy, the original stayed put, and a copy was written onto the receiving disk. But when we moved Boats into a folder on the same disk we moved, rather than copied, the file.

This design suits normal usage: we most often want to copy files from one disk to another, but move a single copy around on one disk.

FINDING FILES

With the ability to move files into folders (and even folders into other folders), it may seem easy to misplace something. But the Mac has a feature to obviate this.

The **Find** command on the File menu lets you find any file on any disk in your computer.

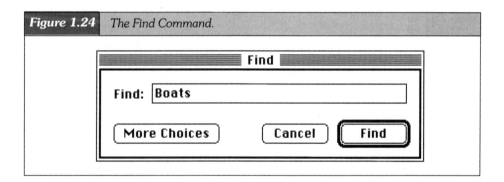

Figure 1.24   The Find Command.

It shows you where the file you want is located, and you can then click on that icon and drag it out of one folder into another, or open it.

CHECKLIST

Make sure that you understand what icons and windows mean. These form the basics of the Macintosh filing system—how we manage the data on our disks. In practicing with these tools, you've learned how to

- open and close windows, and scroll within them,

- use balloon help,

- format and name disks,

- copy files from one disk to another, and

- move files among folders on a disk.

By mastering these concepts, you'll have done more than you think. This is because most Mac programs use the same graphic interface. As we go along, in graphics, word processing, and managing data, your sense of this graphical, visual system will be most valuable.

HELPFUL HINTS

Congratulations! You've done about 90 percent of what Mac users do every day to move around their computers. To practice what you've learned, try making new folders, and moving files or programs into them. You can put folders inside other folders too. Go ahead and play.

The most important thing to understand at this point is not any mass of details about that mysterious computer. Rather, you should realize that the interface, or what you've been working with, *is designed to work with you, not against you.*

The details aren't so important and, in any case, become automatic in just a little while. What you have at your command now is knowledge that the computer in front of you displays what you need to know in a graphic, intuitive format. With a little practice, you can easily grasp and work with it.

Q & A

Q: *I seem to have lost an icon. At least, I can't find which folder I've put it in. I also remember only part of its name. How do I find it?*

A: The **Find** command on the File menu is meant just for this. You only need to type part of the name, and the command shows you everything it finds with a name including what you typed. If the first icon it finds isn't what you want, choose **Find Again** from the File menu. Careful, though: the name or part of it you type has to be exact. If your icon was named "My.Document" and you searched for "My. Doc," you wouldn't find it, since the find request has a space after the period.

Q: *My electronic desktop is even more cluttered than my paper one. Is there a fix?*

A: There are two. The first is the **Clean Up Window** command in the Special menu, which snaps every icon to an invisible grid. Holding down the option key while you choose this changes it to **Clean Up by Name** (alphabetically). Selecting one or more icons and then holding down the shift key while choosing **Clean Up** then moves only the selected icons.

The second way to impose order on chaos is to choose another view from the Views menu. The list views, especially the **By Name** (alphabetically) and **By Date** (most recent at the top), make things easier to find. Personal preference is your best guide.

Q: *My mouse doesn't move very smoothly around the screen.*

A: There are three possibilities here. The first is that the cable connecting it to the keyboard or computer is loose. Be sure that the mouse or keyboard isn't placed far enough away so as to stretch the cable and encourage it to become loose.

The second possibility is that your desk's surface isn't of a kind your mouse likes. The ball on the bottom of the mouse needs a little traction to be turned, and turns erratically if moved on a smooth, polished surface. The solution, and a good idea for the reason below too, is to get a mousepad.

The third possible reason is that the mouse's ball and surrounding cavity has become dirty, and this is a common problem. But it's easy to follow the instructions in your owner's manual and take the ball out, and clean it and the cavity it lives in. This is good preventative maintenance anyway, once a week or so. Using a mousepad keeps your mouse cleaner.

Q: *I want to drag an icon into a folder, but I succeed only in dragging it on top of the folder.*

A: You need to drag the selected icon completely over the folder, so that both show as selected.

Q: *I tend to lose smaller windows behind larger ones.*

A: "Window management" is something of an art. Sizing and positioning open windows so that the ones behind the active window stick out on one side becomes a habit after a while. Or, small utility programs can add a Window menu to programs that lack it, including the Finder. See the note on shareware at the end of this book for a recommendation.

Q: *Should I buy single-sided, double-sided or high-density floppies?*

A: Numbers first: the single-sided disk holds 400K, the double-sided 800K, and the high-density 1400K. For a large file you may need a high-density disk. Otherwise, since floppies tend to get lost or sat on with disturbing frequency, why not have your data distributed over a larger number of lower density disks? The single-sided disks won't hold very much as they're meant to be used, so many people format them as double-sided and use them that way. The reason not to is that although the single-sided and double-sided disks are manufactured the same way, only the double-sided disks have passed the manufacturer's testing on both sides. So it's a little safer to buy double-sided disks.

CHAPTER 2

COMPUTER GRAPHICS

In this chapter, you'll learn how to:

- create graphic images on a Macintosh
- use a variety of painting tools
- save your graphic onto a disk
- work with advanced painting techniques
- copy all or part of a graphic, and paste it into a new file
- use on-line help
- print a file
- work in different graphics modes

For any of you with artistic leanings, Macintosh graphics may be a step into a wonderfully versatile and highly capable medium. You can do so much, so easily and so accurately, with computer graphics, that it's exceptional to find professional graphic art and design these days that *wasn't* done on a computer.

Other advantages abound as well. Art in electronic form can be sent across the country by telephone line to benefit from a colleague's ideas. Of course, you can fax conventional art as well, but that copy isn't as good as the original, while the computer copy is identical to the original.

You can make any number of changes to your art, and then undo some or all of them. There's nothing like trying this or that, then changing it, to give you a sense of what works well.

What if you don't aspire to aesthetic expression in drawing or painting? There's still a great deal of value here, because a graphics program is the best way to learn how to use a Macintosh application (a program that produces something, e.g. a painting or a letter. The system programs that you learned in the last chapter don't produce anything for you; they let you manage the computer and files).

LET'S START

Most programs on the Mac are started by selecting the icon for that program, and choosing **Open** from the File menu—or, as a shortcut, double-clicking on the program icon.

1. **Starting up**. Select SuperPaint and choose **Open** from the File menu, or double-click on the icon. It takes the Mac a moment to read necessary parts of the program into memory.

2. **The painting area and tools**. After the Mac has read the parts of the SuperPaint program it needs, you'll see a screen like Figure 2.1. This is a lot at once, so don't worry. And notice that there's still a menu bar—although there are more menus—and a window with a title bar and zoom, close, and resize boxes, and there are still scroll bars.

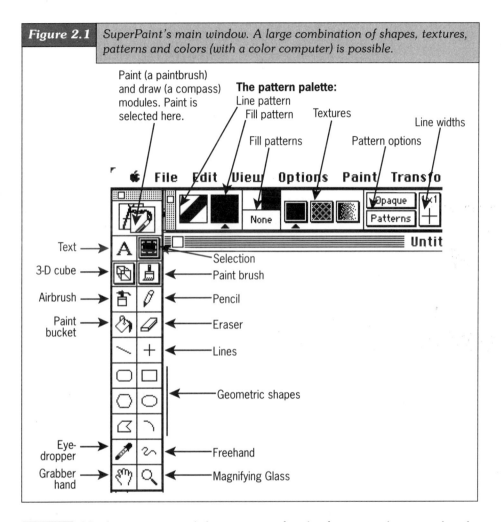

Figure 2.1 *SuperPaint's main window. A large combination of shapes, textures, patterns and colors (with a color computer) is possible.*

 You've just opened this program for the first time, but you already know your way around half of it. This consistency among programs is partly why the Mac is so easy to learn.

N O T E

What's new are painting tools, along the left side of the screen, and a palette of patterns along the top.

3 Select the Paintbrush tool by clicking on its icon.

4 Move your cursor into the painting window, and click and hold the mouse button down.

5 Move your cursor around the window, keeping the mouse button down. Release it when you like what you see.

6 Paint another line or shape in the same way.

7 Go back to the tool palette and choose another tool. Paint something with this.

8 Time for fun. There are lots of tools and patterns. Check out several of them. If you don't like your last step—spilling the paint bucket is common— go up to the Edit menu and choose **Undo**. This feature has saved a lot of people a lot of grief.

SAVING YOUR WORK

Speaking of grief, another reliable source of it in the computer world is losing your work.

In the last chapter, we simply moved files and folders around, and the Macintosh kept track of what we were doing. With SuperPaint and most other application programs, though, we need to save a copy of our work periodically.

This is because what you see on the screen, whether a simple drawing or a doctoral dissertation, is on chips in a part of the computer called *RAM*, or *random access memory.*

This is to say, its present existence is in the form of electrons. Should there be a power failure, or failure of a computer component, the electrons go away and your work goes with it.

There's a simple remedy for it, and your friends' horror stories are almost certainly the result of failure to observe a few easy precautions.

WARNING

The most important precaution is also the easiest: *save often.*

Saving writes a copy of what's in RAM onto a disk. What's on disk is relatively permanent and reliable.

HOW TO SAVE

Go up to the File menu and select **Save**. Since this is the first time you're putting a copy of your work onto disk, the computer has to know things such as a name for the file and where to put it. It asks you in the form of a dialog box like Figure 2.2. This is initially a little confusing, so let's look at some parts of the dialog box:

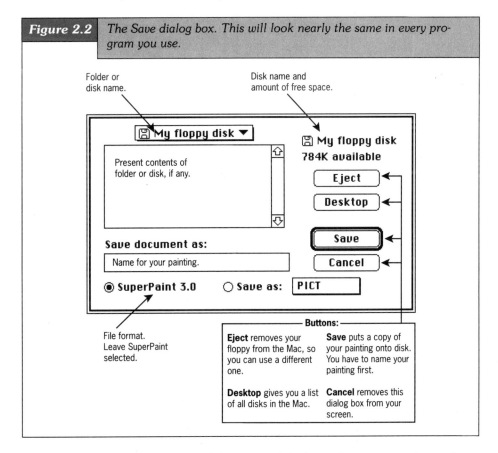

Figure 2.2 The Save dialog box. This will look nearly the same in every program you use.

Folder or disk name.

Disk name and amount of free space.

🖫 My floppy disk ▼

Present contents of folder or disk, if any.

🖫 My floppy disk
784K available

Eject

Desktop

Save document as:

Name for your painting.

Save

Cancel

⦿ **SuperPaint 3.0**   ○ Save as: PICT

File format.
Leave SuperPaint selected.

Buttons:

Eject removes your floppy from the Mac, so you can use a different one.

Save puts a copy of your painting onto disk. You have to name your painting first.

Desktop gives you a list of all disks in the Mac.

Cancel removes this dialog box from your screen.

- At the top right is the name of the active disk drive. On many machines there are two disks to choose from: the hard disk inside, and the floppy you inserted and formatted.

Be sure to save your work onto the right disk, probably your floppy, with your name as the disk name. If this first small box at the top left doesn't show your name, click your arrow on the **Desktop** button to list all of the active drives. Then double-click on your disk name.

- The largest box now lists the contents of your disk (or active folder). It might be empty at this point.

- The next box down is labelled **Save document as:** and here's where you give your file a name. You can call your painting "Rembrandt Redux" or anything else except that file names on the Mac can't be longer than 32 characters, nor can they contain a colon.

- Click in the **Save** box, and you'll be returned to your painting.

- All succeeding saves are much easier. The name and place are determined, and the computer simply replaces the older version of your work with the newer. So successive saves just update what's on disk with what's in memory, and should take about five seconds.

As good habits are as easy as bad ones, please nourish the habit of saving your work often.

ADVANCED PAINTING

1. **More tools**. Back to going wow with the paint tools. Several of them have a neat trick: click and hold on the icon, and a pop-up palette is displayed, with more tools. Click on the one you want, and the tool icon changes to reflect your choice. Try this with the Paintbrush tool. Change this tool back to the original Paintbrush before going on.

2. **More features**. The tools are lots of fun, and the menus have neat stuff. Go to the Paint menu and choose the **Brush Symmetry** command. Click on two or three lines in the symmetry box. In the illustration, we clicked on the diagonal lines to make them heavy, thus active. Click OK, and see what the paint brush does now. This is just a sample of the elegant features you'll find in computer graphics programs.

3. Try a slanted paintbrush with **Brush Shapes** under the Options menu. You can choose a pre-defined brush shape, or make your own, by clicking here

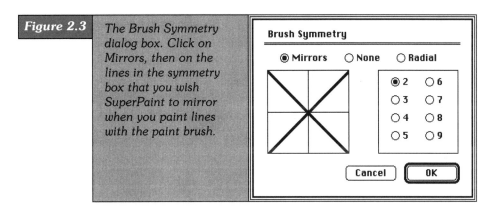

Figure 2.3 *The Brush Symmetry dialog box. Click on Mirrors, then on the lines in the symmetry box that you wish SuperPaint to mirror when you paint lines with the paint brush.*

and there in the magnified view box. Each click you make on a white area changes that pixel (the smallest dot visible on the regular screen) to black. Click on a black pixel to change it to white.

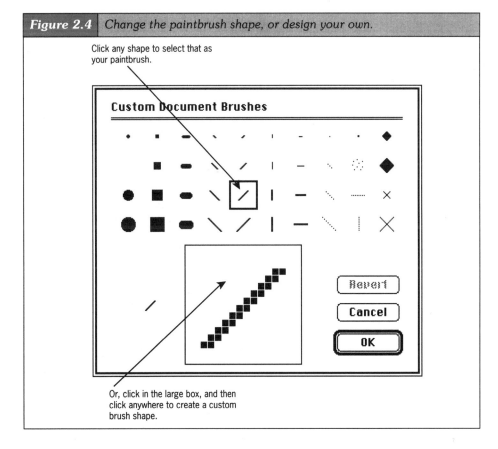

Figure 2.4 Change the paintbrush shape, or design your own.

Click any shape to select that as your paintbrush.

Or, click in the large box, and then click anywhere to create a custom brush shape.

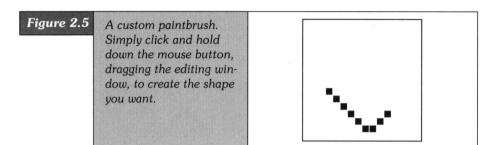

Figure 2.5 A custom paintbrush. Simply click and hold down the mouse button, dragging the editing window, to create the shape you want.

4 **More fun**. Use Fatbits by choosing the Pencil tool, holding down the **Command** key (which, from one Macintosh to another, may have a cloverleaf or Apple symbol, or may say Command) and clicking on the part of the screen you want to enlarge by 8x. To leave Fatbits, command-click on the smaller view on the left side of the painting area.

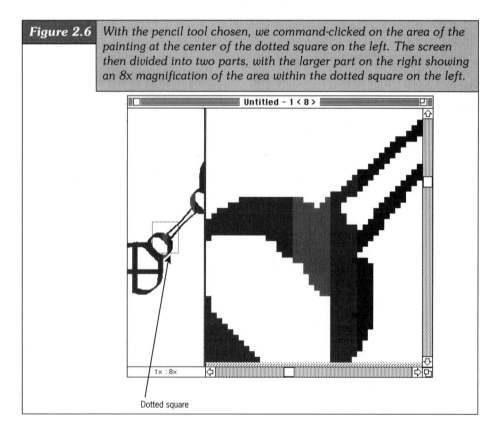

Figure 2.6 With the pencil tool chosen, we command-clicked on the area of the painting at the center of the dotted square on the left. The screen then divided into two parts, with the larger part on the right showing an 8x magnification of the area within the dotted square on the left.

Untitled – 1 < 8 >

1x : 8x

Dotted square

5 **Options**. Many Mac programs use the double-clicking technique for various things. Try this on some tool icons such as the Pencil, Eraser, and Paintbrush. Also, holding down the **Option** or **Shift** keys changes the way some tools draw. Set the Paint Pattern to none in the palette, choose a shape tool, such as the Oval, and then check out the **Paint Multiple** feature under the Paint menu.

6 In general, get a little loose and have a good time. Wonderful for stress.

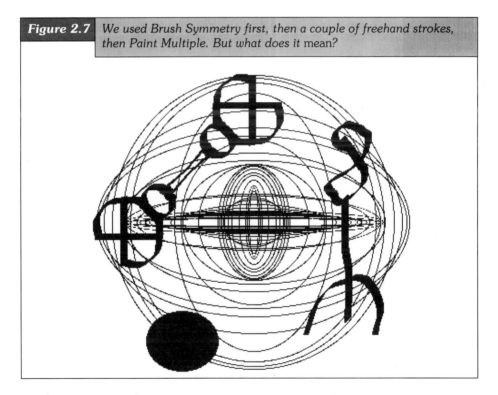

Figure 2.7 We used Brush Symmetry first, then a couple of freehand strokes, then Paint Multiple. But what does it mean?

The other great antidote for stress is saving often.

Your first save was complicated, with the dialog box. Every succeeding save of this file is very easy—just choose **Save** from the File menu, and you're done.

NOTE

We recommend that you nourish the habit of saving at least every five minutes.

SAVE AS

Let's take a break from all of this creative activity to look at a useful feature of the Mac system. Let's say that you've named your painting "Monday Morning." It's fairly good, but you want to add to it, to make a painting called "Friday Night," while keeping Monday Morning intact.

You can do this by using a command on the File menu similar to Save, called **Save As**. This creates a second copy of what you have on the screen, without touching what you last saved to disk.

1 Choose **Save As**, and get the standard Save dialog box, just as though you were saving for the first time.

2 Type a name for your new file, and click **Save**.

You're now working on your new file. The earlier version is dormant on your disk. This feature has several uses. Incremental saves are valuable if you're not sure about the additions you want to make to your painting.

You can also make several versions of one basic document, for different purposes.

SHORTCUT

COPY AND PASTE

Back to your painting, and another very useful feature: you can take just a part of your file, and copy that to a new document.

1 Select the **Marquee**, the tool that looks like a rectangle drawn with a dotted line, which you'll see at the top right of the tool palette, just above the Paintbrush icon. This tool is used to select part of a painting.

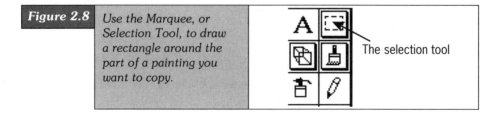

Figure 2.8 *Use the Marquee, or Selection Tool, to draw a rectangle around the part of a painting you want to copy.*

The selection tool

2 Put your cursor at the top left of whatever part of your painting you want to select.

3 Click and drag down and to the right, until the dotted rectangle you've drawn encloses the area you want to copy. Then release the mouse button.

Figure 2.9 *Part of the painting is selected: a line of moving dots describes the rectangle we've drawn.*

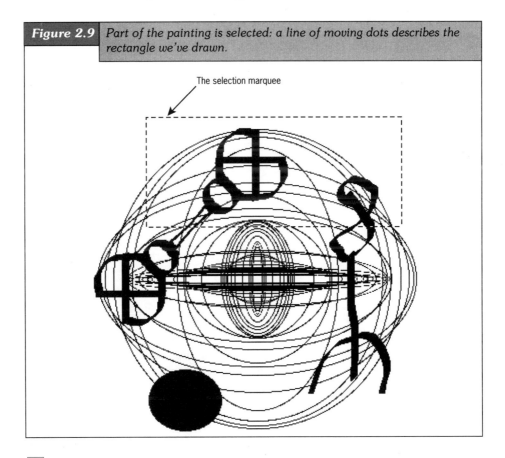

The selection marquee

4 Come up to the Edit menu and choose **Copy**.

5 Choose **New** from the File menu.

Conceptual point here: you can have more than one file open at a time. This is handy for moving data from one document to another, or comparing two versions of some work.

N O T E

6 Choose **Paste** from the Edit menu, to paste this part of your painting into the new (blank) document on the screen.

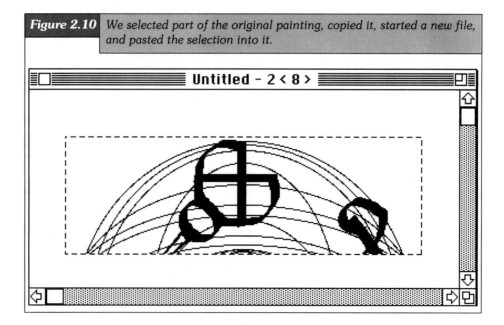

Figure 2.10 *We selected part of the original painting, copied it, started a new file, and pasted the selection into it.*

Untitled - 2 < 8 >

N O T E Copying and pasting uses a part of the Mac's memory called the *Clipboard*. You can move data around any number of times. It gets spectacular when you move something you've painted, or numbers from a spreadsheet, into a paper you're typing. And we almost always do it in the same way as you just did.

Because the Clipboard is memory (RAM, electrons), what's in it doesn't last after you turn the Mac off. So we have another place to store data, one that lives on disk. We call it the *Scrapbook*.

THE SCRAPBOOK

This is an *Apple Menu* item, a small program in the Apple menu, at the far left of the menu bar. These programs are also called *Desk Accessories*.

Their advantage is that you can run them at the same time as SuperPaint, or another large program.

1. Take your cursor up to the Apple menu, at the far left of the menu bar. Click and hold here, and move down to the **Scrapbook**.

2. Scroll through what's there with the horizontal scroll bar below the picture window until you find something you like. Then copy it, using the **Copy** command in the Edit menu (no need to select it—the visible picture in the Scrapbook window is already selected).

3. Click on the close box to get rid of the Scrapbook and use **Paste** to paste the picture you chose into your document.

You would copy something (either painting or text) to the Scrapbook just like to a new document.

ON-LINE HELP

SuperPaint has a nice feature to assist you with menu commands, tools, and other parts of the program. This is its *Help* function, which you'll find under the Apple menu, as the second item. Choose this, and you'll see:

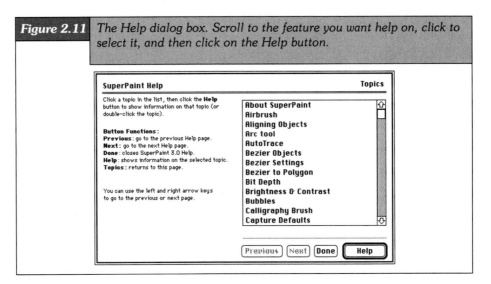

Figure 2.11 The Help dialog box. Scroll to the feature you want help on, click to select it, and then click on the Help button.

This is a useful tool, although the information isn't as complete as what's in SuperPaint's manual. On-line help is a feature of more programs all the time, though, simply because it's immediately there when N O T E you need it.

PRINTING

Well, your painting is complete and anyway it's time for lunch. Let's look at how to print.

1 **Save it first**. Before you print, save your work one last time. A lot of things can go wrong during printing, and most of them take your unsaved work with them.

2 **Check out your printer**. See that it's on, has paper, and is connected to your computer. Specifics depend on how your Macintosh is set up, and what kind of printer you're using. You may need to access the *Chooser*, another Apple Menu item that lets you, logically enough, choose a printer.

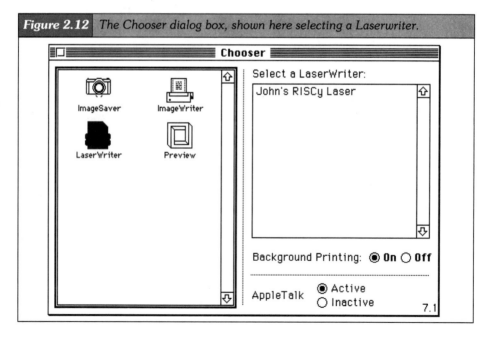

Figure 2.12 *The Chooser dialog box, shown here selecting a Laserwriter.*

With your printer turned on and chosen,

3 Choose **Print** from the File menu. The Mac responds with a dialog box like Figure 2.13, for a Laserwriter. The Imagewriter or Stylewriter dialog boxes read a little differently.

Figure 2.13	The Print dialog box. Standard use calls for one copy, all pages, no cover page, paper coming from the printer's cassette, color/grayscale printing, and the destination is the printer.

LaserWriter "John's RISCy Laser"   7.1.1   [Print]

Copies:[1]   Pages: ⦿ All ○ From: [   ] To: [   ]   [Cancel]

Cover Page: ⦿ No ○ First Page ○ Last Page

Paper Source: ⦿ Paper Cassette ○ Manual Feed

Print: ○ Black & White   ⦿ Color/Grayscale

Destination: ⦿ Printer   ○ PostScript® File

Print Color Bitmaps as: ⦿ Gray (Faster) ○ Color

This is a color document. Please make sure the
"Color/Grayscale" button is selected above.

If an option is currently selected, the little circle to its left (we call them *radio buttons*) are darkened. To change an option, just click on the name of what you want. No need to click in the button itself.

4 **Do it.** Click on the **Print** button, and watch your artistry take shape on paper.

5 **Quitting the program.** After printing has completed, you'll want to leave, or quit, SuperPaint. This command is on the File menu, and is the last one at the bottom. If you have made any changes to your file since you last saved it, the Mac asks you if you want to save these. Click on your decision, then see how the computer erases SuperPaint's palettes and windows, and restores the earlier screen of icons and folders.

Notice that in your disk window, in addition to the icons you saw there before you ran SuperPaint, there's a new icon with the name of your painting.

To retrieve your disk, put your cursor on the disk icon at the right side of the desktop, click on it, and drag it into the Trash. The computer should eject your disk.

What you have on your disk at this point is a copy of a document you made with a program. You can re-open this document on any Mac that has SuperPaint. If you try to open your file on another Mac that doesn't N O T E have SuperPaint, you'll be told that "The application is busy or missing."

All this means is that the other Mac doesn't have the information needed to read your document. It surely has several other programs installed, but those won't help.

So, if you're planning to move a file from one computer to another, check first that the destination computer has the program that you need, or (if you own the program), take it with you.

SUPERPAINT'S DRAW MODE

What you've done already in this chapter is cover the basics of one kind of Mac graphics. It's given you a good sense of how to make illustrations on a computer, and how to **Save As** into a new file, and **Copy** and **Paste** from one document into another.

This last section goes into more advanced territory, something that is of some interest to most everyone, and of great interest if you want to go further with computer graphics.

In terms of computer graphics, there's a major difference between *painting*, what we've done so far in this chapter, and *drawing*, another kind of computer art.

In the paint mode, we created shapes and textures, and all of this art became fixed on the computer screen at the time that we painted it. Just as though it were oil or fresco. On our screen, we can select part of it and move it, just as though we had cut it with a knife.

If you select part of an oval and move it, the paint you've selected moves with your mouse. The figure is no longer an oval.

This is because although you painted the figure as an object, once you finished and clicked the mouse somewhere else, the object lost its integrity, and became simply a collection of black dots on the white screen. So you can select some of those dots and move them.

Draw mode is another way of doing things. When you draw a circle, as opposed to painting one, the object looks exactly the same. But when you select

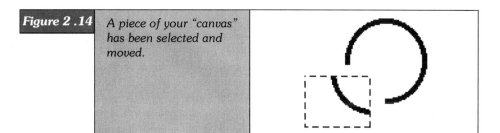

Figure 2.14 A piece of your "canvas" has been selected and moved.

and move something, you can only move the object as a whole. It maintains its integrity.

To check this out, go back into SuperPaint (if you've quit), and:

1 Click on the Compass icon, partially hidden behind the Paintbrush icon, at the top of the tool palette.

 Much of the tool palette changes, to reflect the different features and functions of SuperPaint's draw mode. Note especially that the Selection Marquee of the paint mode has changed to an arrow—the N O T E corresponding selection tool of the draw mode.

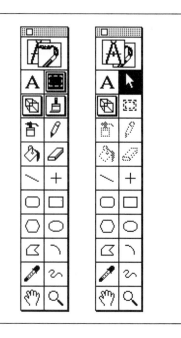

Figure 2.15 The tool palette with the paint brush in front as the top icon (at left) and then compass in front. These represent the paint and draw modes of the program. Note how some other tools in the palette change or gray out when you change modes.

2 Choose the Oval tool, and draw an oval.

The resulting figure has *selection handles*—four black boxes—around it. Reselect the Arrow tool, and:

3 Click and hold with the tip of the Arrow on a handle, and drag it in any direction.

You can change the size or proportions of the oval, but not the fact that it's an oval.

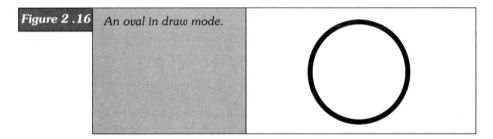

Figure 2.16   *An oval in draw mode.*

The other difference between paint and draw modes is that, since a paint object is a collection of dots, or pixels, it's painted at the resolution of your Mac screen: about 72 dots-per-inch. It prints this way, even on a Laserwriter with a resolution of 300 dots-per-inch.

A draw object, conversely, is stored in your document as a description of an oval, or other shape. When you print, the object appears at the full resolution of the printer.

Note the difference between the ovals in Figures 2.14 and 2.16, for example. The former is rough, or "jagged," while the latter is perfectly smooth.

One looked just as smooth as the other on the screen, but the higher resolution of a laser printer is available to your drawings, not your paintings.

The distinction is remarkable in text, where text you paint again has the resolution of the screen, while draw text benefits from as much resolution as your printer can offer.

So when should you choose paint or draw modes? To an extent, your practice with your own work determines this. Paint offers a much greater variety of textures, and you have complete flexibility over what you select, cut into pieces, and move around. With draw mode, you have higher quality resolution, and you can continue to work with shapes and text after you draw them.

N O T E

Figure 2.17 *Text typed in paint mode can be jagged when you print, while text in draw mode will be as smooth as your printer can provide.*

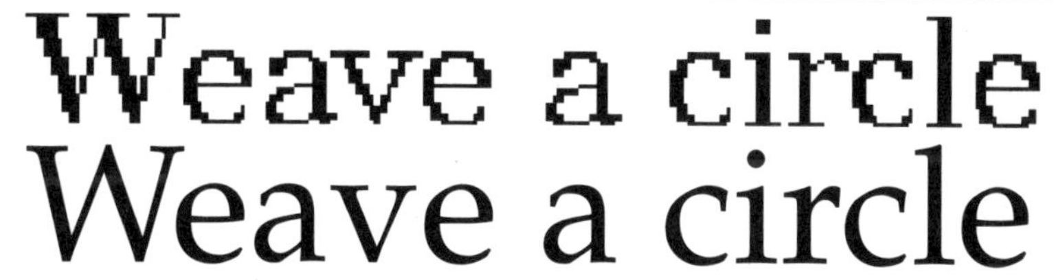

Weave a circle
Weave a circle

BÉZIER CURVES

The precision of the drawing mode is complemented by a tool of remarkable sophistication, enough so that its introduction made it difficult to justify *not* using a computer for most illustration work.

This is a way to draw a curve that carries with it *control points* that let you make highly precise adjustments to the shape of the curve itself—not just its height or width.

Figure 2.18 shows two Bézier curves that are copies of each other. The upper one, though, is selected, and you see added to it straight lines that come out from points on the curve: one at the middle, the others at the end.

Figure 2.18 *Structure of a Bézier curve. The curve on top, an exact copy of the one below it, is selected. Control points let you make precise adjustments to the shape of the curve.*

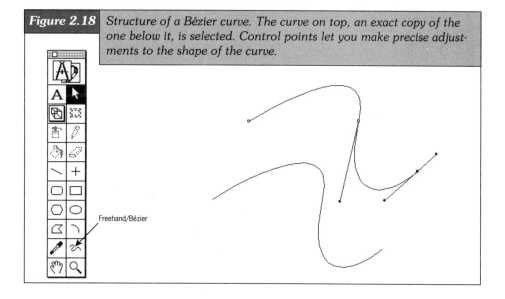

Freehand/Bézier

These lines end in control points. Clicking and dragging any of those points changes the shape of the curve. Moving different points produces varying changes.

In SuperPaint, you begin a Bézier with the Freehand tool in draw mode. Select it and:

1 Draw any shape you like.

SuperPaint takes a moment to calculate a set of Béziers that closely match your freehand path.

In Figure 2.18, we've added lines going from the curve to the control points, for sake of clarity. In SuperPaint, the lines don't appear, but the control points do, as you see in Figure 2.19.

Figure 2.19 *SuperPaint calculated Bézier points for this freehand object. Each point on the curve is either a hinge point (box) or smooth point (circle). The three curve points on the right are selected, thus outlined, and their control points show as diamonds near the curve.*

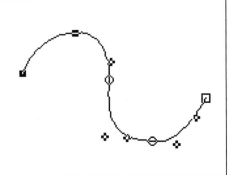

Of the points on the curve itself, SuperPaint distinguishes between *corner* or *hinge points* and *smooth points*. Dragging the control points affects hinge points differently from smooth points.

SuperPaint creates a hinge point where it discerns enough of a change in direction in the freehand drawing. You can, though, select a hinge or smooth point and change it to the other kind.

Depending on how your computer is set up, what you drew may show these points. If not, select it (you'll see the four handles at the corners), and choose **Reshape** from the Draw menu. Your object then looks like Figure 2.19.

2 Click on any point on the curve, and watch its control points appear. Drag these around, to see how you can precisely adjust a curve after you've drawn it.

CHECKLIST

You've explored the basics of computer graphics in this chapter, and learned valuable features of the Macintosh system in general. You should now be able to:

- open an application program and produce graphic work,

- save your efforts to disk,

- use **Save As**, to update successive versions of what you create,

- copy part of your work to a new file or to the Scrapbook,

- access on-line help,

- distinguish conceptually between painting and drawing, and use each mode to its best advantage, and

- print a document.

OTHER CHOICES

SuperPaint's flexibility in using both painting and drawing modes is matched by Canvas, a faster and more expensive program with a larger feature set, and a toll-free number for technical support. Other programs offer either paint or draw, not both.

For painting, take a look at UltraPaint, Amazing Paint, Cricket Paint, or the program that started it all, MacPaint.

More sophisticated effects in gray-scale and color are available with paint programs like PixelPaint, Digital Darkroom, Adobe Photoshop, ImageStudio, and ColorStudio.

In draw mode, there are two broad types: polygon-based designs that have some Bézier functionality, such as MacDraw, or dedicated Bézier instruments such as Adobe Illustrator or Aldus Freehand.

The learning curve for these last two is steeper than for other kinds of drawing programs so, if you choose to learn one, take your time with it and don't expect to master its techniques in a week. Output can be spectacular, though.

At the next level are *CAD (computer-aided design)* programs—say, for the next automobile you make, and imaging and rendering software, for something that looks exactly like a color photograph, except it isn't. Claris CAD and Ray Dream Designer are examples of these decidedly professional applications.

HELPFUL HINTS

While Bézier curve work and technical illustration can be done well with a mouse, other input devices are preferable for paint (or bitmapped) mode. The best for most artists is a *tablet*, on which you draw with a metal pen-like stylus: the tablet's sensitive surface records your motions and pressure.

It's wise to look at the different modes of illustration—drawing, painting, design, imaging—before investing time and money in a choice. More than other kinds of programs we'll learn, graphics programs differ within their genre. The best choice is one only you can make.

At this point, we can't emphasize enough the value of practice. Start a new document, and play with SuperPaint's features. Don't be afraid of the computer or the program. Just save a lot, and use **Save As** several times.

Every minute of what might seem like wandering around in the program is actually important progress in using your mouse, scroll bars, menus, and other features of this intuitive and friendly interface.

Q & A

Q: *How can I remember to save as often as I should?*

A: This is a habit well worth nourishing. Using a kitchen timer as you work is actually a good idea. A competent user saves her file *every time* she stops to adjust the paper on her desk, or to think about what she's just done on the Mac.

Q: *For graphics images that I use often, should I keep them in separate SuperPaint files or in the Scrapbook?*

A: There are advantages to both. Saved in a separate file, they're easier to copy onto a floppy and take to a different computer. Saved in the Scrapbook, your image library is a little easier to get at. Try both, and see what's more convenient for the way you work.

Q: *I printed a graphic both on an Imagewriter and on a Laserwriter. The Imagewriter output looks slightly squeezed horizontally—a circle became an oval. How can I avoid this?*

A: For the Imagewriter to match the Laserwriter as closely as possible, you need to check the **Tall Adjusted** box in the Imagewriter print dialog box. This widens all shapes slightly, so that the oval becomes a circle again.

Q: *I closed a document without saving it. Is there any way to get that graphic back?*

A: No.

Q: *Can I combine paint mode and draw mode graphics in one document?*

A: Yes, and that feature greatly enhances SuperPaint's versatility. Each mode has its own layer, and you can switch from one to the other and put objects next to (or on top of) one another.

SAMPLE EXERCISE

1 Paint anything you like with SuperPaint. Use at least five tools and three fill patterns, but try for more. Your painting should be at least three inches on a side, but feel free to make it larger.

2 Use the Text tool to put your name in a corner of the painting.

3 Switch to the draw mode and add to your work. As you do this, ask yourself which of these different modes seems to appeal to you more.

CHAPTER 3

WORD PROCESSING

In this lesson, you'll learn how to:

- enter word processing data
- use different type styles and sizes
- format text with italic, bold, and other character attributes
- check spelling
- use an electronic thesaurus
- find and replace any text in a document
- create and edit footnotes, headers, and footers
- work with the layout of a page
- work with graphics in a word processing environment
- check grammar electronically
- use outlining to organize your writing

Believe it or not, you've weathered the hardest parts of learning computers. What you've covered in the last two chapters won't be automatic for a few weeks yet, but it's now just a matter of practice. And one of the nicer things about the Macintosh's way of doing things is that most programs share details of operation. You'll load a program, open a document, save changes, and quit in remarkably similar ways from one program to the next.

Now let's look at a kind of program that you, either as a student or professional, may well use more than any other: word processing.

Plenty of people run around thinking that word processing on a computer is a glorified typewriter—if so, it's mightily glorified. Your humble author gave away his IBM Selectric once he had learned to word process, for two reasons:

- Like a graphics program, you can make unlimited versions of one file, undo your mistakes, try lots of things without making anything permanent, save copies on disk and carry them around, send copies to your friends or publisher via telephone line, and produce a perfect copy from disk every time.

- Unlike graphics programs, you have available to you tools and capabilities that writers not using a computer can only dream about. Monet might have seen SuperPaint as a real convenience, but it's questionable whether it would have made him a better painter. But there's little question that a word processing program, with sufficient practice, can make you a better writer.

In this book, we'll be using Microsoft Word, one of the more powerful word processing applications available. Like SuperPaint, it has lots of tools, but we won't switch among them so much. Instead, we start the program and enter text, or edit what we've already written, and then use tools to format, check spelling, find synonyms and so forth. So the keyboard is the locus of our main activity, with other tools available as we need them.

OPENING AND STARTING

[1] Open Word, either by clicking on its icon to select it and then choosing **Open** from the File menu, or by double-clicking on the icon. After a moment, you get a screen and you're ready to type.

NOTE Take a moment, though, to note how similar many aspects of the screen are to SuperPaint. There's a menu bar, an active window with close, zoom and resize boxes and a title bar, and scroll bars at the bottom and right. Note also that the File and Edit menus have many things in common.

Given that this program is designed for a completely different purpose than SuperPaint, it's remarkably user-friendly that so much is similar.

2 **Entering text**. Time to remember how to type. Type a couple of lines, and don't use the **Return** (or **Enter**) key.

Watch what happens to your text when you get to the right of the screen. It *wraps* to the next line for you. No more stopping your train of thought when a little bell rings.

This is a good example of what a computer can do—keep the mechanics out of your way to let you think. Use the **Return** key only to start a new paragraph.

FORMATTING

We can choose the size of what we type, and make a basic change in the shapes of the letters, by choosing which *font* we want. Here are some examples:

Figure 3.1	Fonts and sizes.		
This is Palatino.	10 point	14 point	18 point
This is Helvetica	10 point	14 point	18 point
This is Piegnot Demi	10 point	14 point	18 point

There's quite a variety available on most Macintoshes. As far as heights go, 72 points are an inch. Text in most books and magazines is 10 or 12 point type. Word defaults to 12 point.

If you want to format text you're about to type:

1 Choose a font and size from the Font menu, and start.

But if you want to apply these changes to text you've already typed:

2 Click your mouse in front of any word and, holding the button down:

3 Drag through several words, then release the mouse button.

Note that the text used to be dark on light, but has changed to light on dark. We've *selected* it.

4 Choose another font or size for your selected text, and watch it change to reflect your choice.

This is a common couple of steps in word processing—we first select something, then modify it.

5 Here's a good place to save for a first time. Saving often is a very good idea. Make sure your work goes onto your disk, and ignore the Summary Info dialog box— just **OK** it.

FORMATTING WITH THE RIBBON

Let's do another kind of text formatting, and make some text italic, bold or underlined.

1 Choose **Ribbon** from the View menu. The Ribbon command is at the top of the second set on the list. You should see this displayed at the top of your text window:

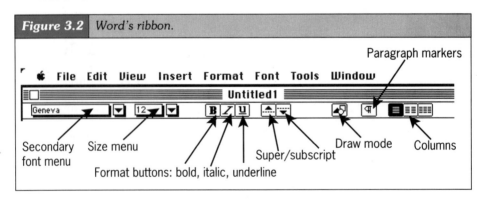

Figure 3.2 *Word's ribbon.*

2 Click on the **Bold** button, and type a couple of more words, then click again on the **Bold** button to toggle that style off. Try the same with italic. Try both. The underline style isn't as popular these days as these other forms of emphasis.

Just as with fonts and sizes, you can select text first and then click a formatting button, to change text already typed.

We'll look at more of this later in this chapter. For now, go back up to the View menu and note that the **Ribbon** command now has a check mark next to it, indicating that it's active. Choose it again, to hide it.

THE RULER RULES

The **Ruler** is another formatting tool much like the Ribbon. Choose it from the View menu also.

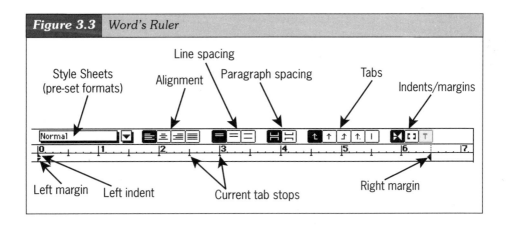

Figure 3.3 | *Word's Ruler*

Another set of formatting icons is displayed along the top of the ruler. Below them you see inch marks, with triangles at the left and right for margins.

To change the margins for text you've already written, select the text and drag the triangles one way or the other. Note that the left triangle is split horizontally into two parts.

Moving the top part allows you to indent each paragraph automatically, without bothering to use the Tab key each time.

The tab sets are several arrows pointing up. These are tab stops of different kinds. The left-most icon, if dragged onto the ruler itself, sets a standard or left tab stop. The next one sets a center, the next one sets a flush-right, the next one (with a dot to its right) sets a decimal tab. (The last icon puts a vertical line where you type the tab key.)

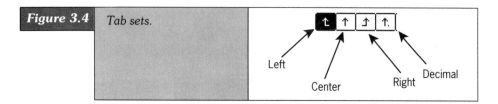

Figure 3.4 Tab sets.

Left Center Right Decimal

1 **Setting tabs**. Drag a standard tab onto the ruler at the 2-inch mark, and a decimal tab onto the ruler at the 4.5-inch mark. Then type the following, with a **Return** after each line, and pressing **tab** where shown:

March: \<tab\>	Expenses \<tab\>	$514.85
\<tab\>	Income\<tab\>	$12.25
\<tab\>	Gambling losses\<tab\>	$14,449.80

Every figure lines up at the decimal point.

2 Drag both of those tab stops off the ruler—just down into the text area—and let go. That erases them, and restores Word's default of left tabs every half inch. Now drag a flush-right tab onto the ruler, at the 4.5-inch mark, and type the following:

Henrietta \<tab\>	Lisa Oglethorpe
The Duke \<tab\>	Ted Hill
His Sister \<tab\>	Susan Elizabeth Thorncastle

3 **Centering and justifying**. The next set of icons on the ruler concerns *justification*. The default is the first icon, which you see highlighted, and which shows a series of lines even on the left and uneven on the right. The second icon represents centered text, the third, right justified, and the last one is full justified (at both the left and right margins), as are most books published today.

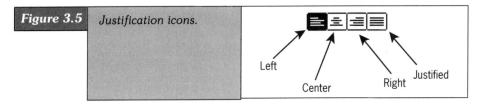

Figure 3.5   *Justification icons.*

Left
Center
Right
Justified

Although full justification has long been considered the most profes-sional in appearance, recent research in reading has shown that left justification, where there are no added spaces between words to make
N O T E   the margins come out even, is easier to read.

Titles, of course, are often best when centered, and you may have reason to use flush-right. For any style—or font, or size, or any other attribute of your text—if you select text first, then format, that attribute is applied to the exist-ing text. If you do not select text first, the attribute you choose is applied to whatever you subsequently type, until you change it.

4 **Spacing**. The next set of icons on the ruler spaces lines of text for you. The first three choose single, 1.5, or double-spacing, and the next two choose closed or open paragraphs. Open paragraphs have an extra space between them, as is common in a business letter.

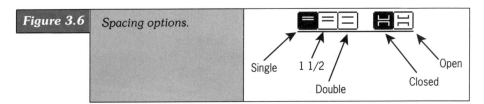

Figure 3.6   *Spacing options.*

Single   1 1/2   Open
Double   Closed

5 Try some of these tools, and then go to the View menu to put the ruler away. As with the **Ribbon**, the command has a check mark next to it if it's active. Many commands toggle like this.

As you familiarize yourself with Word, you may want both the ribbon and ruler showing, to remind you of the features available. For now, though, hide them, simply because it leaves more of the screen for your work.

All of the ribbon and ruler commands are also available through the menus. More and more though, people seem to like tool palettes better than menu com-mands, possibly just because they're more visual.

NOTE Let's take a second for a note on formatting: the ability of the Mac to show you your formatting as it appears when printed is called *WYSIWYG*: "What you see is what you get." It's a couple of orders of magnitude nicer than the way other computer systems go about it by, for example, indicating bold type in a normal shape but in a blue color on the screen. Or a larger font shown in the same size on screen, but yet another color.

Why is bold mapped to blue? Because they both start with the letter B? It's arbitrary and inefficient, compared to working with what you're actually producing.

WYSIWYG is part of another acronym, *GUI*, standing for "graphical user interface"—windows, buttons, and icons. The Macintosh pioneered this way of working, and it's been found to increase both productivity and satisfaction among computer users, for many different kinds of work.

Simply put, the better the computer can show you how your work is going to look, the easier time you have making your work look good.

COPY AND PASTE

This feature, which works just the same as in SuperPaint—except that you're copying text, rather than a graphic object, or area of the screen—is a real timesaver.

1. Find a paragraph of your text you want to copy. Put your cursor at the left of the text, and click, hold and drag to the right and down until all of the text you want is selected.

2. Choose **Copy** from the Edit menu. Then come up to the File menu and:

3. Choose **New**. When you have a blank screen, paste the text. Voilà. Save this new document onto your disk. Give it any name you want. At various times in your computing, you'll note that shorter names are easier to work with.

SHORTCUT There are lots of uses for this. A business may have a standard contract form, and want to enter varying terms and conditions for a particular agreement. By keeping the standard form as one document, and optional terms as other files, you can copy and paste from one to the other, and individualize a contract or other document very fast, without retyping anything each time.

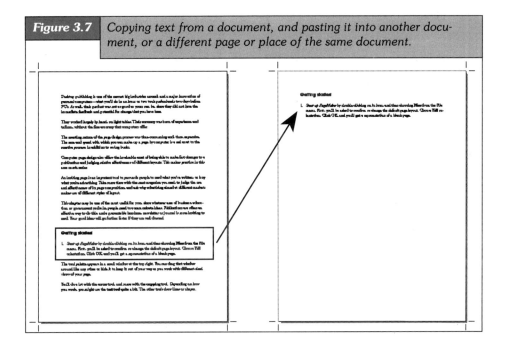

Figure 3.7   *Copying text from a document, and pasting it into another document, or a different page or place of the same document.*

SPELLING

Word processing programs can help not only the look and ease of your writing, but also its quality. That's not as flashy, maybe, but in the end more satisfying.

Word's Spelling Checker finds some (not all) of your mistakes. Why not all? It doesn't know the difference between "there" and "their," or between "too" and "to." But it's a start.

To take a look at this, add some misspelled words to your file: mistakes you'd expect a dictionary to catch.

1 Type "A goood exemple is thes sentence." just as you see it here. Then:

2 Click your mouse to the left of the words you want to spell-check. Word starts at the cursor and moves forward.

3 Choose **Spelling** from the Tools menu. Word finds the first misspelled word, "goood," and shows it to us as in Figure 3.8.

At this point we can decide that "goood" is correctly spelled—it might be a name, for example—and tell Word to **Ignore** its catch. If this word is a

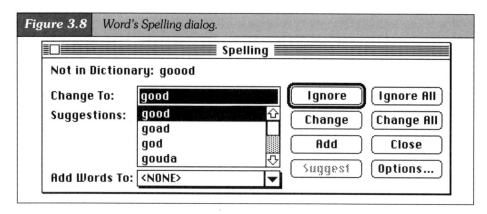

Figure 3.8 *Word's Spelling dialog.*

name we've typed in our document several times, we can tell Word to **Ignore All**.

If we decide the correct spelling is "good," we can have Word **Change** this one instance of it or, if we think the word is identically misspelled at several places, we can have it **Change All**.

If we want to add this word, say a specialized term, to our own User Dictionary, we can click **Add**. The word is then not flagged on subsequent spelling checks.

After we do any of these things, Word then looks for the next misspelling.

At this point, the **Suggest** button has gray rather than black text within it. This means that Word has already given us suggestions, and has no more to add.

Mac programs commonly show a command or button in gray text if it's not available at the time. They change to black when their operation can be performed.

4 **Save those changes**. After a spell-check, or formatting or other changes, is a great time to save your work. The changes you made are in RAM and should be written to disk fairly often.

THESAURUS

Spell checking is fairly straightforward stuff. Going past that, expressive writing is one of the best tools that powerful people have. A good vocabulary is a big part of it.

A capable thesaurus won't provide all of this, but it's a help. And electronically, it's finally easy to use. Let's look at this elegant tool.

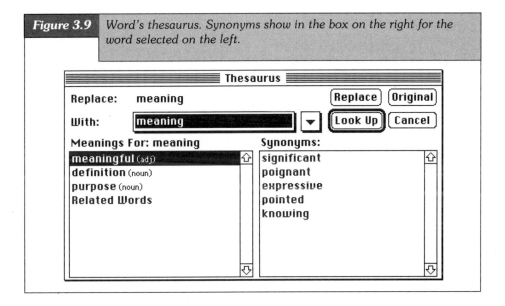

Figure 3.9 *Word's thesaurus. Synonyms show in the box on the right for the word selected on the left.*

1. Add these words to your open document: "The hidden archetypes of meaning."

2. Click your mouse within the word "meaning."

3. Choose **Thesaurus** from the Tools menu.

   A window like Figure 3.9 is displayed with synonyms, of various parts of speech, for the word you chose to check.

4. Peruse the list, noting that changing the selected word in the box on the left gives you a new list in the box on the right. Click **Replace** when you find a suitable synonym.

FIND

In a long document, you'll want to be able to find part of a word, any word or multiple words. Any of these is called a *string*. To do this, go to the top of your document, and choose **Find** from the Edit menu. This dialog box is displayed:

| Figure 3.10 | The Find dialog box. |

```
┌──────────────────────────── Find ────────────────────────────┐
│ Find What: [                                              ]  ( Find Next ) │
│    [Format ▼]                                              ( Cancel ) │
│    [Special ▼]                                            Search:      │
│  ☐ Match Whole Word Only   ☐ Match Case                  [Down    ▼]  │
└───────────────────────────────────────────────────────────────┘
```

This allows you to search for any part of your text. The Format and Special menus let you search for formatting rather than text itself. For example, you could change all instances of underlining to italics.

If you specify **Match Whole Word Only**, your search for "end" ignores "bend," "send," and "depend."

If you specify **Match Case**, your search finds, for example, all occurrences of "BASIC," (a computer language), but not the generic word "basic."

REPLACE

This is a feature that power users like a lot. It lets you utilize shorthand as you write, and then replace it with longer expressions or technical terms.

1. In your document, tell us all about the field of "Agriculture and Life Sciences." Use that long phrase at least three times in your essay. But don't even type it once. Put in some shorthand instead, such as /a. After you're done, go to the top of your document and:

2. Choose **Replace** from the Edit menu. You'll see the dialog box shown in Figure 3.11.

3. Type /a in the Find What dialog box. Type the full title in the **Replace With** dialog box. Then click on **Replace All** and be thankful you don't use a typewriter anymore. Especially if your field is biology or law.

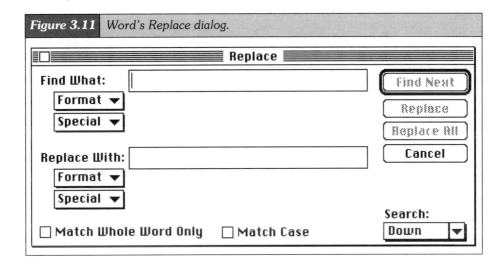

Figure 3.11 *Word's Replace dialog.*

FOOTNOTES

Automatic placement of footnotes in Word is easy and, much more importantly, footnote numbering updates automatically as you enter or delete notes at various points in your document.

When you're at a point in your text you'd like to reference:

1 Select **Footnote** from the Insert menu. You'll see this:

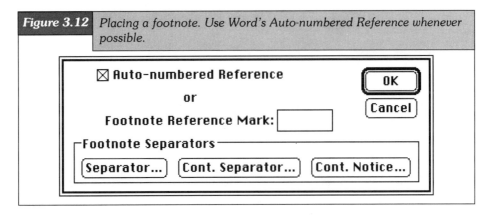

Figure 3.12 *Placing a footnote. Use Word's Auto-numbered Reference whenever possible.*

Word asks you whether you'd like to use its automatic numbering reference, or another of your own. In almost all cases you want to use auto numbering.

Click **OK**, and note that the small window at the bottom of your screen is ready for you to type in your footnote. When done:

2 Close the window by putting your mouse on the thick black bar that separates the vertical scroll bars of the main window from those of the footnote window. Note how the cursor changes shape. At this point, drag that thick bar down to the bottom of the footnote window, or double-click on it, to close the footnote window.

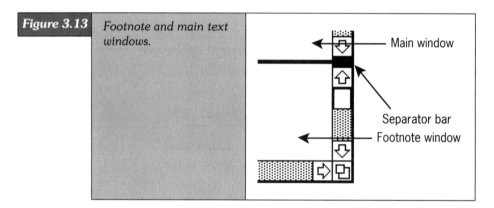

Figure 3.13 *Footnote and main text windows.*

Main window

Separator bar

Footnote window

The especially nice part of footnotes, automatic numbering, is that say you decide to add a note between existing notes 21 and 22. Just go ahead and do it, and Word renumbers 22 to 23.

 Later on, you may want to copy a quote you've referenced as footnote 26 into a new paper. Copy the quote, being sure to include the footnote number. Paste it into your new paper, at a point following footnote 5. Your reference now shows footnote 6, in the body text and in the footnotes.

N O T E

This feature alone is worth a change from a typewriter for any academic work.

HEADERS AND FOOTERS

For longer documents, people often want a few lines at the top or bottom of a page that stay the same on every page.

Choose **Header** from the View menu. The three icons above the typing area will, if clicked, insert page number, date and time. The ruler and ribbon, if you want to display them, work the same way in a header or footer window as in any other window, for formatting.

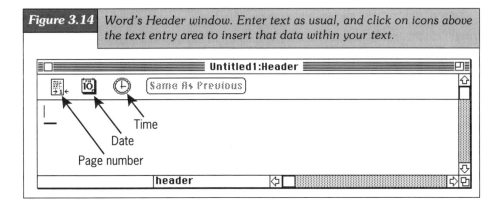

Figure 3.14 *Word's Header window. Enter text as usual, and click on icons above the text entry area to insert that data within your text.*

Footers work just like headers and you can have both on one page. But you won't see either as they'll actually appear in your document unless you're in **Page Layout** view or **Print Preview**.

N O T E

PAGE LAYOUT

Word's normal view shows you your main text, graphics (if you've added any), and nothing else. Page breaks are indicated by a dotted line, and you can display tab, space, and paragraph marks if you want.

When you need a more complete look at your page, you can switch from normal to page layout view.

Choose **Page Layout** from the View menu. Scroll if you need to, and see that your header, footnote and margins now show as they'll appear on the page.

Some people prefer to work in this view all the time, and that's fine. The downside is that scrolling from page to page is slower.

PRINT PREVIEW

Both page layout and normal view show you your document at 100 percent size. Unless your screen displays an entire page, you may want to see each whole page at one glance, to confirm that margins, spacing, type size and such, are really what you'd like to print.

Choose **Print Preview** from the File menu. You'll see:

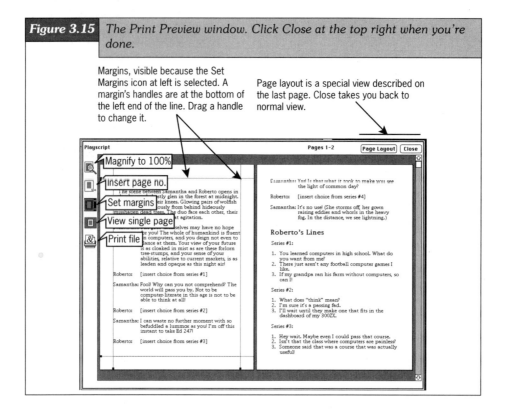

Figure 3.15   *The Print Preview window. Click Close at the top right when you're done.*

Margins, visible because the Set Margins icon at left is selected. A margin's handles are at the bottom of the left end of the line. Drag a handle to change it.

Page layout is a special view described on the last page. Close takes you back to normal view.

INSERTING GRAPHICS

Most word processing programs let you paste a graphic, perhaps something out of SuperPaint, into your word processing document. High-end word processors like this one or WordPerfect have drawing modules built-in.

Word's drawing module is a fairly primitive one, and really is useful only for basic illustration, or last-minute editing of a graphic after you've already placed it in your Word document.

1 Choose **Picture...** from the Insert menu. From the dialog box, select and insert an available graphic.

2 Double-click on the graphic to open it into an editing window:

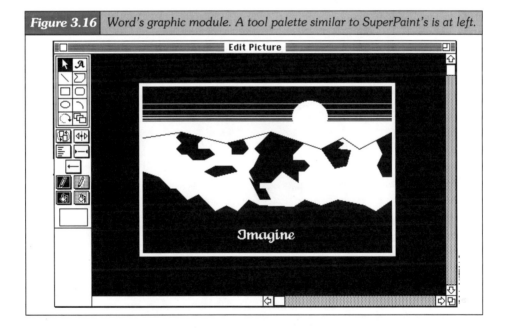

Figure 3.16 *Word's graphic module. A tool palette similar to SuperPaint's is at left.*

Remember that SuperPaint has both a painting and drawing mode of operation. Word's module is draw only and does not offer freehand or Bézier curve tools.

An advantage to a built-in drawing module is that you can prepare graphic work in a program dedicated to it, then import it into Word and scale, crop, rotate, or make other final adjustments to it while you're in the environment that produces the final product.

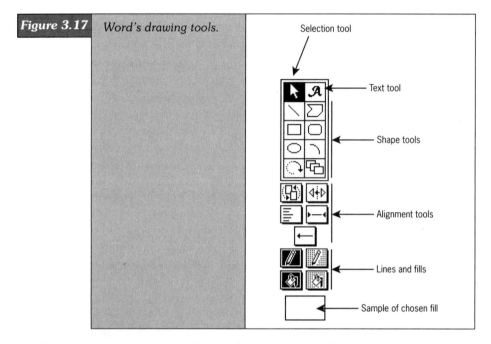

Figure 3.17 *Word's drawing tools.*

Selection tool
Text tool
Shape tools
Alignment tools
Lines and fills
Sample of chosen fill

Or, you can integrate graphics and text more quickly than you can working with two programs. It's certainly a convenience.

HELP!

Online Help is a nice feature that you can call to the screen to answer quick questions about program operation. You can access this help feature in any of three ways:

1. Go to the Window menu and choose **Help** as the first command. You can also go to the Apple menu, choose **About Microsoft Word**, and click on the **Help** button in the copyright notice box that appears. Easy enough. Here's the elegant way: go back to your document and:

2. Hold down the **Command** key which, according to your model of Macintosh, may have an apple or cloverleaf symbol on it, and press the **Question Mark** key. See how your cursor itself has changed to a question mark. Then:

⌐3⌐ Pull down any menu and select any command you want help on. Word goes right to that part of the help file, instead of making you find the topic yourself.

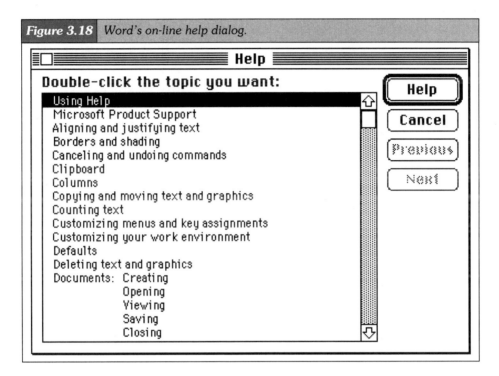

Figure 3.18 *Word's on-line help dialog.*

GRAMMAR CHECKING

This part of Word is a nice help in constructing tight, effective writing. It checks your output against a large number of rules, covering difficulties such as wordy or redundant expressions, inappropriate prepositions, informal expressions, clichés, weak modifiers, and vague quantifiers. Also overlong sentences, like this last one.

Depending on your writing skills, you may want to use this tool often, or you may prefer to use it as an occasional check of writing habits. Some use of it is probably valuable for everyone.

To look at this, put your cursor at the top of your document, and choose **Grammar...** from the Tools menu. You'll see the dialog box shown in Figure 3.19, which, in this case, tells your humble author that he's used a stock phrase.

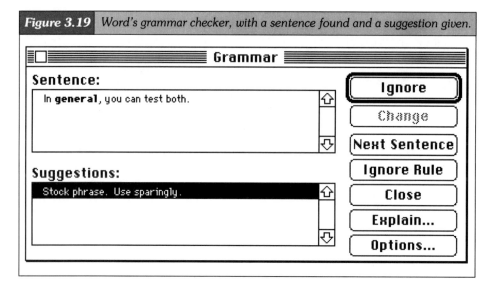

Figure 3.19 *Word's grammar checker, with a sentence found and a suggestion given.*

As you work with this tool, your decisions on the validity and efficacy of its various comments and criticisms depend on your judgment. But options are nice to have.

OUTLINING

Once our writing is spelled correctly, offered rich use of synonyms, and grammatically proper, a larger question comes up. This is one of organization.

Look closely at what you read, and you'll see that professional efforts show careful craftsmanship. Paragraphs follow logically, and each one contains a distinct idea.

A *substantial* help in achieving this kind of quality is offered by computer outlining. Word's oultline module is again an effective tool.

As well, outlining in electronic mode is so fast and easy, it becomes a good way to start almost any piece of writing.

With Word, you can switch back and forth from outline to text at any time, to maintain the good organization of your piece while adding details. To check this out:

1. Start a new document (choose **New** from the File menu).

2 Choose **Outline** from the View menu.

You're given a new ruler, and an icon—an outlined minus sign—appears to the left of your cursor.

3 Type the first line as shown below, and press **Return**.

4 Click the right arrow in the ruler to move your next line to the right.

5 Complete this example, using the right and left arrows.

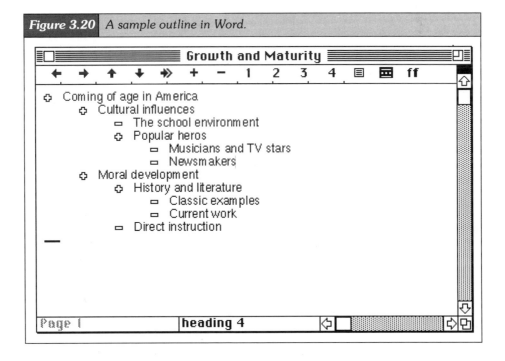

| Figure 3.20 | A sample outline in Word. |

This would be an interesting tool if it only did this much. But an outline in Word is simply another view of a text document, and you can go back and forth between the two views. You can thus reorganize your piece as your thoughts cohere.

N O T E

6 Click and hold on a *heading icon* (plus or minus sign, depending on whether it has subheadings), and drag it elsewhere in the outline.

If your heading has body text with it, such as a paragraph, the whole paragraph moves. Really an effective tool.

OTHER FEATURES

Check out the **Word Count** feature on the Tools menu. This also counts lines and paragraphs.

Try **Find File** on the File menu. You can search for a document by any of a large number of criteria:

Figure 3.21 *Search options from the Find File command.*

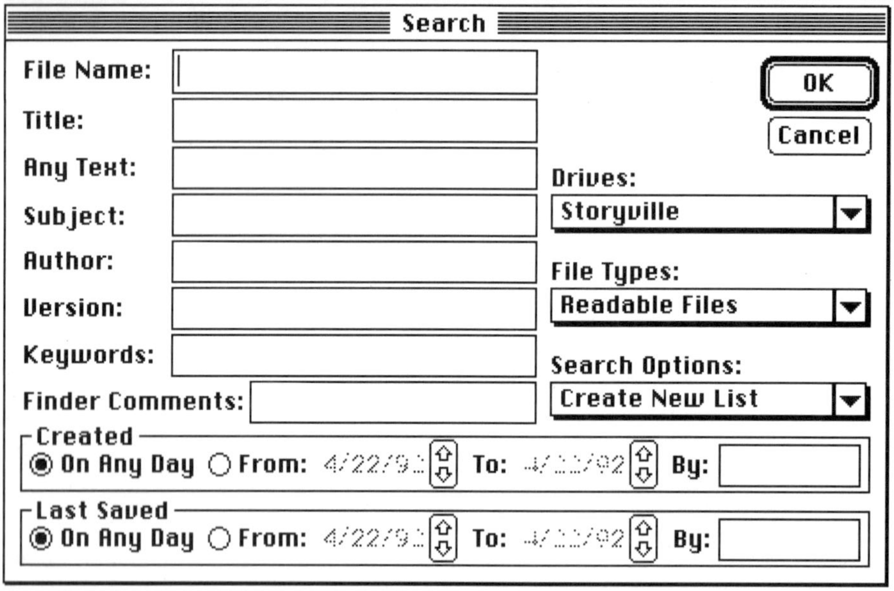

Search	
File Name:	
Title:	
Any Text:	**Drives:**
Subject:	Storyville
Author:	
Version:	**File Types:**
	Readable Files
Keywords:	**Search Options:**
Finder Comments:	Create New List

OK **Cancel**

Created
⦿ On Any Day ○ From: 4/22/9: To: 4/ _ _/92 By:

Last Saved
⦿ On Any Day ○ From: 4/22/9: To: 4/ _ _/92 By:

CHECKLIST

This session has given you all you need for competent and effective word processing. You've covered:

- character attributes and formatting,
- copying and pasting text,
- spell-checking and thesaurus,
- finding and replacing text,
- footnotes, headers, and footers,
- page layout and preview features,
- graphics in a word processing environment,
- grammar checking and outlining.

which is really quite a bit.

OTHER CHOICES

We've learned a popular word processing program, but it's only one of many. The basic operations we've covered here are mostly the same with all of them, but advanced features differ. Which should you buy and use?

Since the market is so big, there's lots of competition and various ideas about which one's really the best. The answer is none of them, since each tool is optimized for a slightly different use. WordPerfect is an excellent tool for serious academic writing, and has elegant page design capability, a comprehensive drawing module, and the best macro feature in town. WriteNow is a clean, fast program that gets in the writer's way very little, but lacks a few advanced features. MacWrite Pro and Nisus are others. One is right for you.

There are more specialized products you may want to look at: More, for example, is a workhorse for many uses. A much smoother and more powerful outliner than what we've seen, effective tree and bullet charts, and extensive graphing capability.

HELPFUL HINTS

When you learned SuperPaint, you of course worked mostly with the mouse, and the keyboard was only occasionally of use. But with word processing, we spend much of our time typing, and use the mouse for a menu command only every so often.

Power computer users like to keep their hands on the keyboard most of the time and, for that reason, Macintosh programs have many keyboard equivalents for menu commands. These do the same thing as using the mouse and the menus, and are often faster. For example, **Command–S** to save your changes. Take some time to practice these.

Word and most other applications list keyboard equivalents next to the command on the menu, as well as providing tables of them in their manuals.

Word also lets you customize menus and keyboard equivalents. You could put a command on a different menu, or give it a new or different keyboard equivalent.

Keyboard equivalents become very useful when you find you're invoking a command a lot, but need to use your mouse every time. Although the mouse is certainly intuitive, there are times when a keyboard command is just faster.

This is partly because we think in different modes, and these are directly related to what we're doing at the time. Thinking in the kind of spatial mode that occurs when we're moving a mouse is different from the more text-based thinking we do at the keyboard.

The experience differs among individuals, but we find that there's an advantage in continuity as well as speed if, when working on the keyboard, we have program commands available there too.

As with choice of programs and graphics modes, the decision here is yours. The name personal computer means more than that it sits on your desk, and others don't use it. It's something that can *work the way you think*.

If you intend to do very much word processing at all, it will be worth your time to learn features such as *glossaries* and *style sheets*, which simplify repetitive tasks and save a lot of time. Accuracy of spelling and consistency of formatting can benefit from these tools. Macros, such as WordPerfect and Nisus have, are also powerful tools towards productivity.

Some writers find they work best in outline mode, moving to full text after their outline is complete and revised. This may not be an easy habit to develop, but many good writers swear by it for organization and coherence. The computer certainly makes it easy enough.

One glaring anomaly in this world of high-tech word processing: the keyboard in front of you. The key layout, called *Qwerty* for the first six letters on the top row of keys, was *designed* to be awkward, to slow typists down, so early manual typewriters wouldn't jam.

Your Macintosh isn't about to jam, but you're using a key map that lets you type only 100 English words from the home row, where your fingers rest. The alternative and ergonomic *Dvorak key map*, by contrast, lets you type 4000 words from the home row.

With Qwerty, you do more work with your left hand, just because more people are right-handed. Dvorak uses the right hand more, but it's surprising how much it alternates the hands, producing a smooth and even flow. This is largely because it places the vowels under the left hand, and the most common consonants under the right. We're using Dvorak to write this book. Wait, there's more.

Studies say that the fingers of the average typist move sixteen miles in eight hours. On the Dvorak map they move one mile. There are portents here for speed and accuracy. Of greater significance, you can type all day without getting tired or, much worse, acquiring a repetitive-motion injury such as carpal-tunnel syndrome.

Free software is available to change key maps. Ask a Mac users' group for Electric Dvorak. Find a users' group per the Tech Note in the Introduction. Some typing tutor programs can teach you the keyboard. But for all its advantages, and an inception in the 1930s, Dvorak's still not too popular—such is (in this case) the curse of a standard.

Q & A

Q: *I choose a different font from the menu, but it doesn't change what I have on the screen.*

A: You have to select existing text for your choice of font to apply to it. Otherwise, your choice affects what you type afterward.

Q: *I click on the Bold or Italic buttons, and there's no effect.*

A: Style choices, like font choices, are applied to existing text only if it's selected first. If you don't select anything first, but click Bold or Italic, that style then governs what you type after you make the style choice.

Q: *I change margin, tabs or alignment in the ruler, and only part of my text changes to match.*

A: Word applies these changes only to the paragraph your insertion point is in, unless you select more than one paragraph worth of text.

Q: *I pasted text, and it appeared in the wrong place.*

A: Text pastes at the insertion point. First click where you want the text to appear, then choose **Paste**.

Q: *The Find option doesn't find what I'm looking for, but I know it's there.*

A: Make sure that you're searching in the right direction. Word looks forward or backward, whichever you tell it to. Also, make sure that you haven't added anything, even an extra space, to what you're telling it to look for.

Q: *I want to delete a footnote. I erased all of the text in the footnote window, but the number still appears in the main text.*

A: The footnote itself is still there, although there's no content to it. Delete the number in your main document, and the note and its text will be gone, and succeeding footnotes renumber to reflect the deletion.

Q: *I want to move a graphic I've inserted.*

A: You can do this only in Print Preview mode. Click and drag to reposition it.

Q: *I placed a graphic, then made some changes to it, and it now has fewer colors than it used to.*

A: Any editing of a graphic in Word reduces the color information to the eight colors available in this program. Consider making all changes in the original graphics program, and then placing it in your Word document.

Q: *The grammar checker flags things I think are silly. What can I do?*

A: This module functions with a list of rules. You can turn off those which cause it to stop at things you don't want to change—passive constructions, for example.

Q: *I like the Dvorak keyboard, but no one else who uses my computer does.*

A: All of the programs that convert a Mac keyboard to the Dvorak map include an easy way to switch back and forth. Put a sign on the computer saying how, to keep everybody happy.

SAMPLE EXERCISE

Enter these two passages: "Playscript" and "Roberto's Lines" as separate documents. Then, with both files open (go back and forth using Word's Window menu), copy your choice of Roberto's lines and paste them into the script. Your finished product should look professional: don't copy the numbers in front of each of Roberto's lines, and be careful with the number of spaces between each character's line.

PLAYSCRIPT

The scene between Samantha and Roberto opens in a desolate and ghostly glen in the forest at midnight. Fog swirls about their knees. Glowing pairs of wolfish eyes dance mysteriously from behind hideously misshapen dead trees. The duo face each other, their movements expressing great agitation.

Samantha: The gods themselves may have no hope for you! The whole of humankind is fluent on computers, and you deign not even to glance at them. Your view of your future is as cloaked in mist as are these forlorn tree-stumps, and your sense of your abilities (relative to current markets) is as leaden and opaque as this night air!

Roberto: [insert choice from Series 1]

Samantha: Fool! Why can you not comprehend? The world will pass you by. Not to be computer-literate in this age is not to be able to think at all!

Roberto: [insert choice from Series 2]

Samantha: I can waste no further moment with so befuddled a lummox as you! I'm off this instant to take the Cornell computer course that produced this book!

Roberto: [insert choice from Series 3]

Samantha: Yes! Is that what it took to make you see the light of common day?

Roberto: [insert choice from Series 4]

Samantha: It's no use! (She storms off, her gown raising eddies and whorls in the heavy fog. In the distance, we see lightning.)

ROBERTO'S LINES:

Series 1:

1. You learned computers in high school. What do you want from me?

2. There just aren't any football computer games I like.

3. If my grandpa ran his farm without computers, so can I!

Series 2:

1. What does "think" mean?

2. I'm sure it's a passing fad.

3. I'll wait until they make one that fits in the dashboard of my 300ZX.

Series 3:

1. Hey wait. Maybe even I could pass that course.

2. Isn't that the class where computers are painless?

3. Someone said that was a course that was actually useful!

Series 4:

1. But—I'd only take it if I could learn to tally up hockey stats.

2. But—my frat's computer is broken—even though it *looked* like a football, last Saturday night about 2 a.m.

3. But—(You can make up an answer here).

CHAPTER 4

INTRODUCTION TO SPREADSHEETS

In this chapter you'll learn:

- what a computer spreadsheet is and how it works
- entering, selecting, and formatting data
- using Microsoft Excel's tool bar
- making formulas to automate and speed calculations
- using on-line Help
- relative and absolute addressing in formulas
- specifics of previewing and printing a spreadsheet
- displaying and checking formulas
- producing different kinds of charts from data ranges

With graphics and word processing, you're at this point as knowledgeable as a large percentage of computer users. With the addition of *spreadsheets*—a structured way of working with numbers—you'll be more accomplished than most people who sit down in front of a PC! So off we go.

Spreadsheets were what gave personal computers their first real start in the marketplace. They demonstrated decisively to a lot of people in different professional or educational situations that the PC was something that anyone could benefit from.

These peoples' vantage point, back in the computer's ice age, was quite different from yours. You've just explored highly sophisticated versions of graphics and word processing conceptions. In the beginning, the advantages these programs had over conventional artists' tools and the ubiquitous typewriter weren't quite so convincing.

Conversely, the difference between a conventional financial, statistical or scientific worksheet, and the electronic versions of each, was enough to settle the question right away. The revolution had rather inauspicious beginnings, though.

Back in 1979 there were a couple of funny guys in a garage in Cupertino, California, who invented and brought to market a novelty called the Apple, and everyone's first question was, "How nice. What do I do with it?"

Of the myriad answers of varying coherence, the best was expressed by the writer of Visicalc, a program that produced what looked like an accountant's worksheet, but with two stupendous differences.

The first was that each *cell*, or area of the worksheet that could hold a number or some words, could also hold a formula that could reference, or access information from, any other cell in the worksheet.

Without formulas, cells are just places to store numbers and text. You could, for example, manually add cell A1 and cell A2 and put the answer in cell A3.

Figure 4.1 *Cell A3 is the sum of A1 and A2. If we change the value in A1, we must manually change the sum in A3 to reflect that change.*

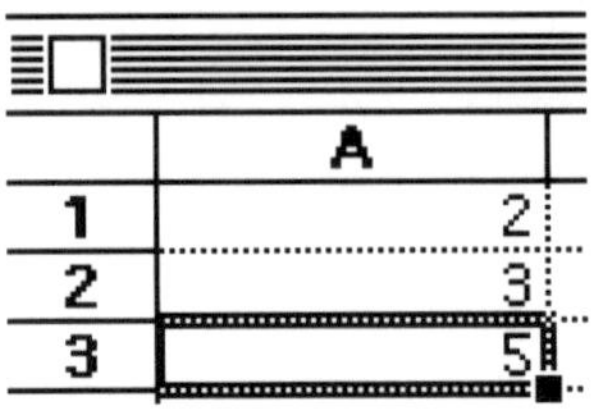

What A3 then contains is a value that could be A1 plus A2, or your sister's street address. Only you know. And if A2 changes, A3 then doesn't mean anything. But on a computer, if what's in A3 is the formula "A1 plus A2," A3 remains accurate. And, if you have another formula in cell H6 that references A3, H6 remains accurate too, and so on forever. It's a pretty good boost in productivity and potential for accuracy.

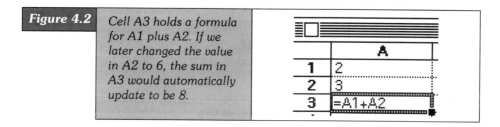

Figure 4.2 *Cell A3 holds a formula for A1 plus A2. If we later changed the value in A2 to 6, the sum in A3 would automatically update to be 8.*

The second reason involves the use of numbers in making predictions. Where the economy goes next year is a function of quite a lot of things, and an accurate forecast is tremendously valuable. By organizing formulas in a worksheet to predict, say, interest rates, you can make changes here and there in prices or GNP and produce any number of "what if" scenarios.

You can also optimize solutions, working backwards from the numbers you want to see, to the numbers you need to have in order to get what you want to see, for instance, to determine affordable interest rates for monthly car payments. This is a powerful tool for allocating resources and minimizing waste. It's a highly visible and specific example of how technology, including computer technology, can really work for the better.

A computer spreadsheet is such an intelligent tool for numbers that you might think it's hard to learn, in some way that graphics or word processing isn't. Wrong. It's all very easy to do and, in terms of raw computing power, *you can do more with a spreadsheet than any other kind of program.* So let's look around Microsoft Excel.

Double-click on the Excel icon to start the application. After the program loads, you should see a screen like Figure 4.3. Notice the similarities, such as windows, menus, scroll bars, and zoom box, to other Mac programs. Now look at the differences: along the top, just below the menus, you'll see the tool bar, and then:

- **Reference to active cell**. With 16 million cells available, this is nice information to have. Depending on where you have scrolled to, the active cell might not be visible in the window.

- **Active cell** (with a thick border around it). Whatever you type is going to go here.

- **Check box**. When you enter information in the active cell, it isn't 'fixed' until you click in this box, or move the active cell with the **Tab** or **Return** keys, or an **Arrow** key.

- **Edit line**. This shows what you've entered in the active cell. Note that depending on how you've formatted your worksheet, the cell itself may not display much of what you've put in it. The edit line shows more, and is generally easier to read anyway.

- **Balloon Help** offers the regular help balloons and, in Excel, is also where you'll find the program's Help feature. (If your Mac is using System 6 instead of 7, Balloon Help won't appear on the menu bar, and Excel's Help appears under the Window menu.) There's also a single help line at the bottom left of your screen.

- **Black rectangles** at the top of the vertical scroll bar and at the left of the horizontal scroll bar. These allow you to split windows so you can look at two parts of your file at once. This is a nice feature common to Microsoft programs.

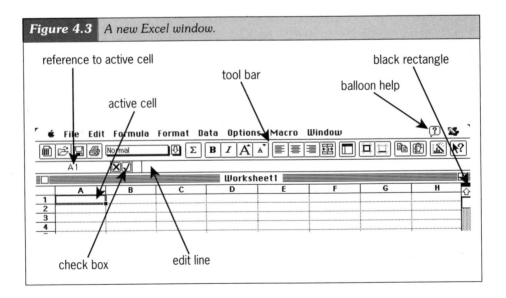

Figure 4.3 | *A new Excel window.*

ENTERING DATA

Note that the worksheet window, below the menus and tools, is divided by dotted lines into several rectangles, or cells, and that each can be identified by its vertical column letter, and its horizontal row number. Thus the cell at the top left is cell A1.

In Figure 4.3, cell A1 is identified as the active cell. If you typed anything at this point, it would go into this cell. Any cell can be active, and it will have the heavier line around it that you see around cell A1 here.

You could then click on another cell, and it would become active. Whatever you typed at that point would go into that second cell.

You could also use your **Arrow** keys, or the **Return** or **Tab** keys, to move from one cell to another.

1 Use your **Arrow** keys to move around the visible part of the worksheet. Another way to move the active cell is just to click on any cell. Note that the cell reference, at the top left, shows which cell is active and the edit line, to the right of the check box, has a blinking cursor—or, if there's data already in the active cell, the edit line reflects this.

2 Type the information shown in Figure 4.4. Don't worry if, when you type a long string of text, not all of it appears in the cell itself. Try to work from the edit line above the worksheet. After you fix the active cell's data by clicking in the check box, what's in A1 spills into B1 if there's nothing entered in B1.

Figure 4.4 *Your first worksheet in Excel.*

	A	B	C	D	E	F
1	My First Worksheet					
2						Category
3	Income		October	November	December	Total
4						
5	Bootlegging		2345.22	1950.86	2640.7	6936.78
6	Bribes		3260.78	3100	2450.1	8810.88
7	Protection		400	400	400	1200
8	Day Job		1500.56	1500.56	1500.56	4501.68
9						
10	Monthly total					
11						
12	Quarterly total					
13						

My First Worksheet

Then save your work—this isn't too soon at all for a Save.

SELECTING RANGES OF CELLS

Now that we have some data, let's format it. The text in cells A1 through A12 would benefit by being in bold type.

The first step is selecting what we want to work with. This is the standard Macintosh paradigm: select something, then choose what to do to it.

The quickest way to select a block of cells like A1 to A12 (such a block is referred to as A1..A12 in spreadsheet land) is to click and drag, much like in word processing.

N O T E

1. Click in cell A1 and hold your mouse button down.

2. Drag to cell A12. When this range of cells shows as selected, release the mouse button.

Another way to select a range is to select the cell in one corner of the block you want to work with. Go to the diagonally opposite corner, hold down the **Shift** key, and click on that cell. Note that this para-

N O T E digm works with a lot of data on the Mac: in Word, for example, you can click to set the cursor in front of a group of words, then Shift-click your mouse at the end of the group.

You can also click on a column letter or a row number to select that entire column or row. Try this. Click in any non-selected cell to deselect the selected area.

Or, you can select the entire worksheet by clicking on cell A0, the top-most left cell in the window (to the left of A and above 1). Try this too.

As a note, since one of the things you can do with large amounts of data selected is quickly erase that data accidentally, it's a good idea to save before selecting much of anything. Then again, it's a good idea to

WARNING save before doing much of anything at all.

New computer users generally get into most of the trouble they get into because they don't save often enough. We wish to reiterate that this is not our fault.

With your data in A1 through A12 (or A1..A12) selected:

1 Choose **Font** from the Format menu. You'll see a dialog box like Figure 4.5:

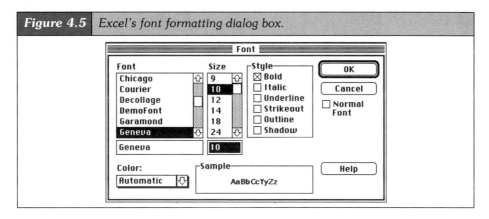

Figure 4.5 | *Excel's font formatting dialog box.*

2 Confirm your choice of bold text by clicking in the appropriate box, and then clicking **OK**.

TOOLS OF THE TRADE

Above the edit line are icons for useful tools for many of the most common ways you'll be manipulating your data. Parts of the tool bar are:

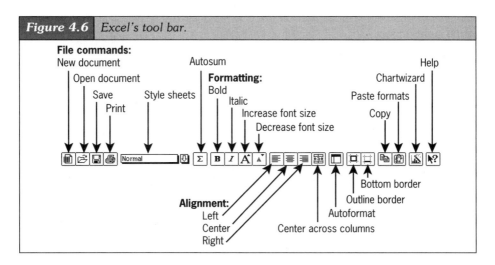

Figure 4.6 | *Excel's tool bar.*

All offer commands that can be addressed more specifically through the menus, but which are immediately available in their most common forms here.

If you don't see the tool bar, go to the Options menu and choose **Workspace**, to display the toolbar.

Let's start exploring these by formatting some more of the data we've just entered.

FAST FORMATTING

Excel gives you a lot of flexibility to format your worksheet, an especially valuable feature when laser-printing files for reports and presentations, but also a useful feature simply for ease of recognition of different parts of your work.

1 Select cells C2 through F3 (or C2..F3), and click on the **Bold** icon in the tool bar.

2 Then click on the **Alignment Center** icon, the middle of the three in that group.

Another nice aspect of formatting is changing column width or row height. These features are available from the Format menu, allowing precision. A quicker way is to position your cursor at the border between two column headings (where the letters are), and see how the cursor changes shape as shown in Figure 4.7, between the column headings A and B.

Figure 4.7	*A formatted worksheet.*

	A	B	C	D	E
1	My First Worksheet				
2					
3	Income		October	November	December
4					
5	Bootlegging		$2,345.22	$1,950.86	$2,640.70
6	Bribes		$3,260.78	$3,100.00	$2,450.10
7	Protection		$400.00	$400.00	$400.00
8	Day Job		$1,500.56	$1,500.56	$1,500.56

My First Worksheet

3 Click and drag either to the left or right, and the columns change width accordingly. Try this on rows also.

Now let's format the numbers as shown in Figure 4.7. We could have typed these dollar signs, but why not just enter numbers, then select a range of cells and format them as currency? To do this formatting, though, we have to go to the menus.

4 Select C5..E8 and, from the Format menu, choose **Number**. Your dialog box should look like Figure 4.8.

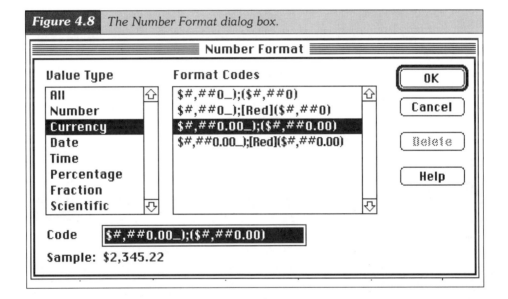

Figure 4.8 *The Number Format dialog box.*

5 Format all of the dollar values in cells C5 to E8 as currency. Use the cents option, as highlighted in the example.

WORKING WITH A WORKSHEET

So far, what you've done could be done with pencil and paper (or at least a fancy typewriter). Here's where we leave the ground. We'll take these income figures and apply formulas to them, both to ensure the accuracy of calculation results (if the formulas are accurate), and to automate copious quantities of work.

If the formulas are accurate? Yes. Not that it's hard to make accurate formulas, but spreadsheets become such great time-savers that lots of people get sloppy with formulas, then wonder how they could make a mistake with a computer.

This points up an old slogan in the computer world: "Garbage in, garbage out." Formulas are easy, but beg to be checked. Let's enter a formula first.

1. Find the total income for October. That would be the sum of cells C5 through C8. Let's put that total in C10. So click in C10, to make that the active cell and so that whatever we enter next is going there.

2. Watch the edit line, and type an equals (=) sign. In Excel, all formulas begin with an equals sign. Type this:

= c5+c6+c7+c8

(no need to capitalize the letters) and then click in the check box just to the left of the edit line.

Wow! and congratulations, you've just entered your first formula.

Half of the point of this is that should you find later that the actual figure for bootlegging for October were not accurate, you could change it, and your total income for October, in cell C10, would change automatically.

N O T E

Slick, but too much typing. So let's use a shortcut to find the total income for November.

3. Click in cell D10, and then on the **Autosum** icon in the tool bar, then in the check box. Excel goes looking for something to add up, and suggests C10, the closest. Nope. Drag through D5..D8, and notice how the formula in the edit line changes to reflect your choice. Now click in the check box. Smooth.

Let's have Excel do even more for us. If the Mac can copy and paste graphics and text, why not formulas?

4. Click in D10, and choose **Copy** from the Edit menu. Then click in cell E10, where we want the totals for December, and choose **Paste**. Voilà, there's the December total.

N O T E Excel gave us the December totals because formulas normally reference the cells *relative* to the cell where you're entering the formula. It moved everything it referenced one cell to the right, because you copied and pasted a formula one cell to the right.

Now we'll put in the category totals. Click in F5, and let's get the total for the category Bootlegging.

Instead of using the Autosum button, this time we'll enter the Total function (or SUM) in the same way we enter Excel's hundreds of other functions:

1 Come up to the Formula menu, and choose **Paste Function**. Scroll down the Paste Function list. Impressive, no?

2 Select **SUM** and click **OK**. Note that the function, properly preceded by the equals sign, is now on the Edit line, with the blinking cursor between the parentheses. Or—

Depending on how your copy of Excel is set up, you may see "(number1,number2,...)," with "number1" selected. Drag through "number1,number2,..." leaving the parentheses, to select this text, and press the **Delete** key on your keyboard.

3 Click and hold on C5 and drag to cell E5. Watch the Edit line as you do this. Click on the check box.

To add formulas for the other category totals:

4 Click in F5 and choose **Copy**. Then drag to select cells F6 through F8. Choose **Paste**. Starting to see how much time this thing can save?

Note that totals you're adding from cells already formatted as currency also show as currency.

5 Put the total for the quarter in F10. It's probably easiest to copy a formula for one of the monthly totals and paste it in F10. Then what we want to do is put this same value in C12. So click in C12, click in the edit line, type *=F10*, and click in the check box.

So whatever's in F10 also appears in C12. This is a simple trick for moving information around a worksheet, especially a large one.

6 Save your work again. **Command–S** is the best friend you have at this point.

A SECOND SECTION

Let's do an expenses and totals section of the worksheet.

1 Scroll down to a blank area of your worksheet, say A15, and enter what you see in Figure 4.9.

Figure 4.9 *The Expenses and Totals section. In cells C28..C31, don't enter text in parenthese; enter formulas that compute these.*

≣☐ My First Worksheet ≣

	A	B	C	D	E	F
15	Expenses					Category
16						Total
17	Food		$125.00	$135.00	$160.00	
18	Housing		$350.00	$350.00	$350.00	
19	Utilities		$45.00	$55.00	$72.00	
20	Fun		$125.00	$150.00	$100.00	
21	Car Payment					
22						
23	Monthly total					
24						
25						
26	Quarterly Financial Report					
27						
28	Gross Profits		(Total income – total expenses)			
29	Income tax rate		(Constant. e.g. 15%)			
30	Tax witholding		(Tax rate * Gross Profits			
31	Net income		(Gross Profits – Tax witholdings)			

2 Total the months and categories. Include the cells that indicate Car Payment, even though we haven't figured that out yet.

This is another fun part of spreadsheets: We can include that payment in a formula and, when the payment data becomes available the formula accurately includes that expense.

N O T E

And now's a good point to save again. You've done quite a bit so far.

It's actually a good idea to save more often than recommended here. Experienced computer users hit **Command–S** almost every time they stop typing to look at something.

At this point, we can figure out the car payment:

1 Enter the data in A36..B38 of Figure 4.10. Then Click in cell C21, in preparation for entering the payment formula.

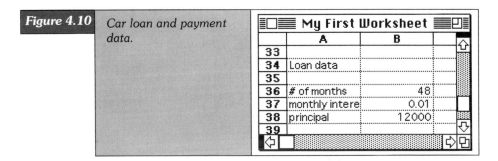

Figure 4.10 Car loan and payment data.

	A	B
33		
34	Loan data	
35		
36	# of months	48
37	monthly intere	0.01
38	principal	12000
39		

2 Look up *Microsoft Excel Help* under the *Help balloon menu*, to learn how to figure the monthly payment.

Figure 4.11 Excel's initial Help window.

You have the raw data already. What you need is the *order of parameters* that the formula argument requires. That's just the order of things we enter in the formula.

So scroll to the Reference section of the first Help window, and then:

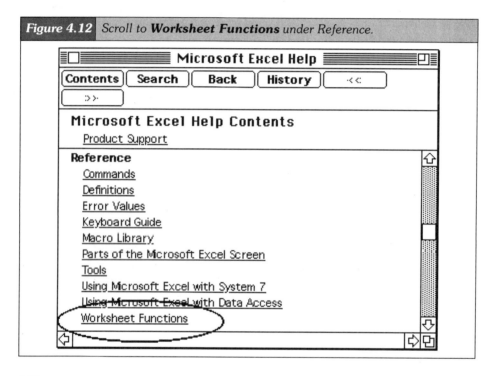

Figure 4.12   *Scroll to* **Worksheet Functions** *under Reference.*

3 Click once on **Worksheet Functions**, once on **Financial Functions**, and then scroll down to PMT().

It tells you that the argument is: PMT (rate, nper, pv, fv, type) and explains what those mean.

4 Exit Help and, with C21 as the active cell:

5 Enter the formula for your car payment by entering =PMT() through pasting the function. Select and remove the text, if any (another description of the order of parameters) between the parentheses, or just click between the parentheses, so that what we enter next goes there.

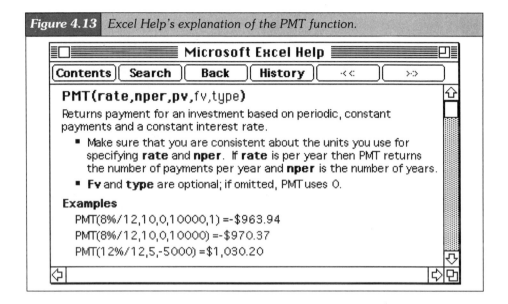

Figure 4.13 *Excel Help's explanation of the PMT function.*

We're going to enter parts to the formula a different way this time: by clicking directly on the cell which holds the value we want to go in the formula.

6 Click on the **monthly rate**, and type a comma.

7 Click on the **number of months**, and type another comma, and then:

8 Click on the **principal**, or present value, of the loan.

9 Click in the check box to the left of the edit line to fix the formula.

10 Now scroll up to see what's in C21. That is the correct payment and, per accounting procedures, it's a negative value. What we want is a positive value to add to other expenses, so:

11 Go to the edit line and add *-1 to the end of the formula (after the last parenthesis) and click on the check box again. The value should change to positive, but stay the same figure.

We're going to copy this formula to get car payments for the other months, but let's be careful here. Remember that our copying and pasting of formulas so far has used the default relative addressing, not absolute addressing. Here's the difference:

Figure 4.14	*Light arrows represent relative addressing; the heavy arrow absolute addressing.*

We wanted October's income total from October's figures, and November's total from November's figures. So we just took the SUM formula in C10 and copied it to D10. D10 then addresses cells in the same relative position as C10's formula does.

The formula for the car payment, in C21, uses data in B36..B38. If we copied C21 to D21, the formula in D18 would address data in the same relative position as C18 does.

But since there's no data in C36..C38, and the data in B36..B38 are valid for all months anyway, we need to make the formula in C21 absolute, so that we can then copy it anywhere and it will continue to reference B36..B38.

We stipulate absolute addressing in spreadsheets by means of dollar signs in front of the cell addresses.

So let's change the formula in C21.

12 Click on that cell, and you should see (on the edit line):

=PMT(B37,B36,B38)*-1

Change that to read:

=PMT(B37,B36,B38)*-1

If you get tired of typing dollar signs, putting your cursor within any cell address and typing **Command-T** toggles the dollar signs (both the first and second ones, independently) on and off.

SHORTCUT

13 Copy this formula to D21 and E21.

14 Put in the category and monthly totals for the expense section. Your Quarterly Financial Report should now be complete.

Sit back for a moment. This is a lot of pretty sophisticated stuff. But what you've just done is master a big part of spreadsheet operation. Relative and absolute addressing are not easy concepts to grasp, so you might want to go through this exercise again sometime this week. Pat yourself on the back for having done this—and never needing to go back to manual calculations again.

PRINTING

Printing from a spreadsheet is much like printing graphics and word processing files, with one big difference. Since spreadsheets can get so large, Excel asks you which part you want to print. So the first step is:

1 **Set the print area**. Select the area of your worksheet you want to print. Then use the Options menu to **Set Print Area**. Note the dotted line around this part of your sheet.

2 Choose **Print** from the File menu and notice that, in addition to the usual items in the dialog box, there's a **Print Preview** below the paper feed options (as well as on the File menu itself, should you want to choose it for one occasion, rather than as a default. Better to leave it checked in the dialog box, though). This is a real time- and paper-saver with spreadsheets.

3 Click on the words **Print Preview** to turn on this check box. Don't click in the box—it takes too much of your time to guide the mouse to it. Click on

Figure 4.15	The Print dialog box, with Print Preview checked.

```
LaserWriter  "John's RISCY Laser"              7.1.1     [ Print ]
Copies:[1]          Pages: ⦿ All ○ From:[    ] To:[    ]   [ Cancel ]
Cover Page:   ⦿ No ○ First Page ○ Last Page
Paper Source: ⦿ Paper Cassette ○ Manual Feed
Print:          ⦿ Black & White    ○ Color/Grayscale
Destination:   ⦿ Printer           ○ PostScript® File
⊠ Print Preview        □ Print Using Color    [ Help ]
┌Print────────────────────────────────────┐
│ ⦿ Sheet      ○ Notes       ○ Both         │
└──────────────────────────────────────────┘
```

the words, and then click **OK**. Excel gives you a view of your print area, reduced as necessary to fit your screen.

[4] When you actually want to print what you see, click **Print**. For now, click **Close** to return to your working document.

DISPLAYING FORMULAS

Another (!) nice thing about electronic spreadsheets is that you can print them showing the actual formulas, rather than the values they produce.

This is especially helpful for error-checking because, with the great savings in time that spreadsheets produce, users tend not to check their formulas enough.

The classic story tells how a company lost over one hundred thousand dollars on a bid because of one error in a formula. Since then, many corporations ask you to print worksheets with formulas displayed so that an associate can check them. To do this:

[1] Choose **Display...** from the Options menu, and select **Formulas** from the resulting dialog box.

You may end up with columns wider than needed to see entire formulas. If so:

[2] Double-click on the line separating two column letters for a 'best fit', or click once on the line and drag to set the desired width.

Figure 4.16 Values are displayed in the illustration on the left; formulas on the right. A label on a calculated number is no guarantee of its accuracy. Checking formulas is one of the most important parts of working with spreadsheet programs.

	A	B
1	Value 1	662
2	Value 2	667
3	Value 3	670
4	Value 4	676
5	Value 5	680
6		
7	Total 1-5	2675
8	Mean 1-5	668.75
9	St. Dev. 1-5	5.85

	A	B
1	Value 1	662
2	Value 2	667
3	Value 3	670
4	Value 4	676
5	Value 5	680
6		
7	Total 1-5	=SUM(B1:B4)
8	Mean 1-5	=AVERAGE(B1:B4)
9	St. Dev. 1-5	=STDEV(B1:B4)

If the increased column widths make your printouts larger than one page, you can reduce the font size for the worksheet, or print it out sideways (in *landscape* orientation, rather than *portrait*).

To do this, go to the File menu, and:

3 Choose **Page Setup**. In the resulting dialog box, note the options for orientation, header and footer, and margins. Then go to **Print Preview** to see how this looks. Note also that you can omit gridlines and row/column headings

Figure 4.17 The Page Setup dialog box.

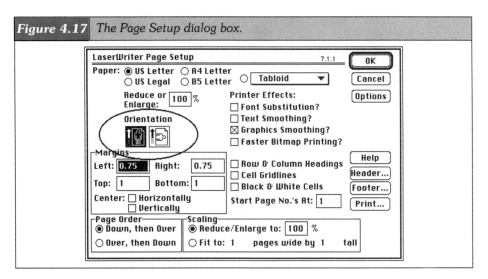

from printing. You can also prevent them from displaying, a choice made by choosing **Display** from the Options menu. What displays and what prints are independent here, something of a departure from Mac WYSIWYG.

GRAPHICS

Here's the most fun part of the Excel program. It also bears on an important fact about information: although the numbers might be valuable and useful, they're often less understandable as numbers than as charts.

Excel lets you take numbers and make charts—and *you can include these charts, as well as the numbers, in your word processing documents*. You can also work up nice presentations, with numbers and graphics for slides or brochures, right out of the Excel program.

It's so easy that users tend to produce charts that are beautiful but not very useful. Have an idea what you want to say with a chart before you make it.

Let's make a presentation, including numbers and chart, of your income for the last quarter. First, let's copy that part of your sheet to a new one.

1. Select cells A1 through F10.

2. Choose **Copy** from the Edit menu.

3. Choose **New** from the File menu, and specify new worksheet.

4. Choose **Paste** from the Edit menu, and save this data to disk.

These are the numbers we'll present. To make a chart:

1. Select the income categories in A5 through A8.

2. Hold down the **Command** key, and drag through the totals in F5 through F8. This is called *selecting discontiguous regions* of the sheet. With these two areas selected:

3. Click on the **ChartWizard tool** in the tool bar. Your selected areas now have dotted lines running around them.

4. Click in the top left corner of A12, and hold your mouse button down.

5 Drag to the bottom right corner of F24, and release the mouse button. You'll see the first of a series of dialog boxes asking you for specifics about your chart.

6 Click **Next** in the **ChartWizard–Step 1 of 5** dialog box. Click **Next** on each of the succeeding series of steps, to choose:

- chart type: **Column**

- format: **1**

- Excel's suggestions for the Sample Chart

- the second set of suggestions. Click **OK**.

Presto. Excel has drawn a chart of the numbers you selected, in the area you selected.

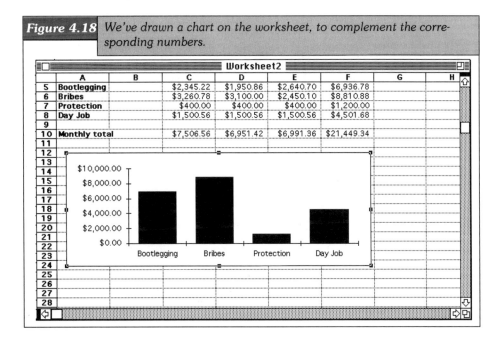

Figure 4.18 *We've drawn a chart on the worksheet, to complement the corresponding numbers.*

Nice, but we wanted a pie chart. To fix that,

1 Double-click on the chart, to put it into its own window. Note that the menu bar has changed as well. Now we can modify the chart.

2 Select **Pie...** from the Gallery menu and choose option 6, which includes percentages, and click **OK**.

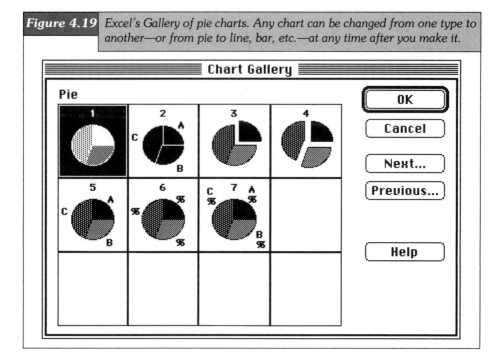

Figure 4.19   *Excel's Gallery of pie charts. Any chart can be changed from one type to another—or from pie to line, bar, etc.—at any time after you make it.*

Pretty nice, but 'twould be better with a legend. So, from the Chart menu:

3 Choose **Add Legend**. There you go—not bad for a day's work. To finish up:

4 Choose **Attach Text** from the Chart menu, and **OK** the resulting dialog box, indicating that you want to attach text to the title. The word *Title* now shows in the Edit line.

5 Double-click on the word *Title* to select it, and type in *Category Totals*. Click in the check box. Then, with the title still selected—it has handles around it, to show it's selected—

6 Choose **Font** from the Format menu and choose what font, size, and style you'd like for your title. Then click in the chart window's close box. You should end up with something like this, pretty professional by anyone's standards:

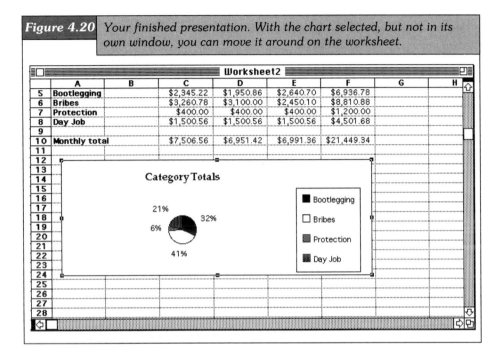

Figure 4.20 Your finished presentation. With the chart selected, but not in its own window, you can move it around on the worksheet.

CHECKLIST

It's hard to overestimate the value of what you've learned today. Business, government and education rely on fast numbers and meaningful presentation to make intelligent decisions. The ability of the personal computer to do so well in this area was historically the largest single factor in convincing people that their desk should have space for one.

Spreadsheet features you can now use include:

- data entry and formatting with dialog boxes and the tool bar,

- formulas,

- cell addressing, relative and absolute, and

- structured graphics.

OTHER CHOICES

Excel's main competitors are Lotus 1-2-3 and Claris Resolve. Both of these and Excel are written to exchange data with Lotus' best-selling spreadsheet for the IBM PC.

Lotus for the Mac has the feature set to match Excel, adds three-dimensionality to spreadsheets, and is a well-designed tool. Resolve is less expensive but also noteworthy and is, like Lotus, a newer entry in the marketplace than Excel. Choice of program in this area is a difficult one.

Q & A

Q: Is there a shortcut to select the entire worksheet? I want to do global formatting.

A: Click in cell A0, so to speak—the blank box above row 1 and to the left of column A.

Q: My screen doesn't show the tool bar.

A: Choose **Workspace** from the Options menu, to give you choices about what Excel displays.

Q: I want to format my numbers as currency, but the Format command doesn't work.

A: As in word processing, you have to select first, then format.

Q: Excel is representing my formulas as text.

A: For Excel to recognize a formula as such, it needs to begin with an equals sign.

Q: I enter a formula in a cell, and then get "REF!" or "NUM!" as a result.

A: Your formula makes an incorrect reference, or it attempts to divide by zero. Be patient and methodical when checking formulas.

Q: *I'm having trouble printing, and getting the parts of the worksheet I want on one page.*

A: Changing font size (or the font selection as well) can help here. So can using the landscape orientation.

Q: *When selecting cells, when do I use the Command key or the Shift key?*

A: Selecting a range, and then holding down the **Shift** key to select further, works as in Word: you'll select everything between the original selection and your more recent choice. The **Command** key, conversely, lets you select discontiguous regions—groups of cells separated by other cells you don't want to select.

Q: *My chart seems too small for the size window I give it.*

A: Excel makes good use of white space, an important feature in presentation. Simply put, charts and numbers are easier to comprehend if there's empty space around them. Matching chart size to the numbers behind it takes practice—formatting the numbers as larger is one option.

SAMPLE EXERCISE

Start a new worksheet to hold and present data about an interest of yours that *doesn't* relate to finance. Since spreadsheets are stereotyped to finance, many computer users lose sight of their myriad other applications—a shame, because almost any time you have a list with more than one column, a spreadsheet can do that for you. Clubs, collections, car repair records… and then see how helpful formulas and charting can be.

CHAPTER 5

ADVANCED SPREADSHEETS

In this chapter you'll learn:

- Balloon help for spreadsheet use

- multiple worksheets

- linking two worksheets to a third

- combining worksheets

- working with split and multiple windows

- naming and locating spreadsheet regions

- attaching notes to worksheet cells

- altering variables to predict outcomes

- solving backwards from an outcome to its components

- advanced charting functions

- macros

- multitasking

- publish and subscribe

In the last chapter, we looked at an application that you might use more in a business environment than any other. Excel is also an especially large and complex application, but current trends in software are producing programs like these—there are enough features for everyone, and so many that most users don't explore all of the application's possibilities.

This chapter explores some of Excel's advanced features, for two reasons: first, it's such a useful tool, and second, it demonstrates that with applications like Excel (and FileMaker Pro, which we'll look at in the next chapter), there's simply a great deal that these programs can do.

ON-LINE HELP

In the last chapter, we looked at Excel's context-sensitive help, available from System 7's Help Balloon menu (or Window menu for a Macintosh on System 6), and noted Excel has a second Help function, in the form of one-line guides at the bottom left of the screen. Excel has a third kind of help, the help balloons themselves like those in the Finder. To use these, Balloon Help must be turned on.

1 Start up Excel in the usual way.

2 Choose **Show Balloons** from the Help Balloon menu.

3 Move your mouse over, for example, Excel's tool bar. You should get informative balloons about that tool or part of the screen.

Note that all tools are still operational. The process of drawing balloons slows operations down a little, though, so users usually turn Show Balloons off after they learn a program.

MULTIPLE WORKSHEETS

Assume that you are a Superintendent of Schools, and are preparing budget proposals to present to the School Board for your elementary school and high school, reflecting a target increase for the coming year of 5 percent. The principals of your two schools, Auburn and Cedar Ridge, have prepared two Excel worksheets for your use.

1 Enter, save and close these two worksheets, as shown below.

Figure 5.1 | *Estimated budgets for two schools.*

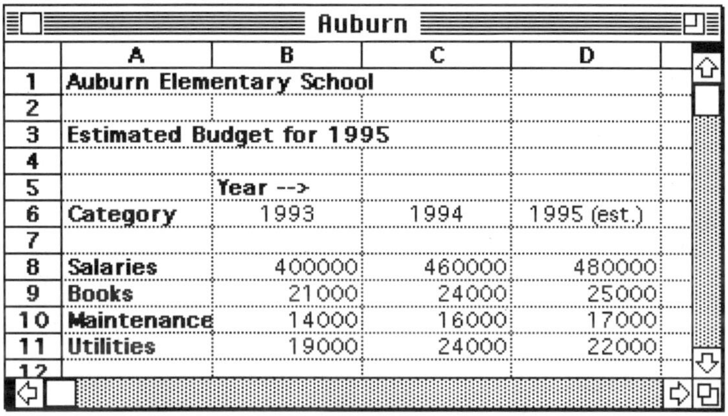

Auburn

	A	B	C	D
1	Auburn Elementary School			
2				
3	Estimated Budget for 1995			
4				
5		Year -->		
6	Category	1993	1994	1995 (est.)
7				
8	Salaries	400000	460000	480000
9	Books	21000	24000	25000
10	Maintenance	14000	16000	17000
11	Utilities	19000	24000	22000
12				

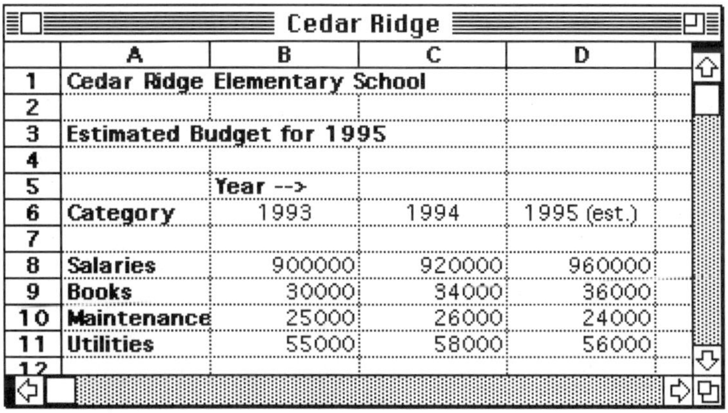

Cedar Ridge

	A	B	C	D
1	Cedar Ridge Elementary School			
2				
3	Estimated Budget for 1995			
4				
5		Year -->		
6	Category	1993	1994	1995 (est.)
7				
8	Salaries	900000	920000	960000
9	Books	30000	34000	36000
10	Maintenance	25000	26000	24000
11	Utilities	55000	58000	56000
12				

At this point, let's say that these two worksheets have been prepared for your use, and are on your disk.

All you have to do now is find them, and it's sometimes easiest to do that in the Finder, the part of the Macintosh we covered in chapter 1. It uses windows and icons to show what's on disks and in folders, and to copy files from one place to another.

The Finder has another function, that of searching all of the disks in a computer for a certain file. We looked at this in Chapter 1. What's important to realize now is that this tool is available to us, no matter which program we're in, by switching back to the Finder for the search.

SHORTCUT

[2] Make your Excel window(s) smaller than screen size—especially, leave some room on the right, where the Finder shows disk icons.

[3] Look at the very top right of your menu bar. Since you're presently in Excel, you'll see a miniature version of its icon, as in Figure 5.2.

Figure 5.2	*The Excel icon (left) and Finder icon (right), as seen at the right of the menu bar when these programs are active.*		

[4] Click on that icon, and you'll see a menu drop. You'll see a list of open applications, programs currently running, and the Finder is one of them.

The Finder is always running. Right now, Excel is in front of it on your screen, much like one window in a program can be in front of another window of the same program.

N O T E

[5] Choose the **Finder**, to bring it to the front of Excel. The Finder's miniature icon now shows at the right of the menu bar, again like Figure 5.2.

[6] Use the **Find** option from the Finder's File menu to locate the Auburn and Cedar Ridge files. Move them both into the same folder, if they're not already together.

[7] Select one of them and then, holding down the **Shift** key:

[8] Click on the other to select it as well.

We call this *Shift-clicking*, and use it a lot on the Mac to select multiple items.

[9] Choose **Open** from the File menu (or type **Command-O**).

This amazing machine goes from the Finder back to Excel, and opens both of these Excel files. This is a great 'power feature' that experienced Mac users just love.

Now that the individual schools' worksheets are open, let's make a new sheet for your consolidated budget.

1 Start a new worksheet, and type in the information you see in Figure 5.3. Column A is a bit narrow for your use so, after entering the data, widen it by double-clicking on the line in the column headings (between A and B), so that the contents of A3 ("Target increase=") is completely visible in the cell.

2 Save this worksheet. This isn't too early to save it. Call it *Con.Budget*.

Figure 5.3	*Your Consolidated Budget worksheet.*

Con.Budget

	A	B	C	D	E	F
1	MacDonald County Schools: Consolidated Budget Predictions for 1995					
2						
3	Target Increase=	0.05				
4						
5		Year -->				
6	Category	1993	1994	1995 (goal)	1995 (est.)	
7						
8	Salaries	1300000	1380000			
9	Books	51000	58000			
10	Maintenance	39000	42000			
11	Transportation	85000	88000			
12	Utilities	74000	82000			
13						
14						

3 Enter a formula in D8 to give us the goal for salaries for 1995, which will be the 1994 figure plus the target increase of 5 percent. This is =**C8*(1+B3)** where (1+B3) amounts to the present value plus the increase, or 1.05 percent.

We want this calculation in D9 through D12 too, but if we just pasted it as is, we'd end up with the same problems with relative addressing we found in chapter four. So,

4 Change the formula in cell D8 so that B3 reads B3. Just click in **B3** in the formula, and type **Command-T**. Copy it, and paste it into D9 through D12. Just select the range D9..D12, and choose **Paste**.

Note that a single dollar sign before B3 (or before the 3) would not work for our purposes—that would hold only the vertical (or horizontal) component absolute, while we need both components absolute.

While we want B3 to be an absolute reference in this formula, we do *not* want this for C8, so that the pasted formulas accurately address the various categories of expenditures.

5 | Enter *Total Budget* in A14. Enter a formula that totals expenditures in column B. If you like, you can click B14 and then click **Autosum** in the tool bar, but note that Autosum suggests the range B8..B13, while your layout has left B13 blank. Fine, but should you later enter a number in B13, the total in B14 includes it.

This can spell either convenience or disaster, so it's good either to change the formula, or keep in mind Autosum's way of doing things.

6 | Copy this and paste it into C14:E14. For these formulas, relative addressing is just what we want.

7 | Save again at this point. You've done a lot already.

Here's a good place for what's called a Power User's Tip. If you ever want to make a lot of money fast, publish a book of these tips. Computer users go crazy over them.

SHORTCUT

This tip is: what if you make a mistake in a formula—one of your references is wrong, say, and you can't find it. You could if you had another five minutes but, just at this moment, you need to do something else with the worksheet. For example, you may need to help someone who's just called on the phone.

Excel won't let you do anything else until that formula's right—so edit out the equals sign, and make it into text. The cell just displays the botched formula as though it were text and, when you have time, you can come back and fix it.

Back to business: let's look at how we can greatly magnify the power of a worksheet, by linking two or more together so that they can literally talk to each other.

LINKING WORKSHEETS

1 | Look at Excel's Window menu. You should have three open worksheets at this time. What we're going to do is *link* information from the Auburn and Cedar Ridge worksheets into your Consolidated Budget.

Rather than just copying information, linking creates a *dynamic relationship* between cells in different worksheets, so that should the Auburn sheet later be revised, that alteration updates your
N O T E Consolidated sheet automatically.

2 Bring the Consolidated sheet to the front with the Window menu.

3 Click in E8, and we'll enter a formula that links to the estimated salaries for the Auburn and Cedar Ridge schools.

4 Type an *equals* sign and then, with the Window menu,

Figure 5.4 *Linking data from the Auburn and Cedar Ridge sheets into the Consolidated worksheet.*

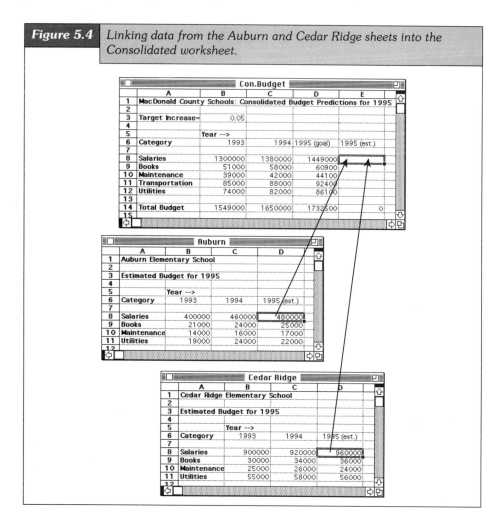

5 Bring the Auburn sheet to the front and click in its cell D8.

6 Bring Cedar Ridge to the front, and click in D8.

7 Then click in the check box to complete the formula. This brings Consolidated to the front again, and E8 should be the sum of D8 for both schools' worksheets.

Linking data is a powerful way to use a spreadsheet. Take a moment to review what you've just accomplished. Repeat the steps if you don't understand the concept behind this.

8 Repeat this for Books, Maintenance and Utilities.

Entering data in a linked worksheet is the same as entering data in any other worksheet:

9 Increase the 1994 figure for transportation by 5 percent in your Consolidated sheet, since transportation is not included in each school's sheet, to complete your estimated costs for 1995. The formula for this is **=C11*1.05**.

An elegant feature worth a quick look is how Excel maintains links, whether documents are opened or closed.

1 Close your Con.Budget worksheet, saving changes.

2 In Auburn, change D8 to $520,000. Close it, saving your change.

3 Open Con.Budget again. Excel asks if you want to update references to unopened documents, in this case Auburn. Click **Yes**.

Excel knew that you had changed Auburn, and that the change would reflect in Con.Budget. This works only as long as you don't change the name or location of Auburn, since that's how Excel identifies the links between worksheets.

As well, Excel gives you the option to open any sheet linked to the one you're working with, by the Links option on the File menu. But why have all links open all the time? It just takes up memory.

Rather than link separate worksheets, another way is to combine small sheets into one large one. This option doesn't let others update the smaller pieces to a big puzzle, and it gives the user the additional headache of having to navigate around a larger worksheet (although Excel has several features to make navigation easier).

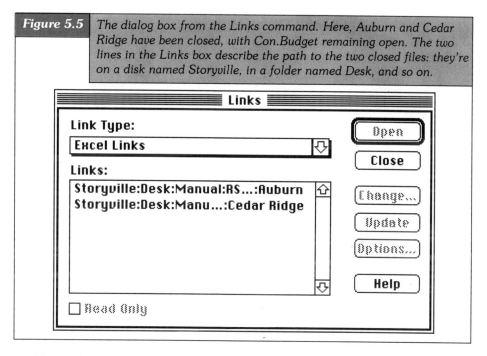

Figure 5.5 | The dialog box from the Links command. Here, Auburn and Cedar Ridge have been closed, with Con.Budget remaining open. The two lines in the Links box describe the path to the two closed files: they're on a disk named Storyville, in a folder named Desk, and so on.

But earlier versions of computer spreadsheets didn't allow a linking structure, and many users learned to combine smaller sheets into larger ones. So let's combine ours.

1. Open Auburn and select the range A1:D13. Do this either by clicking in A1 and dragging to D13, or by clicking in A1 and Shift-clicking in D13.

2. Copy this, then bring Con.Budget to the front, activate A17 and select **Paste**. Excel pastes from the top left.

3. Do this for Cedar Ridge, pasting from A33.

Now, even though the Auburn and Cedar Ridge sheet information is contained within Con.Budget, the links in Con.Budget remain with the separate schools' sheets. We need to change this.

So let's revise some formulas. We'll simply go back to estimated salaries in the Auburn and Cedar Ridge *areas* of Con.Budget, and include those in the formula in E8 in Con.Budget.

Overall, an easy maneuver. The only difficult part might be scrolling from one point to the other without getting lost. A major difficulty with large worksheets is seeing what you need to at one time. Con.Budget, in a real implementation, could easily be larger than your screen. Two useful features here are *split windows* and *multiple windows*.

1 Look at your scroll bars. Just above the top arrow on the vertical bar, and just to the left of the left arrow on the horizontal bar, are the two small black rectangles used to split windows, as shown in Figure 5.6.

Figure 5.6 *Black rectangles to split windows.*

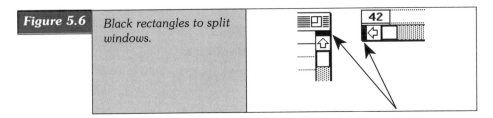

2 Click on the rectangle in the vertical bar, and note how the cursor changes. Drag down to about the middle of your screen. Excel has split the window, and you can scroll these two panes vertically, independently of each other.

3 Do the same thing with the rectangle on the horizontal bar. Move this to about the middle of your screen. You now have four window panes, and can scroll to move around each.

Figure 5.7 *One worksheet, shown in four independently scrollable windows.*

Con.Budget

	A	B	C	A	B	C
1	MacDonald County Schools: Consolidated B			MacDonald County Schools: Consolidated B		
2						
3	Target Increase=	0.05		Target Increase=	0.05	
4						
5		Year -->			Year -->	
6	Category	1993	1994	Category	1993	1994
7						
8	Salaries	1300000	1380000	Salaries	1300000	1380000
9	Books	51000	58000	Books	51000	58000
1	MacDonald County Schools: Consolidated B			MacDonald County Schools: Consolidated B		
2						
3	Target Increase=	0.05		Target Increase=	0.05	
4						
5		Year -->			Year -->	
6	Category	1993	1994	Category	1993	1994
7						
8	Salaries	1300000	1380000	Salaries	1300000	1380000
9	Books	51000	58000	Books	51000	58000
10	Maintenance	39000	42000	Maintenance	39000	42000
11	Transportation	85000	88000	Transportation	85000	88000
12	Utilities	74000	82000	Utilities	74000	82000
13						

Some word processors have windowing capabilities too. They're a convenience for word processing, but necessary for serious spreadsheet work.

The other way to increase your access to a large worksheet is by creating a separate new window of the same document:

1. From the Window menu, choose **New Window**. Your new window is displayed in front of the old one. To move among the various windows you can create, use the Window menu to bring one to the front, or:

2. Choose **Arrange**... from the Window menu to have Excel make an arrangement for you of your choice—try **Tiled** for now. Then pull down the Edit menu, where the second item (just past the *extremely valuable* first item, **Undo**), is the command to repeat your last action: in this case, select **Repeat New Window**. Do this, then choose **Arrange All** from the Window menu again.

3. Revise your formulas for column E of Con.Budget so that they now reference Auburn and Cedar Ridge information not on their separate sheets, but from their areas of Con.Budget.

As a general rule when entering formulas, try to use Paste and the mouse, rather than typing. Saves lots of mistakes! Speaking of **Save**...have you lately?

N O T E

NAMING REGIONS

Another way to navigate is to give an area of your worksheet a name. You can name a cell you use often, such as the Target Increase value (B3) of Con.Budget. You understood "Target Increase" much faster than "B3," right?

1. Select B3 and use **Define Name** from the Formula menu to name this cell "Target_Increase." (The underlined space between the two words is necessary because Excel doesn't like range names with spaces in them. Excel does, however, prompt you to name the cell with the text in the cell to the left or above, if any.)

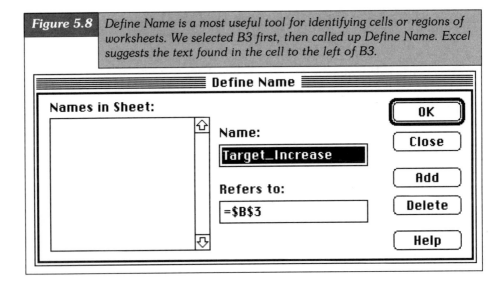

Figure 5.8 *Define Name is a most useful tool for identifying cells or regions of worksheets. We selected B3 first, then called up Define Name. Excel suggests the text found in the cell to the left of B3.*

2. Now select D8 and select the reference to B3 in the edit line (just double-click on it). With that selected, choose the **Paste Name** command in the Formula menu, click **Target_Increase**, and click **OK**. Then click in the check box to confirm this change in the formula.

In a large sheet, you could name all sorts of key cells, then construct formulas using **Paste Name**. At any point your formulas would tell you, in plain English, just what you're doing. This practice also obviates a major source of errors.

N O T E

You can name a range, or selection of cells, just as easily, in order to make that area of your sheet easier to find.

3. Select the part of Auburn's budget that you pasted into Con.Budget (A17:D29) and name it Auburn. Then use **GoTo** under the Formula menu to move to that section of Con.Budget. Downright spiffy.

NOTES

Excel allows you to attach a note, something like a Post-It note, to any cell. This is useful to include non-printing information to yourself or to others who will be using your worksheet.

1. Select A8, and choose **Note** from the Formula menu. Click in the Text Note window, and type *includes new positions*. Click **OK**.

2. Click cell A1, and choose **Find** from the Formula menu. In the dialog box, type *new positions* in the Find What box, and click on **Notes** in the Look In box. Click **OK**, and Excel goes to the cell containing that note.

3. If you had the same word, or string of characters, in more than one note, you could find the second occurrence by choosing **Repeat Find** at this point from the Edit menu.

THE WONDERFUL WORLD OF 'WHAT-IF?'

We've covered what Excel can do for us as long as we're doing all of the thinking, low-level as well as high. But a different order of magnitude in the usefulness of personal computers comes along when we let them do the low-level thinking, freeing us to spot trends and make decisions.

To begin with, one of the nicest features of electronic spreadsheets is that, by altering one variable, you can predict the effects of several different possible outcomes.

In school budgets, different banks' home mortgage offerings, or any number of scenarios, your ability to make a cogent decision depends on being able to see results of calculations that include several changing factors. Let's do some of this with our school budgets:

1. Bring Con.Budget to the front.

2. Change the 5 percent target increase to 3 percent, then to 10 percent. Watch column D as you click on the check box in each case.

If you have constraints in one category of expenditure, and wish an overall target increase for planning purposes, this is one way to find it.

THE SOLVER

So far, we've put in numbers and looked at the calculated result. What if we were shooting for a result, and wanted to know the numbers needed to reach it? We'd be calculating backwards from the solution to its components, and Excel can do this rather well.

This type of calculation is trivial where our paradigm is linear, but considerably more complicated where it is non-linear, for example in cases of diminishing returns.

Say your company makes widgets. As you increase advertising, profits increase but by a diminishing amount. Somewhere along the curve, there's an optimum amount of advertising for your widget. Let's find it. Our marketing model is:

Unit sales = 12 * (Advertising + 5000) ^0.5

so that advertising adds to the baseline of 5,000 units people will buy anyway, but with diminishing returns. Ten thousand dollars in advertising yields 5,511 units sold, $20,000 yields sales of 7,115 units, while $50,000 returns sales of 10,553 units. What's optimum?

Our complete model is shown in Figure 5.9. We want to maximize the value of B11 by changing, in this instance, the value of B7. So:

Figure 5.9	A marketing model. Is the advertising expenditure optimum?

	A	B
1	Unit Sales	=12*(B7+5000)^0.5
2	Revenue	=B1*B14
3	Sales Costs	=B1*B15
4	Gross Margin	=B2-B3
5		
6	Sales Force	6500
7	Advertising	
8	Overhead	=0.11*B2
9	Total Costs	=SUM(B6:B8)
10		
11	Product Profit	=B4-B9
12	Profit Margin	=B11/B2
13		
14	Product Price	100
15	Product Cost	65
16		

1 Start a new worksheet, type in this model, display *values*, and:

2 Open **Solver** from the Formula menu. You'll see a dialog box like Figure 5.10.

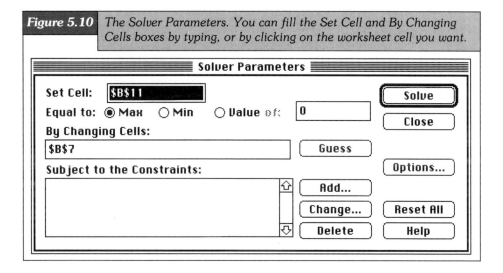

Figure 5.10 *The Solver Parameters. You can fill the Set Cell and By Changing Cells boxes by typing, or by clicking on the worksheet cell you want.*

Drag the dialog box out of the way of your marketing model if you need to and, with the cursor in **Set Cell**:

3 Click in cell B11 of your worksheet. The absolute reference to that cell appears in Set Cell.

4 Set Equal to at **Max**.

5 Click in **By Changing Cell**s, then click in cell B7 of your worksheet.

6 Click on the **Solve** button at the right, and watch the fun.

You should have reached a solution of $15,737.

This is a nice tool to have. If you like, you can solve for more than one variable at a time. You can then go back to the "what-if" paradigm, this time with a multi-dimensional perspective on the situation. Tell your competitors not to play too much golf.

GRAPHICS

As previewed in the last chapter, a particularly nice feature of spreadsheets is their ability to create graphs and charts from your data. Nice, because good charts can convey meaningful information much better than the numbers themselves.

Bring your Con.Budget sheet to the front again with the Window menu. We'll try a 3-D column chart of Books, Maintenance, Transportation, and Utilities.

1. Select these cells, using the **Command** key to select discontigous regions: A6; A9..A12; D6; D9..D12; E6; E9..E12.

2. Click on the **ChartWizard** tool in the tool bar. Note that the cells you've selected have shimmering marquees around them.

3. Draw a rectangle on your worksheet below the numbers, to cover about A16 through F40. You can move it later. The first of the ChartWizard dialog boxes appears.

■**Step 1:** Click Next to confirm the cells you've selected.

■**Step 2:** Double-click the 3-D column chart type.

■**Step 3:** Double-click chart type 6.

■**Step 4:** Here's your sample chart. Check that the radio buttons for **Data Series in Rows**, **Use first row for Category (X) Axis Labels**, and **Use first column for Series (Y) Axis Labels** are all selected. Click **Next**.

■**Step 5:** See that **Add a legend?** is not selected. Click **OK**. Your chart appears as part of the worksheet, with handles around it. Note the icon row at the bottom of your screen, should you wish to change chart types.

At this point, the chart is part of the worksheet. It can be moved or resized, but not edited. To do that,

4. Double-click on the chart. It reappears in its own window, and the menu bar changes to list options appropriate to graphics.

5. Add a legend from the Chart menu. We didn't add a legend as part of the ChartWizard sequence because we wanted a better look at our chart first.

6. Click the chart text tool (fourth from the right on the bottom row of icons). Then click in Excel's edit line.

7 Type *Estimates in these categories are lower than the goal figures*, and click the check box. This text appears in your chart, with handles around it.

8 Move and reshape this text so that it is on two lines, and is displayed at the bottom of your chart.

9 Click the close box of the chart window, so that the graph once again shows as part of your Con.Budget worksheet.

By now your effort should look something like Figure 5.11, except of course that you probably didn't name it "Figure 5.11" when you saved it. What did you name it when you saved it?

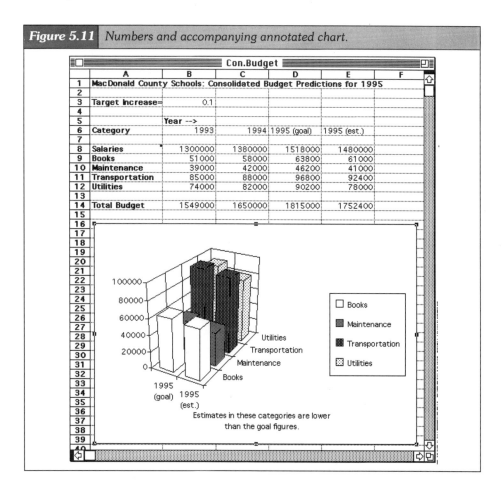

Figure 5.11 *Numbers and accompanying annotated chart.*

While you've just made a nice presentation, you can also move charts or numbers right into a word processing or desktop publishing document. Inclusion of graphics in a larger report does a lot for readability **N O T E** and interest, and for your ability to convey meaning concisely and well.

When you do that, one thing to consider first is the finished size of the chart that you want. It's best to resize a graphic in the original program, rather than letting the receiving program worry about it.

Here's how to move a chart into a word processing document:

1 Double-click on the chart to put it in its own window.

2 Use the resize box to make your chart an appropriate size.

3 From the Chart menu, choose **Select Chart**.

4 Use the **Copy** command from the Edit menu to copy your chart to the Clipboard.

5 Open the Scrapbook, and paste your chart there.

When in a word processing or desktop publishing program, you can paste a chart from the Scrapbook into your paper, just like anything else. Proofs for this book were done entirely on a Macintosh, copying, for example, Figure 5.11 from Excel into a page design program such as you'll learn in Chapter 8.

MACROS

Here comes one of the more sophisticated parts to Excel, or to computer usage in general. Up to now, you've done everything step-by-step, and have gone through many steps twice to repeat an action after making some change to relevant data.

For example, if you were making several charts, each to reflect some change in the worksheet information—graphing several 'what-if' scenarios, for instance—you'd select the ranges of cells you wanted to graph, then go through all the steps of creating a chart.

Why not tell the program the sequence of steps you wanted it to perform each time? Have it *record* that sequence, and *play it back* for you on command? This is actually a kind of programming, called a *Macro*.

Let's try ⟋ ur graph-making, to automate the procedure of creating a chart. Let's tr rt this time, and let's create it in its own window. We can paste it onto t et later on. So, close the chart window presently open and, with it bac vorksheet with handles around it, press the **Delete** (or **Backspace**) ke it from Con.Budget. Let's make a chart macro.

1 Select the cell to graph. (This is the step we do not want to auto-mate, since we' ng the data to be graphed each time.) For this exam-ple, select all of t ture categories, and the 1995 estimated figures.

2 Come up to the u, and choose **Record...**. Excel asks you for a name for your ma r than "Record1," let's try "Pie.Chart." Put a period rather than a veen the words, as spaces won't work.

Excel also asks you ɔard equivalent—**Option** and **Command** key—so that you ca 's macro just by typing simultaneously Command, Option, ar ʲ. It suggests *a*, and that's fine. Next, we want to store this mac n-global Macro Sheet, as should be the default. Click **OK**.

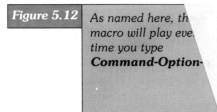

Figure 5.12 As named here, th macro will play eve time you type **Command-Option-**

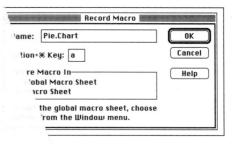

Excel is now recording what you are e your time, as it's only each step that's recorded, not the time in b

3 Choose **New** from the File menu, an art from the dialog box. Click **OK**. A bar chart is displayed in a r ʲ.

4 Choose **3-D Pie** from the Gallery menu. ype 6.

5 Add a legend.

6 Choose **Stop Recorder** from the Macro n e the existing chart, then test your new macro. Select the expend ategories and 1995 goal figures, and type **Command–Option–a**. Hey there. You've just done some computer programming.

There are many kinds of macros in different programs. All are great time-savers and, more importantly, can minimize mistakes because the steps taken are less prone to the errors that humans tend to make when performing repetitive tasks.

SHORTCUT

But they can also *create* mistakes if not thought through carefully.

Keep macros short and sweet, so they do only a few steps. You can later combine, either by chaining or nesting macros, so that one larger macro plays several small ones.

The big advantage here is that should you later decide to make a change in one step, you only need to re-record the one small macro that contains that step.

7 Save your macro. From the Window menu, choose **Macro1**. Save this onto your disk—the default name is fine. Now look at what you've got:

Starting in A1, you should see this sequence:

Pie.Chart (a)	Your title (command equivalent)
=NEW(2,2)	Choosing **New** with the second option: Chart
=GALLERY.3D.PIE(6)	Choosing **Gallery**, **3D-Pie**, then the sixth option
=LEGEND(TRUE)	This step added the Legend
=RETURN()	Macros always end with a **Return**

There are four things of interest here:

- You can go to a macro you've recorded and edit it, once you know the code. This is a very handy time-saver.

- You can learn that code by recording some macros, and then looking at what you've done.

- You can take only the macro document, which you've just saved onto your disk, and take it to another computer that uses Excel. Open that macro sheet and use the macros you've created to work with other data.

- You can have several macro sheets: one for your income statement, another for your balance sheet, and open and close them as needed.

WARNING

Here's a big tip, though: The major mistake people make with macros is that they record one, and then go off and play it, or do something else, without stopping the recording! Remember that Excel records everything you do until you turn the Macro Recorder off.

MULTITASKING

Now that you know how to use both Excel and Word, let's look at a big step up in PC operation: how to use two programs at the same time. This is not just so that you can work up a spreadsheet for a while, then do some word processing. Rather, you can include numbers or a chart from Excel in your Word document much faster, by having both open at once.

Allowing multiple programs open at once is automatic—you can open a program and then simply open another one. To test this:

1️⃣ Open a chart in Excel.

2️⃣ Click on the small icon in the Application Menu at the far right of the menu bar. You'll see a menu drop, which shows you the programs currently running. Choose the **Finder**.

Figure 5.13	The Excel icon (left) and the Finder icon (right), as they appear on the Application menu.		

3️⃣ Open Word, and type a few lines like what you see in Figure 5.14. Press **Return** twice, to move the cursor to open space in the document.

4️⃣ Go back to the application menu, at the far right of the menu bar, and switch back to Excel.

5️⃣ Select your chart, and choose **Copy**.

6 Switch back to Word, and paste the chart there. Figure 5.14 shows this sequence.

Figure 5.14 *With both Word and Excel running, we created a chart in Excel using the Auburn worksheet. Then we copied it, switched to Word, and pasted it into our document.*

We could also use the Scrapbook, or System 7's Publish and Subscribe capabilities. Publish and Subscribe would create a dynamic link between the two files. If we should revise the chart in Excel, the Word file would automatically update to reflect the change.

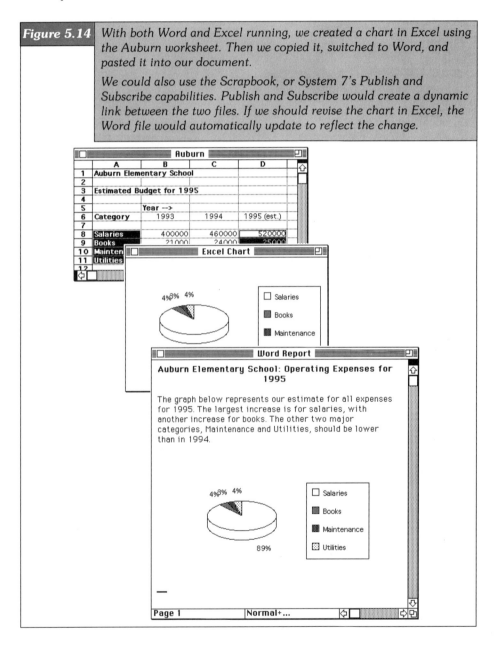

This is quite a bit faster than using the Scrapbook, and opening and quitting each program in turn. But there's a *much* more sophisticated version of this routine, available only in System 7. The difference is this: in the preceding sequence, you copied and pasted a chart as a graphic, and that graphic is then fixed in your Word document, even if you or an associate makes a change in the original chart.

What if you could *dynamically link* the Excel chart to the Word file, so that if a later change were made to the chart, it would automatically update the Word file?

In other words, you could *publish* the chart, and the Word file would, as it were, *subscribe* to it. If the chart changed and were, so to speak, a later *edition*, the Word file that subscribed to the chart would include that later edition.

Here's how to do this.

1 Switch to Excel, and select your chart.

2 Choose **Create Publisher** from the Edit menu. You'll see:

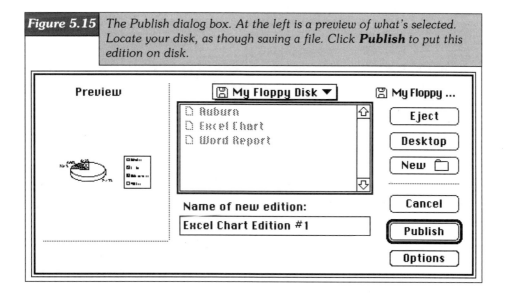

Figure 5.15 *The Publish dialog box. At the left is a preview of what's selected. Locate your disk, as though saving a file. Click **Publish** to put this edition on disk.*

Check that the **Preview** is what you want, and follow normal Mac desktop steps to publish this.

This is called an *edition*, and will be available to every program using System 7's publish and subscribe technology.

3 Switch to Word, put your cursor where you want this edition to appear, and choose **Subscribe** from the Edit menu. You'll see:

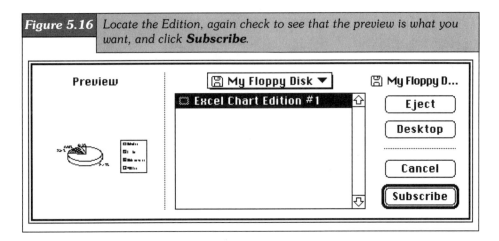

Figure 5.16   *Locate the Edition, again check to see that the preview is what you want, and click **Subscribe**.*

4 Again locate the edition, and subscribe to it.

The visible results match Figure 5.14, but there's a big difference. The chart in Word updates automatically whenever the chart in Excel is revised.

This procedure doesn't require that both programs be open at once. We did it that way this time to look quickly at how it works. But once an edition is published and subscribed to, the subscriber updates every time it is opened.

To be sure, this feature requires that all of the subscribing documents—any number of them—be on the same disk as the publisher, or on the same network. Or keep the publication on your floppy current with the Excel chart on computer 1, and insert it in computer 2 before opening the Word document subscribing to that edition.

You could do this just as easily going the other way: you could publish something in Word. Excel has a text box feature, and you could subscribe it to the Word file. Or, you can publish a document in one program, and subscribe to it in other files in that same program. Excel doesn't need this, with its linking capabilities, but you might find it useful in Word.

For example, you're doing a catalog full of detailed descriptions of merchandise. Your specialists in different areas would be working up capsule depictions.

You could go ahead and put the overall catalog together with their first drafts, and when their work was finished yours would be too.

Publish and subscribe offers substantial potential especially for group efforts on a computer network. Say your graphics department on the fifth floor is doing the illustrations, marketing on the second floor is making the worksheets and charts, and you're putting it all together.

At any point in your work, your efforts are current with everyone else's. And you won't miss a crucial revision in some numbers because the interoffice mail was late.

Note that as of this writing, not all Mac programs use publish and subscribe yet. If you're preparing to buy a program and want to use this technology, check first to see whether it's included.

CHECKLIST

As you've seen, there's a lot of features in a spreadsheet program. After this second chapter with Excel, you've learned to:

- work with multiple worksheets,
- link worksheets,
- work with split and multiple windows,
- name cells and regions and add notes,
- solve for different variables,
- use 3-D graphics,
- make macros,
- work with multiple open applications (multitask), and
- publish and subscribe.

HELPFUL HINTS

The key here, as before, is practice. Once you learn the features, though, tutorials tend to be less useful than cooking up a project of your own.

If you can design a worksheet to fit your business or a course you're taking in anything from economics to statistics to genetics, you're finding program tools that meet your needs. This kind of personal involvement gives you a sense of active exploration of the program, and you'll do a lot very quickly that you can be proud of.

Especially quickly, if you work with multiple programs open. Your Mac can open several programs at once, depending on the model and how much RAM it has. Mac power users run a bunch of programs at once: graphics, word processing, page design—why not?

You most often see Mac power users in the store, waiting while technicians install more RAM in their Mac. How much RAM is enough? We think it's like money: You think that if you have just a little bit more, you'll have enough.

Anyway, at this point you can add "Competent on electronic spreadsheets and computer multitasking" to your resume. You fought and beat both graphics and macros, and you can do high-quality and useful work with spreadsheets, and can multitask effectively. So take the weekend off—you've earned it.

Q & A

Q: *Is there a shortcut for changing relative cell addressing to absolute?*

A: In the Edit Line, click the address you want to change, and press **Command-T**. You'll see that this toggles from completely relative, to first address absolute, then second, then both. Keep pressing **Command-T** until the address is right.

Q: *I can't see all of the data I've entered in some cells.*

A: The column isn't wide enough. Put your cursor between the column labels, for instance, A and B, and click and drag to change the column width.

Q: *Linking cells among different worksheets doesn't work.*

A: You need to start in the worksheet you want to link to. Type the equals sign to begin the formula, and then go to other worksheets for their data.

Q: *I've linked data from other worksheets into the active one, but I'm not getting the correct result.*

A: If you linked the cells correctly, the problem's most likely that you moved, or changed the name of, the sheet you're linking from. Excel then has no way to determine where your source data is.

Q: *I'm constructing a large worksheet, and am having trouble finding parts of it.*

A: Naming cells or regions, linking together smaller sheets, or using split or multiple windows all help. The linking feature to connect smaller sheets is often the most useful.

Q: *I recorded a macro for my worksheet, and it ran fine at the time, but I can't access it now.*

A: You've closed the macro sheet, a separate document that stores macro instructions. You may have done this simply by quitting Excel and starting again later. Open the macro sheet from the File menu, as you would any other document. That's an important concept—macros aren't saved within the worksheet in which they were created.

Q: *I can't subscribe to a chart I published earlier.*

A: It may not be on a mounted drive—that is, on a disk your Mac can find. If the disk is available, finding the publisher is a matter of searching for its name, as with any other file.

SAMPLE EXERCISE

Create a new worksheet in Excel, and make a chart from it. Publish the chart. Then open Word, enter some text and then subscribe to the Excel chart. Format your Word document for a professional and pleasing appearance. Then go back to Excel and make changes, save them, and note how they are reflected in the subscribing Word file. Remember that as long as the disk you saved your publication on is available to your Mac, all editions you make continue to subscribe to it. Data is then forever current. Consider the possibilities.

CHAPTER 6
DATABASES

In this chapter you'll learn how to:

- create a database and enter records
- change the design, or layout, of on-screen and printed data
- set up automatic data entry
- generate reports
- find and sort data by a variety of criteria
- pre-define values and constraints, for speed and accuracy
- use formulas in calculated fields
- create custom reports including graphics
- add macro, or scripting, functions

After number crunching, database applications were the first major use of computers in the business world. A *database* is simply a collection of orderly information—where "orderly" is something you define and structure.

Examples of paper databases are the telephone book, a recipe file, and the library card catalog. On a computer, a database gains orders of magnitude of flexibility and power over the paper examples, and offers a great tool for almost any area of endeavor.

Today we'll learn an exceptionally flexible and elegant Macintosh database called FileMaker Pro, and how we can *make information work for us*.

But since FileMaker's flexibility is supported by one big structural difference from the other Mac programs we've learned, it's a little confusing at first. Let's get the concept.

WHAT'S DIFFERENT ABOUT A DATABASE?

The other programs give you a place to start work—SuperPaint gives you a blank painting area, Word a new sheet of paper, Excel rows and columns of empty cells. These programs *provide an environment* for you when you start them up.

FileMaker is different—the first thing you do is build your own environment. This is because there's quite a difference between a phone book and a recipe file, even though they're both structured information.

The phone book, for one thing, has a different kind of information than the recipe file. We define one kind of information (which we call a *field*) in the phone book as a name, and another kind of information as an address.

Recipe card files, as well, have fields for names, ingredients, and cooking time. In fact, the first thing we do when beginning a database is figure out what kinds of information, or fields, we want to include.

Our second question is where these fields are going to go on a page, or card. The New York City telephone book puts all of the names at the left, and phone numbers at the right. The phone book on my desk puts four boxes on each page, with a name at the top, address in the middle, and phone number at the bottom of each box. Their *layouts* are different.

Similarly, my recipe card file has a different layout than *The Starving Student's Cookbook*, even though the data for the recipes, especially the good ones, is similar.

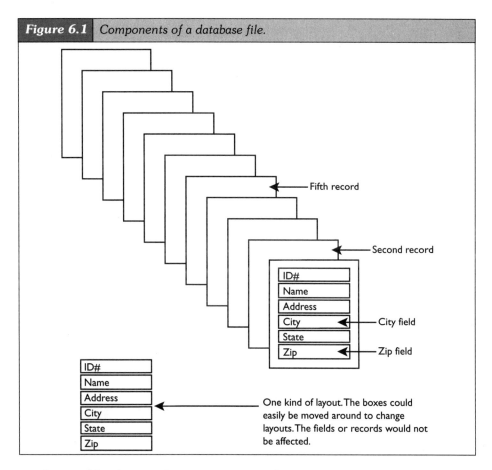

Figure 6.1 | *Components of a database file.*

Fifth record

Second record

ID#
Name
Address
City ◄─── City field
State
Zip ◄─── Zip field

ID#
Name
Address ◄─── One kind of layout. The boxes could
City   easily be moved around to change
State   layouts. The fields or records would not
Zip   be affected.

In a cookbook, a single recipe is a *record*.

So when we start FileMaker Pro, we'll keep fields and layouts in mind, plus the records, that together make up a database. FileMaker has us handle these three parts in separate modes:

- The **Field Definition** mode allows us to create and edit fields, but we won't be able to see the data in those fields. In the phone book example, we would work with kinds of information such as name and address, rather than any actual information of those types.

- The **Layout** mode is how we place fields on the screen, or the printed page. We can put Address to the right of Name, or below it. Again, while I'm in this mode, I can't see any actual addresses.

■ The **Browse** mode is FileMaker's term for the mode we use to enter and retrieve records.

A record in the phone book is all of the information on one person—her name, address, and phone number.

In the Browse mode, I can find anyone's address, or sort addresses by street or zip code. But I can't change fields or layouts unless I go into those other modes.

When using FileMaker or any database, the most important thing to remember is what mode you are in. It sure saves headaches.

CREATING A DATABASE

1 Double-click the FileMaker Pro icon. In the first dialog box:

2 Click on **Desktop** and then on the name of your floppy, which you of course inserted in your computer a minute after you turned it on. Then click the **Open** button. Be sure you're creating this file on your disk.

3 Then click on **New** in this dialog box, as in Figure 6.2, to create a new data file.

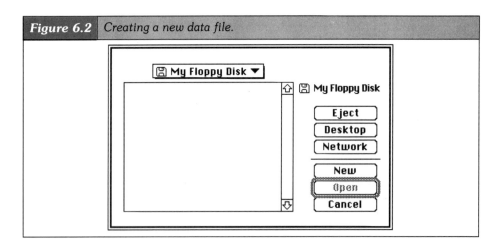

Figure 6.2 Creating a new data file.

In the second dialog box, shown in Figure 6.3:

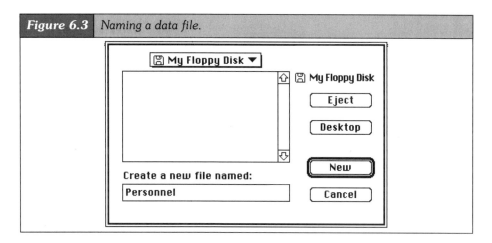

Figure 6.3 | *Naming a data file.*

4 Type in *Personnel* for the name. Confirm that the name and disk drive are correct, and click **New** again.

5 Define fields for your data file, as in Figure 6.4. Start with *ID#*, and define that as a field of the number type.

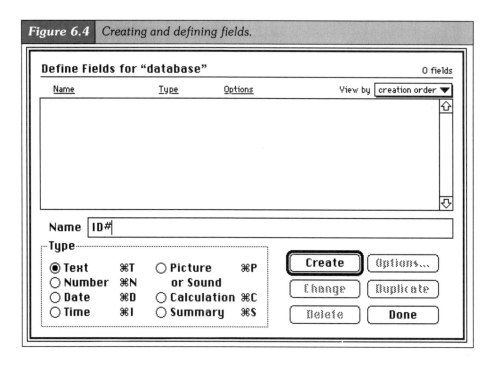

Figure 6.4 | *Creating and defining fields.*

6 Define these other fields, and their types, as in Figure 6.5. After you type the name for a field, and press **Create**, just go ahead and type the name for the next field.

Figure 6.5	A List of fields.	Field Name	Type
		ID#	Number
		First Name	Text
		Last Name	Text
		Street	Text
		City	Text
		State	Text
		Zip	Text
		Phone No.	Text

7 Click **Done**.

When you leave the Field Definition mode, FileMaker takes you back to the mode you were in last. In the case of a new data file, it takes you to the Browse mode. The word Browse is displayed on the bottom area of the active window, just to the right of several icons, to confirm this.

This is where we do most of our work. In Browse mode, we can look at any record, such as any individual name and address in our personnel file. We enter all data, edit it, sort it, or find one or more records while we're in Browse mode.

Since this is a new file, you're now in the first (blank) record. The book icon at the upper left, as in Figure 6.6, tells you how many records there are in this file and which record you are on.

Enter the data for the *first record only* shown in Figure 6.7.

Use the **Tab** key to move from field to field. Pressing the **Return** key adds lines to the field guide.

If you accidentally press **Return**, press **Delete** to remove the extra line, and then use the mouse to first de-select and then re-select the field. (The line stays until you de- and re-select.)

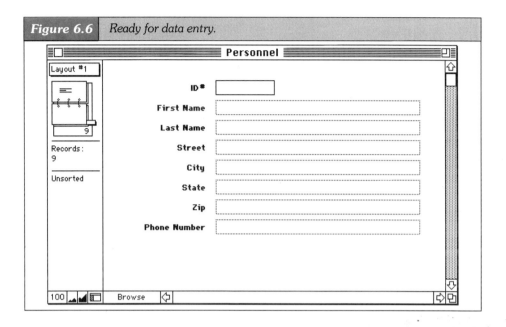

Figure 6.6 | *Ready for data entry.*

Figure 6.7 | *Records to enter.*

ID#	First Name	Last Name	Street	City	State	Zip	Phone
1382	Molly	Jones	122 Adelphi St.	Ithaca	NY	14850	277-7251
2120	Kay	Green	25 Seaview St.	Dryden	NY	13053	845-1350
3855	David	Harris	705 Court St.	Ithaca	NY	14850	276-1800
4996	Daniel	Green	17 Eddy St.	Ithaca	NY	14850	276-7043
5033	James	Chapin	65 North St.	Auburn	NY	13021	771-9050
6280	Lisa	Schmidt	27 Seaview St.	Dryden	NY	13053	845-2901
7407	Nancy	MacMillan	43 Lynn St.	Ithaca	NY	14850	277-8641
8761	Catherine	Harris	705 Court St.	Ithaca	NY	14850	276-1800

LAYOUT

With one record entered, let's change the layout:

1 Choose **Layout** from the Select menu, or click on **Browse** at the bottom of the window, and a menu drops. Or type **Command-L**. In keyboard-intensive work like this, Command-key equivalents are time-savers.

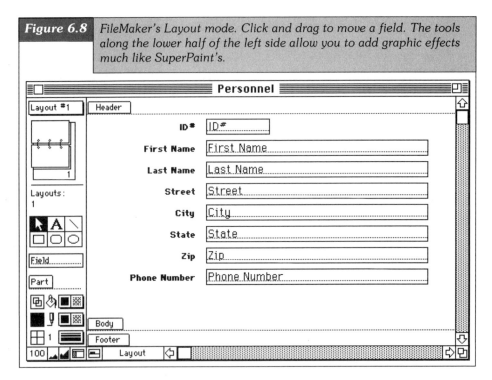

Figure 6.8 *FileMaker's Layout mode. Click and drag to move a field. The tools along the lower half of the left side allow you to add graphic effects much like SuperPaint's.*

In layout mode, you can rearrange the fields (or boxes) that hold names and addresses. You can also add another arrangement of fields:

2 Choose **New Layout** from the Edit menu, or type **Command-N**.

3 Choose **Standard**, as in Figure 6.9, name it *Address Book*, and click **OK**.

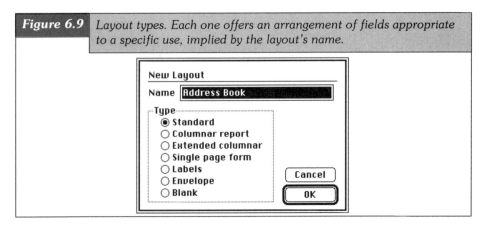

Figure 6.9 *Layout types. Each one offers an arrangement of fields appropriate to a specific use, implied by the layout's name.*

After you add a layout, the book icon at the top left lets you scroll among the different layouts you have. In Browse mode, the same book scrolls among the records in the file. Note Figure 6.10.

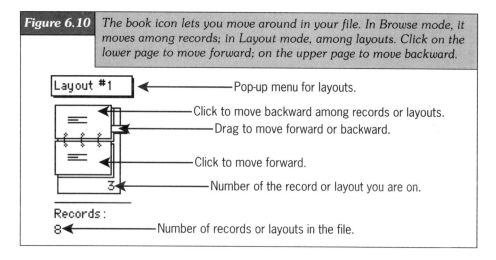

Figure 6.10 *The book icon lets you move around in your file. In Browse mode, it moves among records; in Layout mode, among layouts. Click on the lower page to move forward; on the upper page to move backward.*

Layout #1 ────── Pop-up menu for layouts.

────── Click to move backward among records or layouts.
────── Drag to move forward or backward.

────── Click to move forward.

3 ────── Number of the record or layout you are on.

Records:
8 ────── Number of records or layouts in the file.

At this point, the book icon tells you that you now have two layouts. You could scroll among your layouts. But since both of them are identical at the moment, let's change the new one.

We do this by clicking on a field to select it, and then dragging it around, or resizing it with the handles at the corners—much like object handles in SuperPaint's draw mode. A lot of tools in various programs share design and functionality. This makes learning much easier.

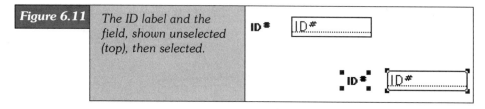

Figure 6.11 *The ID label and the field, shown unselected (top), then selected.*

ID # ID#

ID # ID#

You can also change the text format and style options for a field when it is selected. You can select multiple fields by Shift-clicking, or using a selection rectangle—again, much like in SuperPaint.

Note that the bold text next to the fields is just a label—not part of the data. This supplemental information makes data entry more convenient.

Move an entire object by clicking and dragging in the middle of it. Resize it by clicking and dragging a corner handle.

4 Shorten the First Name field, and move the last name field up onto the same line. You have to shorten it as well, so it will fit. See Figure 6.12.

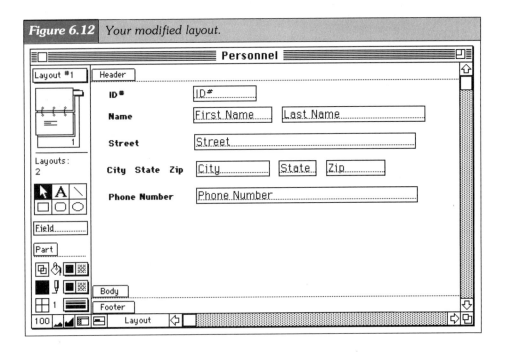

Figure 6.12 *Your modified layout.*

5 Change the text label for this line to *Name*. Do this by using the text tool (denoted, as in SuperPaint, by an A). Choose this, click your text cursor in the middle of the "First Name" text, drag to the left to select the word "First," and press **Delete**.

6 Move and resize the State and Zip fields so they are on the same line as City. Shorten the fields so they all fit.

For more precision in moving things around, select an object and press a directional **Arrow** key on your keyboard. Each press moves the selected object one pixel. This feature is becoming standard in Mac programs, SHORTCUT thank goodness.

7 Move the Phone Number field up to fit underneath the other fields. Move the text labels after you move the fields.

8 Return to the Browse mode by the Select menu, or the menu at the bottom of the window, or by typing **Command–B**.

Your first record, for Molly Jones, hasn't changed at all in terms of the field definitions or the data in them, but the layout of the fields has changed.

We've now been in each of FileMaker's three modes. You can see how changes made in one mode don't affect what you've done in the other two. It's frustrating to forget this and try, for example, to find data while in layout mode.

Automatic Entry

FileMaker automates several aspects of data entry for you:

1 Choose **Define Fields** from the Select menu, and click on the State field, as in Figure 6.13. Click on the **Options** button.

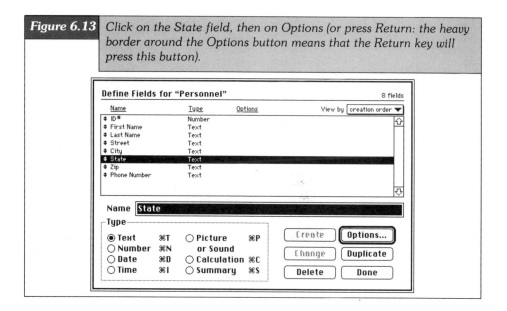

Figure 6.13 *Click on the State field, then on Options (or press Return: the heavy border around the Options button means that the Return key will press this button).*

2 Click on **Data** and type *NY* (See Figure 6.14). Click **OK**, and when you're back in the dialog box shown in Figure 6.13, click on **Done** to return to Browse mode.

Figure 6.14 *Entry options for a field.*

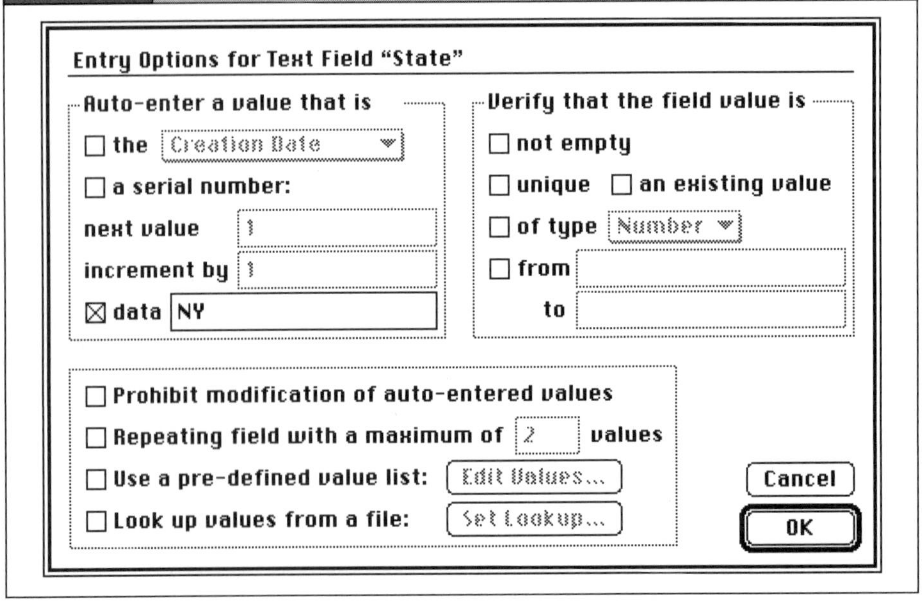

Entry Options for Text Field "State"

┌─ **Auto-enter a value that is** ─┐   ┌─ **Verify that the field value is** ─┐

☐ **the** | Creation Date ▼ | ☐ **not empty**

☐ **a serial number:**   ☐ **unique**   ☐ **an existing value**

next value | 1 | ☐ **of type** | Number ▼ |

increment by | 1 | ☐ **from** | |

☒ **data** | NY | **to** | |

☐ **Prohibit modification of auto-entered values**

☐ **Repeating field with a maximum of** | 2 | **values**

☐ **Use a pre-defined value list:** | Edit Values… | [**Cancel**]

☐ **Look up values from a file:** | Set Lookup… | [**OK**]

---

3 Enter the rest of the records shown in Figure 6.7. For each new record, choose **New Record** from the Edit menu (or type **Command-N**). Within a record, use **Tab** to move from one field to the next, **Shift-Tab** to move back.

If you need to move from one existing record to another, click on pages of the book icon at the top left of the window, or click on and drag the bookmark. Or, type **Command-Tab** to move forward or **Command-Shift-Tab** to move back.

N O T E

Here's a good place to discuss a major conceptual difference between databases and the other kinds of programs we've worked with. Since with a database you mostly enter and manipulate data, rather than make many changes in it as you do with word processing, spreadsheets, or graphics, *FileMaker saves for you automatically, at short intervals.*

REPORTS

With databases, we do three basic categories of things to data: enter, manipulate, and report it.

A report is really just another layout, but one that's meant to be printed, or used on the screen for quick overviews of records.

Since we don't need to put every field in a layout, we can make up a list of our personnel with, say, just their first names and phone numbers. It's a handy list for informal use.

1. Go to Layout mode, and create a new layout (choose **New Layout** from the Edit menu or type **Command-N**). Give it the name *List* and choose **Columnar Report** as the type.

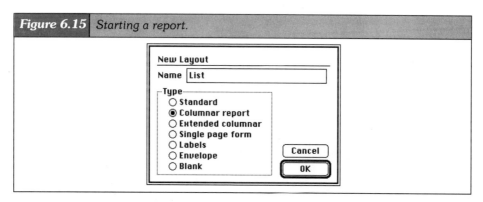

Figure 6.15 *Starting a report.*

Make up a list layout containing seven fields, like Figure 6.16. From the field list in the box on the left:

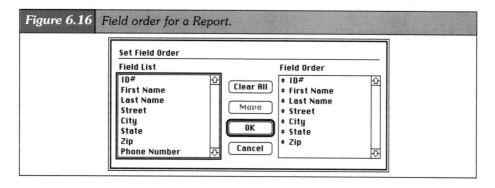

Figure 6.16 *Field order for a Report.*

2. Click on the field you want to appear first on the list. We've chosen First Name. Note that with something selected in the box on the left, the **Move** button in the center is now dark.

3. Click on Move. The First Name field appears in the Field Order box on the right.

4. Repeat this for the other five fields shown in the Field Order box. As a short cut, you can double-click on a field name to move it.

5. Click **OK** to return to Layout mode. Make sure that **View as List** on the Select menu is selected—has a check mark beside it. You should see something like Figure 6.17.

Figure 6.17	Beginning of a list layout. Note the Header, Body, and F... (Footer) boxes at the left of the data area. These are the parts of the layout.

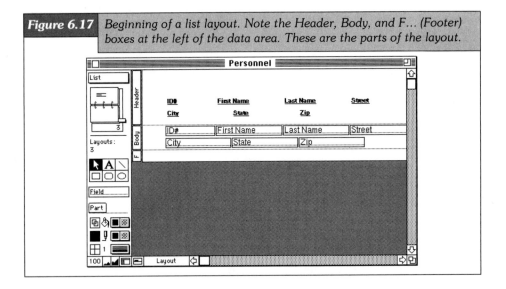

6. Oops. We didn't want to include ID numbers in this layout. Click on the ID# field and then Shift-click on its label, to select them both. Press **Delete**.

7. Drag each label up to the top of the *Header* part of the layout, and put them closer together, so that they fit on one line, as in Figure 6.18.

8. Click toward the bottom of the Header box (at the left of the Header part). This selects it. Drag it up so it allows only room for the single line of labels. Also make the *Footer* box as small as possible.

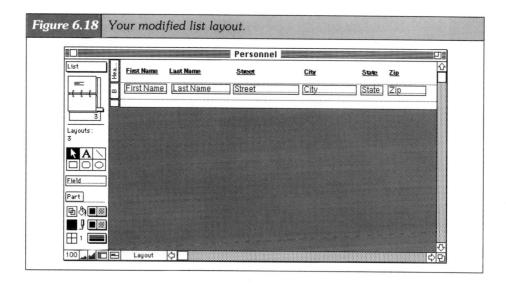

Figure 6.18 Your modified list layout.

9 Do the same for the fields, and for the body part of the layout. It should now look like Figure 6.18.

10 Return to Browse mode. Your records should show on the screen as in Figure 6.19.

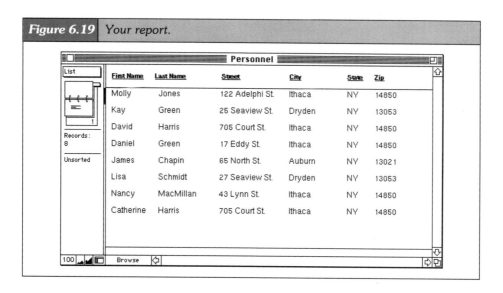

Figure 6.19 Your report.

If any of the records are cut off at the end (someone's last name only partially shows, for example), this is because the layout for that field isn't big enough. Go back to layout mode, and lengthen that field a little.

A list is a nice way to display the part of your data you want to use. Remember that all of the data you entered in each record is still there, even though ID and phone numbers aren't displayed in this layout.

NOTE

See that at the bottom right of the loose-leaf book icon at the top left of the window, there's the number 1. And, just to the left of the word "Molly" in the first record, the twin vertical lines are filled in.

You're at this point in record #1, even though you can see all the rest as well.

FINDING BY CRITERIA

A large part of database use is finding information. When we use the telephone book database, the find criterion we have is generally just a complete name. With the phone book in an electronic database, it would be just as easy to find all of the people whose first names are Kay and whose last names begin with a letter between A and M and who live in a zip code lower than 14000.

Not to mention all of her neighbors in lower than 14000 who drive a late-model car, like pizza, and go to a movie a week. Demographers and advertisers can't get enough of this.

1 Choose **Find** from the Select menu, or type **Command-F**.

2 Click in (or **Tab** to) the second field, and type =*green*. There is no need to capitalize.

3 Click on the **Find** button at the left of the window, or press **Return**.

FileMaker shows you the first record it's found, and the number of records that contain your criteria is displayed below the book icon to the left of the data, as in Figure 6.21.

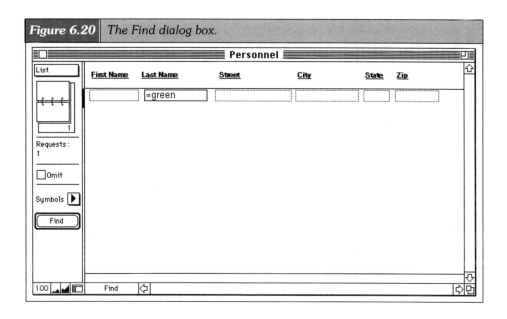

Figure 6.20 | The Find dialog box.

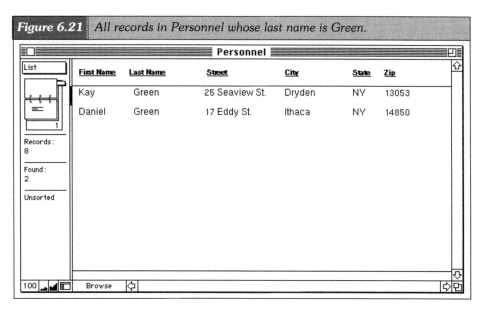

Figure 6.21 | All records in Personnel whose last name is Green.

Since we're in a list layout, with each record on a single line, FileMaker is able to show us more than one record. Had we been in our original layout when we went to find the last names of Green, we would see only one record at a time. We'd then simply scroll through the records.

As info, the equals sign told FileMaker you were looking for an exact match.

If you had not typed the equals sign, you'd have gotten everyone whose last names contained "green."

This points out that even as nice a program as this one only gives you what you ask it for. Always take a critical look at what you put in and what you get out. Garbage in... garbage out.

4 Choose **Find All** from the Select menu to get back to your complete list after finding something.

5 Find these records:

- All of the people who live in Ithaca.

- All of the people whose first name starts with D.

- All of the people with zip codes lower than 14000. Hint: use the < symbol from the Symbols submenu you get by clicking on the Symbols icon at the left. Your find criterion should read <14000.

Finding the first set after the second set doesn't find a subset of the first set, or all of the people who live in Ithaca *and* whose first name starts with D. To search for multiple criteria, put them in the initial
N O T E search mask. (Figure 6.20 is a *search mask*. You could put something in every field in the mask, and the Find would then be those records that satisfied every criterion you entered.)

SORTING

The other primary way to manipulate information in a data file is sorting. FileMaker lets you sort by, for example, last name and then sort by first name. All of the people whose last name is Smith would then be alphabetized by their first names, as in the telephone book.

In database lingo, the telephone book has two *levels* of sort. Sometimes more levels are desirable—the redoubtable Macintosh database Double Helix has 32,767 levels of sort.

We won't use that many today, though.

1. Choose **Sort** from the Select menu. You'll see a dialog box something like what you used to move fields into a layout. Here, though, we're telling FileMaker which field we want it to sort by.

2. Click on **Last Name**, and then on **Move**. Last Name appears in the Sort Order box.

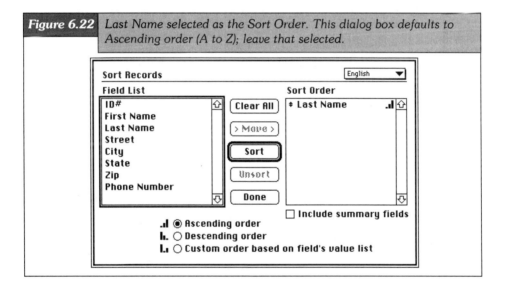

Figure 6.22 *Last Name selected as the Sort Order. This dialog box defaults to Ascending order (A to Z); leave that selected.*

3. Click on **Sort**. FileMaker sorts the records as requested.

But note that within the last names, FileMaker didn't change the order of first names as entered. So the alphabetical sort isn't complete.

4. Again choose **Sort**, and click **Clear All** to clear the sort order. Then select Last Name as the *primary key*, and First Name as the *secondary key*—just select Last Name first, and First Name last, so to speak, as in Figure 6.23. Try it now.

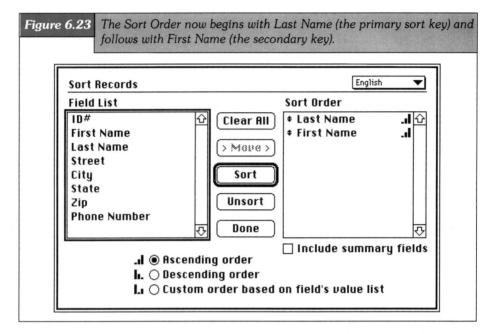

Figure 6.23 *The Sort Order now begins with Last Name (the primary sort key) and follows with First Name (the secondary key).*

See how FileMaker has sorted all of the records by last name, and then without changing the order of last names, has sorted the records within each last name by first name.

This is useful if your records share a lot of data, such as the name Smith, or residence in a city. Multiple levels are, though, useless when you're sorting by a unique field, such as an ID number, as the primary key. All other keys are then meaningless. Similarly, if you're using ID number as the third key, no succeeding key will have any effect.

Speaking of ID numbers, call up the Sort command again, click **Clear All** to clear the Sort Order, double-click on ID Number in the left box to move it to the right, and then sort by this criterion. It should work just fine, even though the ID number field isn't part of this layout.

Why should it have to be? You might want that sort, perhaps if ID number correlated with seniority or department, but you might not want to have your screen or paper cluttered with the ID numbers themselves. Or ID numbers might also be confidential access codes you don't want to print needlessly. Fairly elegant stuff.

ADVANCED FEATURES

While what we've looked at so far would suffice for much basic data manipulation, it's at this point that applications like FileMaker take off.

Why limit ourselves to handling data that we've entered, when a good database can produce calculations, updating automatically each time we add a record, and thereby go a long way towards *managing* information as well as *providing* it.

In this section, we'll have FileMaker calculate several fields for us, and make things easier for us in other fields.

1 Go into layout mode, and select layout 1. As with many parameters of the program, this selection stays in place until you change it.

2 Choose **Define** from the Select menu. We're going to add some fields to your datafile.

NOTE

For some of these fields, we'll provide a list of entry options. Then when we enter data in these fields, either a list pops up with choices or FileMaker checks our entry for accuracy.

These features have two advantages: they save us typing time, and are also good ways to prevent mistakes.

3 Create a field called Position (of the Text type).

4 Click on **Options** in the **Field Definition** dialog box. You used this dialog box to auto-enter the state when you originally entered data. We now want to enter a list of possible occupations for our personnel.

5 Click on the option **Use a pre-defined value list**, as shown in Figure 6.24. Figure 6.25 pops up automatically.

6 Enter the possible occupations as shown in Figure 6.25. You'll need to press **Return** after each entry.

This list pops up when we enter the occupation for each record in Personnel. It beats typing it *every* time.

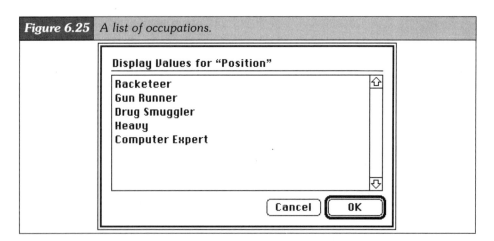

Figure 6.24 *Click on "Use a predefined value list:" from the Entry Options dialog box.*

Entry Options for Text Field "Position"

Auto-enter a value that is
- ☐ the [Creation Date ▾]
- ☐ a serial number:
- next value [1]
- increment by [1]
- ☐ data [ ]

Verify that the field value is
- ☐ not empty
- ☐ unique ☐ an existing value
- ☐ of type [Number ▾]
- ☐ from [ ]
- to [ ]

- ☐ Prohibit modification of auto-entered values
- ☐ Repeating field with a maximum of [2] values
- ☒ Use a pre-defined value list: [Edit Values...]
- ☐ Look up values from a file: [Set Lookup...]

[Cancel] [OK]

Figure 6.25 *A list of occupations.*

Display Values for "Position"

Racketeer
Gun Runner
Drug Smuggler
Heavy
Computer Expert

[Cancel] [OK]

[7] Next, define a field called Annual Salary (of the Number type), and again go to the **Options** dialog box. But instead of a list here, we want to enter a range within which we know all salaries will fall. That way, we won't go putting extra zeros on someone's paycheck. It's our money, and FileMaker's going to keep it that way.

8 Click on the word **from**, as in Figure 6.26, and type those figures where shown. Then **OK** this.

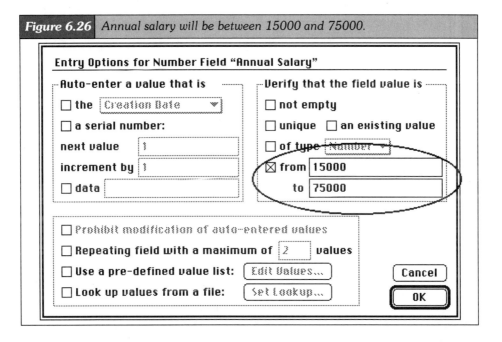

Figure 6.26 *Annual salary will be between 15000 and 75000.*

9 Define a Marital Status field (text), and make the entry option a pre-defined value list of two possibilities: M or S.

Now we're going to get a little fancy, and define a field so that FileMaker calculates, on the basis of what it finds elsewhere, what to put into that field.

10 Define a field called Benefit Rate. Make this a calculated field, as shown in Figure 6.27.

You'll see a dialog box like Figure 6.28. First, though, let's look at what kind of calculation we're going to do.

Remember that we have a Marital Status field which, for each record, is going to be either M or S, per the list. For payroll purposes, we want this new field, Benefit Rate, to be .3 if the person is married, and .2 if she or he is not.

The equation is:

If (Marital Status="M",.3,.2)

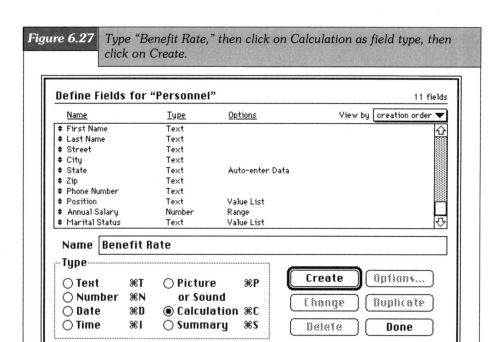

Figure 6.27 *Type "Benefit Rate," then click on Calculation as field type, then click on Create.*

and the commas have special meaning, in relation to the "If" starting the equation. If FileMaker finds an M or, to put it another way, *if* this If function is *true*, the program returns a value of .3 for the Benefit Rate. If the If function is *false*, it enters .2 in this calculated field.

We call this an "if..., then, else" kind of equation. If the proposition is true, we *then* get what's after the first comma. Or *else*, we get what's after the second comma.

Enter this formula this way:

11 Scroll through the list of functions on the right side of the Calculation dialog box until you find:

If (test,result one,result two)

12 Double-click on this, and see that it appears in the box below. It's much better than typing, as it obviates mistakes.

13 Double-click on "test" to select it.

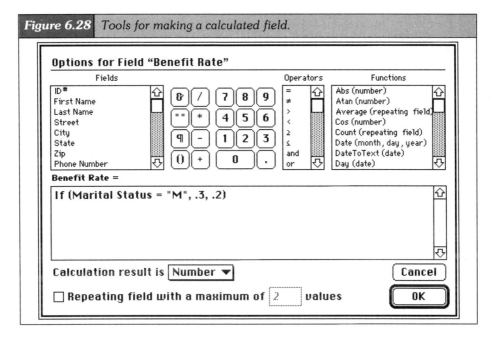

Figure 6.28 *Tools for making a calculated field.*

14 Double-click on the field Marital Status from the list in the box on the left. Scroll if you need to. The field name now shows as the test.

The importance of double-clicking on a field in a list rather than typing field names is that if you typed "Marital Status" and spelled it even a little differently, FileMaker wouldn't know what you wanted to do. Garbage in....

15 Click just after the words Marital Status in the formula, and then double-click on the equals sign in the list of operators.

16 Click on the button in the calculator showing double quotation marks. The quotes land in the calculation box, and your cursor lands between them.

17 Type a capital *M*.

18 Drag to select the words "result one," and then go to the calculator. Click on the decimal point and the numeral 3. All right, type .3 if you really want to.

19 Similarly, replace "result two" with .2.

20 Click **OK** when your screen looks like Figure 6.28. You've got the idea.

21 Define the other calculated fields as shown in Figure 6.29.

Figure 6.29	Formulas to enter.
Tax Rate	**If (Annual Salary < 30000, .15, .28)**
Monthly Pay	**(1 – Tax Rate) * Annual Salary / 12**
Benefits	**Annual Salary * Benefit Rate / 12**
Taxes	**Annual Salary * Tax Rate / 12**

When your field definitions look like Figure 6.30,

Figure 6.30	Resulting field definition.

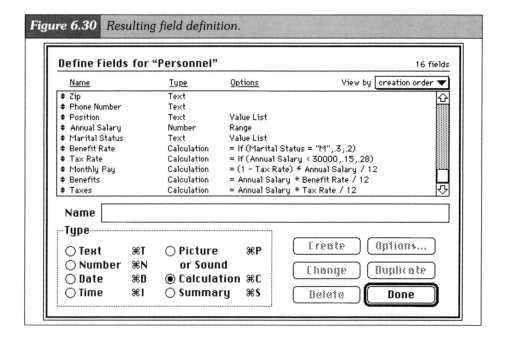

22 Click **Done** to return to Browse mode. We're almost done with the design of this datafile, but we need to format a few fields.

23 Go into Layout mode, and click on the Position field. You'll see handles appear around it.

24 Choose **Field Format...** from the Format menu. You'll see Figure 6.31.

25 Click on **Use Field's Value List...**, and click and hold on the boxed words **Pop-up List**. You'll see a menu drop.

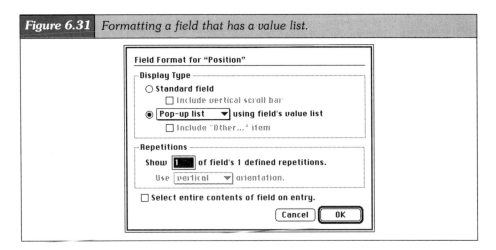

Figure 6.31 *Formatting a field that has a value list.*

Field Format for "Position"
—Display Type
○ Standard field
  ☐ Include vertical scroll bar
● Pop-up list ▼ using field's value list
  ☐ Include "Other..." item

—Repetitions
Show [1] of field's 1 defined repetitions.
Use [vertical ▼] orientation.

☐ Select entire contents of field on entry.

[Cancel] [OK]

26 Drag to **Pop-up Menu**, and release the mouse button. Click **OK**.

27 Format Marital Status the same way.

28 Select the Monthly Pay field, and choose **Number Format...** from the Format menu.

29 Format this field to display a decimal number, with fixed digits after the decimal point as 2, and to display the notation Currency.

30 Select both the Benefits and Taxes fields (click on one, then Shift-click on the second), and format them this way too.

Go back to Browse mode, and:

31 Enter the data from Figure 6.32. Click and hold on the pop-up menus to get the value lists—drag to the one you want, and release the mouse button.

Figure 6.32 *Updates to records.*

ID#	Position	Annual Salary	Marital Status
1382	Your choice	40000	S
2120	Your choice	35000	M
3855	Your choice	30000	M
4996	Your choice	35000	S
5033	Your choice	15000	S
6280	Your choice	35000	M
7407	Your choice	20000	S
8761	Your choice	75000	M

You'll need to click outside your last entry for the calculations to appear.

After you enter the first record, stop to look at the calculation results. Do they look accurate?

Until you gain experience knocking off formulas, make sure one doesn't knock you off first. Spot-checks are most helpful here, as in spreadsheets.

Custom Reports

A common and powerful use of databases is to produce any kind of piece of paper where some of what's printed on it is the same for all copies, and other parts are specific to one person or event. Examples are pay stubs and form letters. Imagine sending a form letter to all the advertisers who send you form letters!

Rather than be so esoteric here, though, we'll design a pay stub for our personnel datafile. This is a good example of the flexibility of a database's layout mode.

1. Go to Define mode, and create a field called Whole Name. Define it as a calculated field, and specify **Calculation Result is Text** below the formula area in the calculation dialog box.

2. Enter the following formula, made up of the First Name and Last Name fields, plus the punctuation. Use the mouse as much as you can, choosing from the field list and the calculator keypad area. Put one space between the quotes:

First Name&" "&Last Name

A calculation that returns text may seem strange at first, but look at this. Whole Name is a calculation of First Name, *one space*, and Last Name.

If we didn't have this nicety, we'd have to make the First Name field long enough in this layout to show longer first names.

This would leave a gap between the first and last names of those with shorter first names. Anything printed this way would simply look unprofessional.

3. Create another new field and call it City State Zip.

Make the calculation result text here too, and enter this formula:

City&", "&State&" "&Zip

Again, keep one space between quotes (or after the comma following "City"). Go back to Browse mode.

4 Make a new layout. Name it Pay Stub, and choose **Blank** as the type.

5 Drag fields from the toolbox onto the layout, as you see in Figure 6.33.

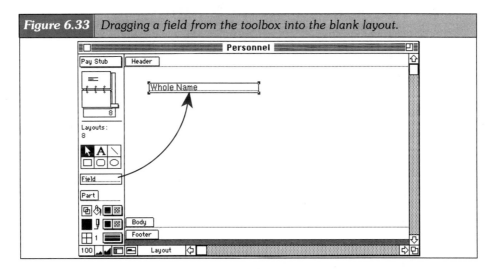

Figure 6.33 *Dragging a field from the toolbox into the blank layout.*

6 Scroll to the fields you want, as in Figure 6.34. De-select **Create Field Label**, and click **OK**.

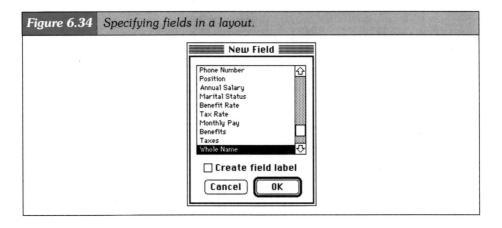

Figure 6.34 *Specifying fields in a layout.*

7 Create sufficient space in the header for a title. Think of something fun. Make the title and labels with the text tool in the toolbox.

8 Format all text (as opposed to fields) with a different font. Figure 6.35 shows Palatino. The title shown is 24 point.

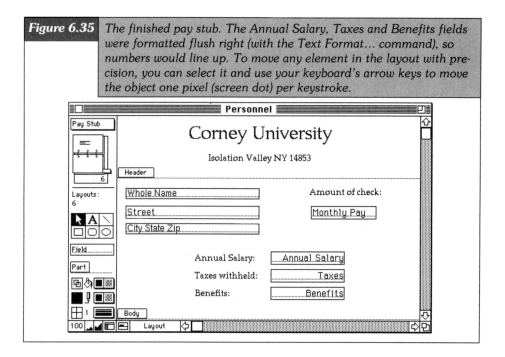

Figure 6.35 *The finished pay stub. The Annual Salary, Taxes and Benefits fields were formatted flush right (with the Text Format... command), so numbers would line up. To move any element in the layout with precision, you can select it and use your keyboard's arrow keys to move the object one pixel (screen dot) per keystroke.*

9 Check to see that all currency fields are formatted as such, with two digits past the decimal point.

For more complicated forms, you can certainly use the same field more than once in a layout.

SCRIPTS

FileMaker, like Excel, has a built-in language to automate repetitive tasks, and assiduous use of such features is one mark of the accomplished computer user. So let's look at FileMaker's implementation of macros, which this program calls *scripts*.

These are less complex than what you learned with Excel. Each script in FileMaker does a small, predefined action, which can save time, or facilitate another user's work, or both. Scripts can be combined with other scripts. Let's make a couple.

First, by way of setup:

1. Do an alphabetical sort, with last name as the primary key, and first name as the secondary. Then go to the list layout. OK, we're set.

2. Choose **ScriptMaker** from the Scripts menu. You'll get a dialog box like Figure 6.36, showing what scripts were already made for this document, if there were any, and your cursor will be in a title box, ready for you to name the script.

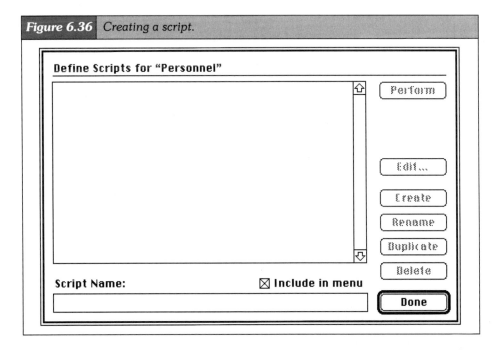

Figure 6.36 *Creating a script.*

Define Scripts for "Personnel"

	Perform
	Edit...
	Create
	Rename
	Duplicate
	Delete

Script Name: ☒ Include in menu

Done

3. Type *Alpha List* for the name of the script, and press **Create**.

You'll get a dialog box like Figure 6.37, showing you script functions available. FileMaker has suggested, in the box on the right, several of the functions available from the box on the left. We want to keep most of these, but we don't want this set of automatic steps to include printing the list, so:

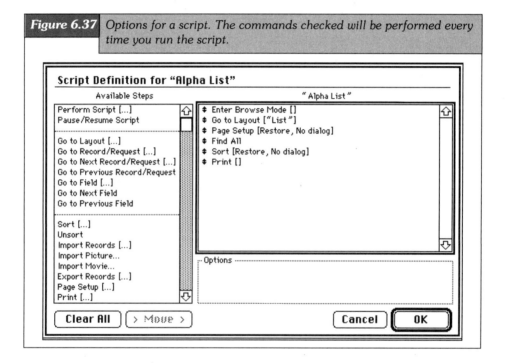

Figure 6.37 *Options for a script. The commands checked will be performed every time you run the script.*

4 Click on **Print [ ]** to select it, and click **Clear** at the bottom of the window.

5 Click **OK**, and then click **Done** to return to the file.

As further setup:

7 Sort by ID number, and switch to the Pay Stub layout.

8 Make another script, and name it Payroll. Again, clear the print command. **OK** and be **Done** with this.

9 Pull down the Scripts menu, and note that you have two new menu commands: **Alpha List** with **Command–1** next to it, and **Payroll** with **Command–2**.

10 Choose each command, and see how you can select either layout and at the same time sort your data with the sort order most useful for that layout.

This works for about anything that FileMaker can do. You can also make life easier by first making small script modules, and then chaining or nesting different ones as you need them.

Scripting is especially handy for a data file, since computer documents like this are more likely to serve multiple users than an average SuperPaint graphic, Word letter, or even most spreadsheets.

It's also most often the case with databases that the user may be unfamiliar with most computer operations. Their work may require them to sit down at a computer only occasionally and pull certain information out of the data file.

It's just this sort of scripting automation that could allow the instructions for the occasional user to read something like: *1. Double-click on "Client File" icon. 2. Choose "New Clients" script. 3. Get list off printer.*

You might have done that by having FileMaker take today's date from the Mac's clock and subtract from that the date the client was signed up. Your script does a find in that calculated field for all records with values less than 30, sorts by zip code and then name, goes to a list layout and prints it.

Your office mates would think you're pretty good on a computer. Then again, you are. Once more you've learned a major program in a chapter. This has been a productive effort because, on odds, a database of some sort may be the computer application you use most in college or business in almost any area.

It's not just having information or using it in the form in which you got it—it's managing it. In the information age, this is good stuff to know.

CHECKLIST

Your tour through a computer database has taught you:

- how to use records, fields and layouts,

- automated or regulated data entry,

- finding and sorting by criteria,

- calculated fields with if-then statements, and

- custom reporting.

all of which offer insight into an area of major power for the personal computer. It's literally true that what sits on a desk today can do what needed a mainframe ten years ago, and an army of clerks ten years before that.

In our exercise, we only hinted at the value this kind of program has for data in large quantities. Why not keep employee records for your company of 50,000 this way? It's fast and accurate. Make lots of backups, though.

OTHER CHOICES

FileMaker is an easy and elegant tool for these uses. Its major competition is Panorama, a similar product except that it's built for speed. It accomplishes this by keeping all records in RAM instead of on disk, as FileMaker does. The tradeoff is that, for most PC systems, RAM is more limited than disk space, limiting with it the number of records you can have in one file.

Both FileMaker and Panorama are called *flat-file managers*: you have all fields for one record in one file. Imagine a more complex program, with which you could have two different files on employees, for example: one file would have fields containing non-sensitive information, the other might have employment and salary history.

Access to the second would be limited but, when used, the program could *relate* one file to the other, and any two fields, each from one file, could be viewed, or made part of calculations, as though they were fields in one file.

Such a relational database is more complex in use but can offer great power. Look at Double Helix, Helix Express, Fourth Dimension, Omnis, or Foxbase as a next step in exploring information management on the Macintosh.

HELPFUL HINTS

As with many kinds of programs, finding a project to learn FileMaker on is especially helpful. And especially easy, since there's a use for a database almost everywhere you look. No organization these days can live very effectively without one.

When you have a chance, you might want to explore *mail merge* (also called *print merge*), in which a database and word processor work together. You can customize 100 letters to clients or friends with data from FileMaker, to look like each letter was an individual effort. Two programs working together this way add an order of magnitude to the flexibility and power now available to you.

Q & A

Q: *I seem to get lost in FileMaker.*

A: Unlike many other programs, FileMaker (and databases in general) are *modal* in design. When you're in one mode, such as Layout, you can't perform some functions without switching modes first.

Q: *I'm in Browse mode, in a list layout, and can only see a few of my records.*

A: You performed a Find, and now can see only what matched your criteria. Choose **Find All** to see all your records again.

Q: *It's difficult to position fields and their labels precisely in a layout.*

A: The invisible grid that makes objects jump from point to point as you drag them is most often a help, but gets in the way of fine positioning. The best solution is to drag objects to approximately where you want them, and then use the **Arrow** keys on your keyboard to move, one pixel per keystroke, the objects into place.

Q: *How do I save in FileMaker?*

A: The program saves for you, either after there's been no input for a minute or two, or after a specified number of minutes. You can set this in the Preferences dialog box, but the default—save on idle—is fine for most purposes.

Q: *I think I've lost some data.*

A: This is hard to do in FileMaker. You may have had a system or hardware malfunction or, more likely, your data is still there but just hidden in one of several ways. Review this chapter's discussion of different modes, change layouts, and use the **Find All** command.

Q: *My calculated fields don't work.*

A: You have to specify exactly what you want FileMaker to calculate. For example, placement of commas and quotation marks are important in If functions. In general, try to click or double-click on as much as you can in the Options dialog box, rather than typing formulas. As a special note, make sure that if you want the calculation result to be text, that you so specify it.

Q: *I was working with a datafile when my computer crashed, and now I can't open the file.*

A: FileMaker has a nice **Recover** feature, on the File menu, to dig data out of a corrupted file. Follow its instructions carefully, and you should be able to recover records, especially, which are most often more important to recover than are layouts. With this as with any program, though, the importance of backing up data can't be emphasized enough.

Q: *I'm in a layout like the Pay Stub in this chapter, and want to edit some field names.*

A: You can't do this in layout mode. You can edit labels or miscellaneous text, but you'll need to go to field mode to change field names.

Q: *My script doesn't do what I programmed it to do.*

A: Until you really get the hang of scripting, it's best to keep them short, test them first, and then build larger scripts from these smaller ones. It's a powerful and versatile tool, so don't give up easily.

SAMPLE EXERCISE

Take some data you already have—from work, a club or a hobby, anything that's intrinsically interesting—and put it in a datafile. Try to separate data into as small chunks as possible. For your CD collection, for example, be sure to put artist and title into different fields. Sort, find, and print your data. You may well find collections more useful, because you now have access to what's in them that you didn't have before.

CHAPTER 7

CONCEPTUAL NAVIGATION AND HYPERCARD

In this chapter, you'll learn about a program that supports a different kind of thinking and expression, valuable for planning, presentation and education. You'll be able to:

- make a HyperCard stack

- add buttons and link them to stacks and cards

- work in HyperCard's background layer

- work with text in fields and add graphics

- use HyperCard's scripting language for impressive special effects

This is the point in this book where we do something really new. What we've done up to now has of course been using new tools, but our results have been similar to what we produced before computers.

SuperPaint, for example, gives you a lot of both options and fun when you paint. But you're still working with the equivalent, high-powered though it is, of a paintbrush or drafting tools. Word processing, with all of its spell-checking and fonts, is placing Roman letters and Arabic numbers on the equivalent of a sheet of paper. You may never go back to a file cabinet after using FileMaker, but the analogy still applies.

What we're going to look at now is not another new and improved tool for an existing idea, but a new idea itself or, more precisely, a *radical conceptual innovation*.

There are two points of interest in a radical innovation: first, no one can predict its appearance and second, it's hard to recognize it for what it is. Invention of the airplane and submarine, for example, were not radical innovations, and so many people, Jules Verne among them, were able to predict their appearance.

The airplane and submarine were new things or tools, but not new ideas, because people had watched birds fly and fish swim for some years prior to figuring out how to do mechanically what these animals did naturally.

The wheel, by great contrast, was a radical conceptual innovation. No one could have predicted its invention, as the philosopher Karl Popper points out, because to do so would be to invent it. No one could have thought of what the wheel did and how, and described it, without thereby inventing it. Such is the nature of a new idea.

The second thing about new ideas is that their value is so hard to recognize. One great story concerns the inventor of the Xerox machine—granted, not a radically new idea, but new enough. Ask your stockbroker if she wishes she had bought Xerox stock at its initial public offering, or if she actually prefers going to work every day. Then tell her that the original Xerox machine was built in the inventor's bathtub, because he couldn't get funding to develop it properly.

Why not? Because no one saw the value of it. The inventor, so the story goes, was a draftsman in a patent office who got tired of reproducing drawings all day. He came up with his idea and went to his company for development funds. His boss said, "Why do I need this machine? That's what I pay you for."

What we're going to look at is a radically new idea in software—and its value may be hard to appreciate at first. The concept was described in 1946 by

Vannevar Bush, and the software was developed by Bill Atkinson, one of the Mac's most creative designers, and released in 1987. Not bad.

What it does is mimic *how we think*, or can think. Ever leave your house thinking about one thing, and arrive at work or class thinking about something entirely different, and wonder how your thoughts managed to take such a complex path? We think in association, or by linking, and many educational researchers consider that creativity is in large part the ability to make more links, and less direct ones. The very process of finding meaning in something is often just linking it to other things.

But the best links are often the hardest to see. Dreams and other symbolic modes of thought sometimes help. The discoverer of the benzene ring could not figure out the molecule's structure, until he had a dream one night of a snake biting its tail.

Conscious thought is not that much different. Brainstorming, a large part of which is random association, is a good example. And psychologists know the value of free association.

The great epistemologist Gilbert Ryle, one of the first to figure out what *mind* really is, thought that this associating or linking couldn't take the linear path we suppose it does. He wrote that once Euclid had his theory, he could explain it logically, step-by-step. But the steps he took before he had it were, Ryle said, closer to a "wrestling and wriggling" of thought—explosions of associations, so to speak.

HyperCard is *simply a way to make links*. Of course, we did that with Excel and FileMaker, but those were highly structured links, while HyperCard is as unstructured and flexible as you can be. Hypertext, the concept, is no more and no less than the idea that anything can link to anything. HyperCard, the program, is a tool to do this.

Its metaphor is stacks of cards. Each card can have graphics on it, or text or both. HyperCard has painting and writing tools to make the content of a card nearly anything you want.

These cards can have buttons on them, much like buttons in dialog boxes, but this time you choose what a button does when you click it. You can produce animation and sounds, and you can give the user choices: click one button or another to run right or left, literally or figuratively, in a maze or a learning program that you can design and build yourself.

The point is subtle. Every choice, every idea, has a result—the user can explore something at her own pace and in accord with her own interest. Hopefully someday more education, whether in school or business training, will work this way.

THE BASICS

When you start most programs by double-clicking on the program icon (rather than a document icon), you're given a new work area. FileMaker asks you to open an existing database, or structure a new one.

HyperCard's a little different. Every time you double-click on the program icon, you go to a 'home base' of sorts called the *Home card*. This starting point facilitates your moving around to other cards in one *stack* or several stacks.

The Home card is part of the *Home stack*. Every card is in one stack or another.

Figure 7.1	The Home Stack.	

You move around in HyperCard primarily by clicking buttons, and the Home card has several, each for a different card or stack. One button might take you to a game, another to a tutorial, a third to an address book.

You can navigate with menu commands as well. They're on the Go menu. Two you'll use often are Home, which takes you to the Home card, and Recent, which shows you miniature views of the forty-two most recent cards you've been on.

To start, while you're still in the Finder:

1. Make a copy on your floppy of the Home stack that comes with HyperCard. You'll be making changes to the Home card as we go, so best not to change the original.

2. Double-click on your Home stack. This takes you to the Home card in that stack.

At this point, you have access to several other stacks, through the buttons for them on the Home card.

Note that your cursor has changed from an arrow to a pointing hand. This indicates that you're in Browse mode. Like FileMaker, HyperCard's Browse mode is where we look at things.

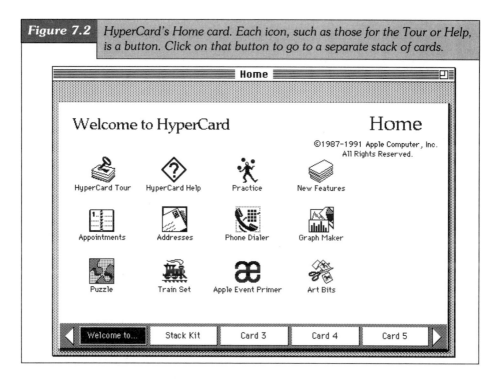

Figure 7.2 *HyperCard's Home card. Each icon, such as those for the Tour or Help, is a button. Click on that button to go to a separate stack of cards.*

Figure 7.3 *HyperCard's Hand cursor. Click on icons (buttons) with this.*

Let's take a quick look at the HyperCard Tour stack, the one at the top left of the group.

[1] Click once with your Hand cursor on the **HyperCard Tour** button.

Depending on your computer's setup, you may get a standard open dialog box, asking you where this stack is.

You'll then get a nice introductory screen, and the instruction to click your mouse anywhere to begin.

[2] Click your mouse, and you go to the next card, with a text introduction. It just seems to be a change in display.

3 Click again, and the two buttons (which, this time, look like buttons) give you the choice between Looking at or Working with HyperCard.

Time out. Note that the program is giving you a choice of ideas. Not much of one in this case, but the concept is important.

4 Click on the **Section 1: Looking at HyperCard** button.

The next and succeeding cards have an arrow or two at the bottom right. Click on the **Next** arrow for the next several cards, to follow the analogy of a rolodex file.

Note, though, what happens when you get to the card demonstrating how the cards can go in a stack. Animation is a HyperCard specialty, and very easy to do.

5 Continue with the tour, for a succinct overview of what it's like to browse through an interesting, interactive stack.

Make sure you understand what the Go menu does. Especially, test going to Home, and then back to where you were. Choose **Recent** to see thumbnails (miniature views) of the path you've taken. Click on a thumbnail to go to that card.

MAKING STACKS

This book takes up where the tour leaves off. In our exercise, we'll make new stacks, add text, graphics, and buttons, and make those buttons do things.

Since we first need to give ourselves permission to do all of this neat stuff:

1 Choose **Home** from the Go menu to go back to your Home card.

2 Press the **Left Arrow** key on your keyboard. You should see a card like Figure 7.4.

The levels 1 through 5 are access privileges to the program. As the capsule descriptions show, each higher number lets you make more changes to stack components. Let's do this right:

3 Set your user level to 5 by clicking on it.

4 Press the **Right Arrow** on the keyboard to go back to the Home card.

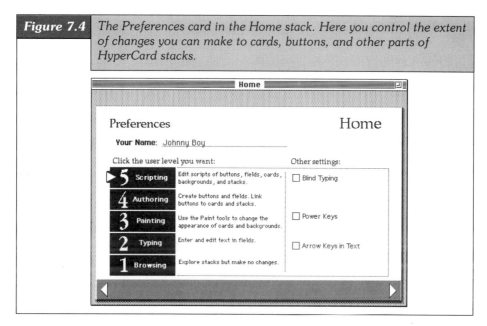

Figure 7.4 *The Preferences card in the Home stack. Here you control the extent of changes you can make to cards, buttons, and other parts of HyperCard stacks.*

Note that while on the Preferences card, we were in the Home stack, not the Home card. Hereafter when we say Home, we'll mean the card.

Speaking of stacks, though, let's create one. We do this in just the same way as creating a new document in any Mac program:

[1] Choose **New Stack...** from the File menu (not New Card from the Edit menu). You'll get:

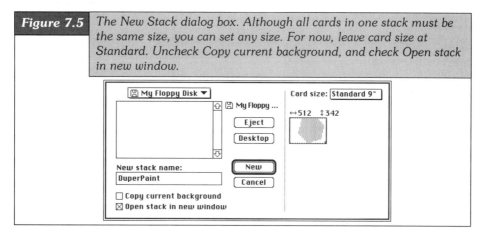

Figure 7.5 *The New Stack dialog box. Although all cards in one stack must be the same size, you can set any size. For now, leave card size at Standard. Uncheck Copy current background, and check Open stack in new window.*

This stack will be a small paint program, using HyperCard's graphics tools. So navigate to your floppy, choose a name you like ("DuperPaint" isn't too bad), set other options to match Figure 7.5, and click **New**.

Your new stack now has one card, and it's blank.

2 Click on the Tools menu. You'll see the palette shown in Figure 7.6.

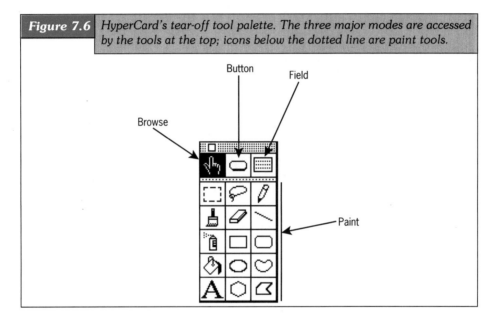

| Figure 7.6 | HyperCard's tear-off tool palette. The three major modes are accessed by the tools at the top; icons below the dotted line are paint tools. |

You'll see also that the top left icon, the **Hand** tool (or the Browse tool), is selected. We'll get to the **Button** and **Field** tools in a little bit.

For now, note an interesting thing about this menu: You can *tear it off the menu bar*, and put it anywhere on the screen. To do this:

1 Click and hold on the Tools menu.

2 Drag your mouse away from the menu bar. Note the dotted line following your mouse.

3 Release the mouse anywhere on the screen. HyperCard's tool palette should stay open, as in Figure 7.6. Elegant.

4 Put the Tools palette in the painting window and, while watching the menu bar, click on any paint tool. See how menus are added to the bar, to reflect the paint mode.

5 Tear off the Patterns palette, in the same way. Your card, while blank, should resemble Figure 7.7.

Figure 7.7 *Your new stack, with paint and pattern palettes torn off and placed within the drawing window.*

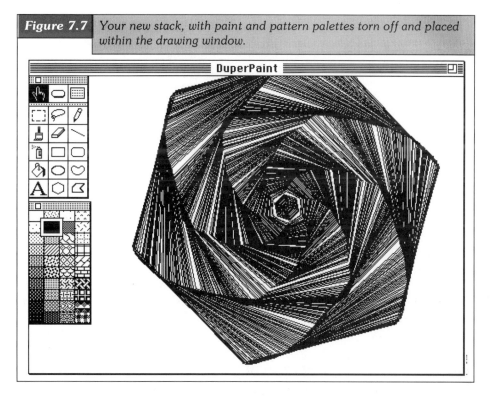

You can now go ahead and paint something. Note the many choices in the Paint and Options menus. Also, try double-clicking on some of the paint tools, to access other options. Double-clicking on the Hexagon tool, for example, lets you change the number of sides of objects this tool paints.

Should you for some reason be interested, the object in Figure 7.7 was created in one mouse drag with the hexagon tool, and **Draw Multiple** selected from the Options menu.

BUTTONS AND THINGS

Now that we have a neat little painting program (actually, one with some impressive features), let's go back to the Home card, and *make a button* that goes to this stack, just like the HyperCard Tour button went to the Tour stack.

1 Go Home, either by the Go menu, or by pressing **Command-H**.

Let's see what's behind one of these buttons. We do this by holding down the **Command** and **Option** keys while clicking on a button.

2 Hold down the **Command** and **Option** keys, and click on the **HyperCard Tour** button. You'll see something like this:

```
on mouseUp
    go to stack "HyperCard Tour"
end mouseUp
```

with perhaps some more added, depending on your exact version of things. But what's important to us is these three lines. They're simply a set of instructions beginning with "on mouseUp"—that is, when you release your mouse button after clicking on the Tour icon.

The next line, in plain English, tells HyperCard to go to the Tour stack. The third line tells HyperCard that it shouldn't do anything else as a part of this mouseUp sequence.

This is a *script*. It's a set of instructions to HyperCard written in English, but with some conventions, telling it what to do.

NOTE

All of the animation, sounds, and special effects that you found when you took the tour were done with scripts. It's easy with a little practice, and lots of fun.

In fact, we'll have HyperCard write our first script for us. But first, to make a button:

1 Click on the Button tool.

See how the appearance of your Home card has changed. There's now a solid line around each button, as in Figure 7.8.

2 Choose **New Button** from the Objects menu. You'll see a moving dotted line (a *marquee*) around the new button in the center of the card.

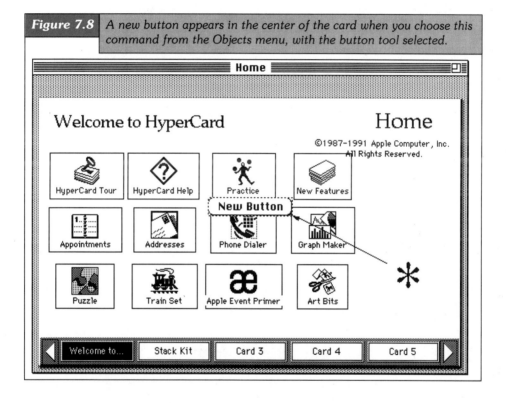

Figure 7.8 *A new button appears in the center of the card when you choose this command from the Objects menu, with the button tool selected.*

3 Click on your new button, and drag it off to the right, where there's blank space on the card.

Remember that in FileMaker and in SuperPaint's draw mode, you could reshape a rectangle by clicking on a corner handle and dragging.

It's the same thing here, except that there aren't handles on the corners of the button's rectangle. Reshape using the right lower corner.

4 Reshape your new button until it's about the same size as the buttons to its left.

Hmm. It still doesn't look as nice. So make sure your button is still selected (a marquee around it), come up to the Objects menu, and:

5 Choose **Button Info...**. You'll see Figure 7.9:

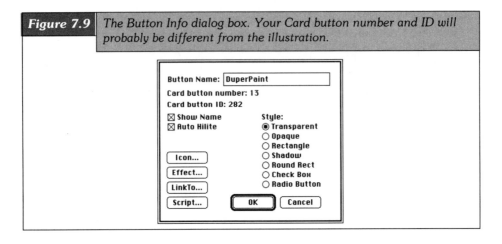

Figure 7.9 *The Button Info dialog box. Your Card button number and ID will probably be different from the illustration.*

6 Type *DuperPaint* for the name, and leave **Show Name** selected. Also select **Auto Hilite**. For Style, choose **Transparent**.

7 Click on the **Icon...** button at the left of the dialog box. You'll get Figure 7.10. Choose the one shown as selected, and click **OK**.

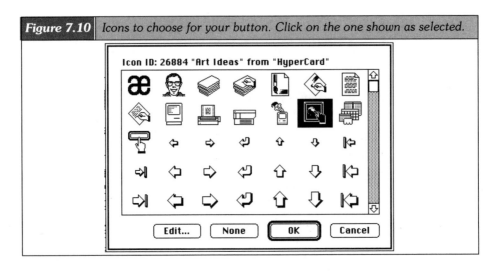

Figure 7.10 *Icons to choose for your button. Click on the one shown as selected.*

You're back to your Home card, with a shimmering marquee around the **DuperPaint** button. Double-click on it to get Figure 7.9 back.

8 Next, click on the **Effect...** button, and choose **Iris Open**. Click on **Slow**, and then click **OK**. This is going to look nice.

Now that it's going to look nice, we want to make it do something. Remember that when we looked at the script for the HyperCard Tour button, we saw it contained instructions to go to another stack.

LINKING

In the trade, we say the button is *linked* to that stack. We want to link our new **DuperPaint** button to the stack of that name. Go back to the **Button Info** dialog box, and:

1 Click on the **Link to...** button. You'll get the **Link to:** dialog box, which HyperCard calls a *windoid*.

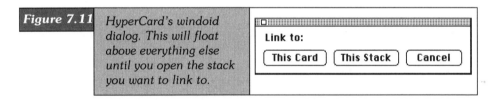

Figure 7.11 HyperCard's windoid dialog. This will float above everything else until you open the stack you want to link to.

It just asks you which card, or stack, you want to link your button to. It floats above all other windows until you use it. So, without clicking on any of its buttons, let's open your DuperPaint stack.

2 Choose **Open Stack...** from the File menu, and navigate to DuperPaint. With that stack open:

3 Click on the windoid's **This Stack** button.

Bingo. You've just linked your button to a stack.

4 Go Home, and click on the Browse (Hand) tool in the Tools menu. Back in Browse mode:

5 Click on your new button to verify that it takes you to DuperPaint. Pretty slick, especially with the Iris Open effect. Go Home again, and hold down on the **Command** and **Option** keys and click the button, to see the script HyperCard wrote for you.

It doesn't tear off the Tools and Patterns palettes for you, yet. We'll figure that out in a bit.

Stop for a moment to think about what you've done. In the Tour stack, much of the fancy effects you saw were done by linking buttons to cards. Now you know how.

PUTTING IT TOGETHER

Let's make a complete stack, with graphics and buttons. We'll also include text, in a mode HyperCard calls *Fields*. The example given is a simple book to teach children the alphabet. Don't worry, it's easy.

To make it even easier, we'll put some of the objects in the background. This HyperCard feature lets you add graphics or buttons or things to a stack so that they are the same on every card.

As you saw in the tour, every card in HyperCard can have two layers: the *Card layer* and the *Background layer*. Both layers can have graphics, buttons and text. You switch between the two by choosing **Background** from the Edit menu, or pressing **Command–B**.

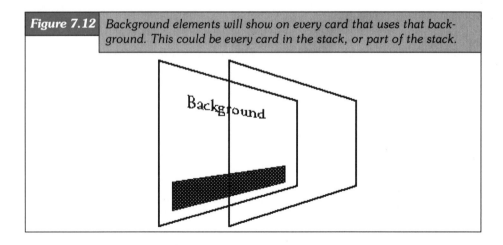

Figure 7.12 *Background elements will show on every card that uses that background. This could be every card in the stack, or part of the stack.*

Take a moment to go through stacks available to you, to find a background you like. Our example is called "My Book," and we'll show an open book background, but any kind of decoration or border you want will work.

When you find something you like:

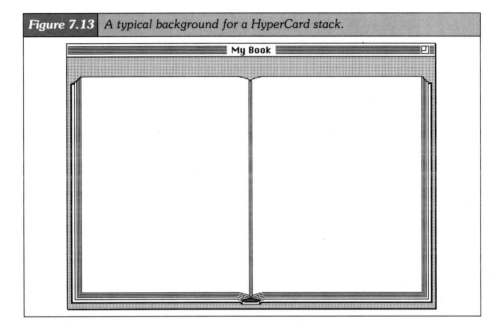

Figure 7.13 *A typical background for a HyperCard stack.*

1 Choose **New Stack** from the File menu, locate it on your floppy disk, and name it My Book.

Be sure that **Copy Current Background** is checked.

You'll get a display similar to this:

First, be sure that you're in the card layer, not the background layer. You do that by looking at the menu bar. If the whole menu bar is bounded by slash marks, you're in the background. Select the **Background** command from the Edit menu, so as to uncheck it, and return to the card layer.

Figure 7.14 *The Menu bar in Background mode.*

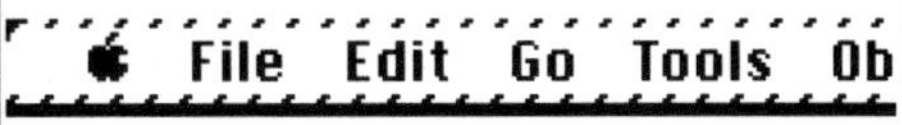

 File Edit Go Tools Ob

We're now on the first card of our new stack. Let's start with a title.

2. Choose the **Text tool** from the tool palette. (This is the large letter A.)

3. Pick a font and size you like from the **Text Style...** command on the Edit menu. Note that the dialog box is labeled **Paint Text Style**.

4. Put your cursor on the right page, if you have a book background, or in the center of another decorative display.

5. Type a title for your stack. Perhaps "My Book," but you can use something else if you want to. Add your name and maybe the date.

 What you've just typed was paint text. Just like the paint mode of SuperPaint, this kind of text is real text when you type it, but once you do something else, this text becomes 'fixed' just as though it were

N O T E paint on canvas. You can select it and move it or erase it, but you can't edit it as text.

We're going to enter the rest of the text in this stack in another way, so that you can edit it as text—or search for a string, much like in a word processor. We do this using HyperCard's *Field mode*.

Just like buttons or graphics, you can put text fields either on a card or the background. Let's put some fields in the background, so they're immediately available on every card we make.

6. Choose **Background** from the menu bar. The slash marks around the Edit menu bar confirm your choice.

7. Select the **Field tool** from the tools palette.

8. Choose **New Field** from the Options menu.

A new field is displayed in the center of the window, just as your new button was.

9. Click on the lower right hand corner of the field, and reshape and resize it until it's a square, about 0.75-inch on a side.

10. Move the field to the center top of the left page, or the equivalent in another background.

11. Make two more fields, and size and position them so all three are as shown in Figure 7.16. Leave a little room at the bottom of the left page.

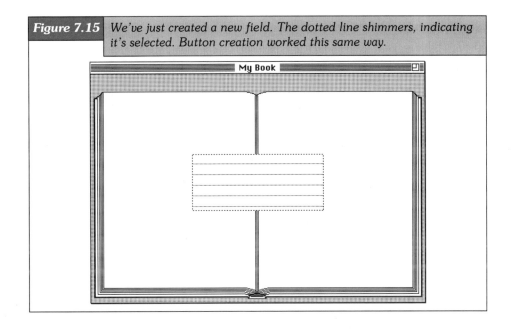

Figure 7.15 We've just created a new field. The dotted line shimmers, indicating it's selected. Button creation worked this same way.

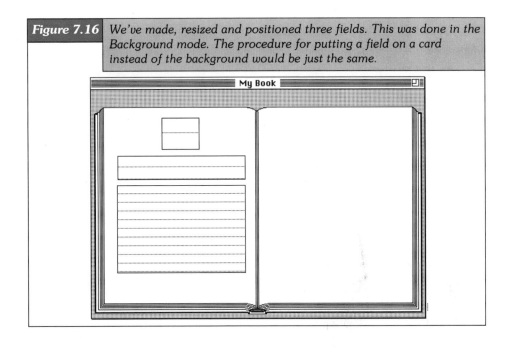

Figure 7.16 We've made, resized and positioned three fields. This was done in the Background mode. The procedure for putting a field on a card instead of the background would be just the same.

Next, let's format the type style and size of each field.

12 Click on the top field to select it, and choose **Field Info...** from the Options menu.

13 Click on the **Transparent** radio button in the Field Info... dialog box. Then click on the **Font** button, and make this top field 24 point, with your choice of font.

14 Make the middle field transparent and 18 point, and the bottom field transparent and 12 point.

15 Select the **Background** command on the Edit menu again, to come back to the card layer. Your title should reappear. Then choose the Browse tool from the tool palette.

Note that your fields have become transparent. Move the Hand icon over the fields, and see how it changes to a text (I-beam) cursor, ready for text entry.

ADDING GRAPHICS

Now for some content to the stack. What we want on the right pages of our book are graphics starting with successive letters of the alphabet.

1 Choose **New Card** from the Edit menu.

Now, let's take a tour through what graphics are available to you, or you can paint your own with HyperCard's tools. Probably the easiest place to get graphics is from the Art Bits stack that comes with HyperCard.

Access this stack by going Home—there's a button for Art Bits. To return to your stack, you can use the Recent option. Or, make a button on your Home card that links to your new stack.

If you're looking through Art Bits, HyperCard's Find command is a big help. Rather than go card-by-card:

2 Choose **Find** from the Edit menu. Then just type what you're looking for; the cursor is already between the quotes. Then press **Return**. Press **Return** again to find further instances of what you specified.

3 Find a graphic whose name starts with A. We've chosen Aardvark from the Art Bits stack.

4 Using HyperCard's Lasso tool, select your first graphic, and copy it. (Don't cut it.)

5 Go back to your stack.

6 Paste the graphic. With it still selected, move your mouse over it, until the icon changes to an arrow, and drag the graphic over to the right page or area.

7 Go back to Browse mode, and enter something in the text fields equivalent to Figure 7.17.

Figure 7.17   *The first inside page of My Book.*

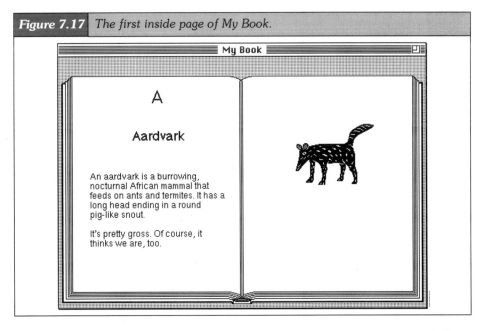

You need locate only the top field with your mouse. Then you can tab from field to field.

8 Make a new card, and repeat this for the letter B.

Let's leave the alphabet for the moment, and get fancy. We'll want an index for our book, one which, in HyperCard's inimitable fashion, lets us go to what we find in the index just by clicking on it.

9 Make another card, and enter text in the second and third fields, as you see in Figure 7.18.

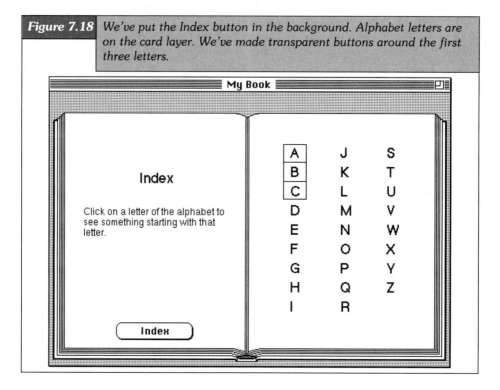

Figure 7.18 *We've put the Index button in the background. Alphabet letters are on the card layer. We've made transparent buttons around the first three letters.*

10 List the letters of the alphabet on the right-hand page, using the Paint Text tool. The example was done in 18 point Helvetica.

11 Switch to the Background layer, and we'll make the **Index** button.

12 Select the Button tool and choose **New Button**. Drag it to where you see the Index button in the example.

13 Choose **Button Info...** (or, as a shortcut, double-click on the button), name the button, and press **Link to...**.

14 Press the **This Card** button on the link windoid.

HyperCard understands that it's the present (Index) card you want to link to, even though you're presently in the Background layer.

Let's add buttons to letters of the alphabet on the Index card. Go to the card layer, and:

15 Make a transparent button over the letter A. Make it transparent, and turn off the **Show Name** attribute. Don't link it just yet.

Now for one of HyperCard's great shortcuts:

16 Hold down the **Shift** and **Option** keys, and drag this button so that it covers the letter B. You've just copied a button. The copy has its own attributes, though, so it has a separate link.

17 Link the Index buttons for the letters A and B to their respective cards. Go back to Browse mode and see that these work. Then check the scripts for these buttons, to see how HyperCard has done them for you. Most often, you don't need to keep track of card ID numbers—just show HyperCard the card you want to link to.

SCRIPTING

Writing your own scripts is the gateway to the real power of HyperCard, called *Hypertalk*. A quick example of this: why have the Index button on the Index card? When the user of your stack is on the Index card, she's not likely to want to press that button.

Let's put a script in the Index card to make the Index button invisible when the user is on that card. So go to the Index, and:

1 Choose **Card Info...** from the Objects menu, and then click the **Script** button.

2 Type this script in the script window. As with any respectable programming language, HyperCard indents the appropriate lines automatically, if you don't make a typing mistake (lack of proper indentation is a good check for typos):

```
on OpenCard
        Hide bkgnd button "Index"
end OpenCard
on CloseCard
        Show bkgnd button "Index"
end CloseCard
```

3 Close the script window by clicking on the close box, and **OK** changes. Test your script by going to another card (the Index button should be showing) and then returning to the Index card (the button should be hidden).

4 Add this same script to your title card.

To complete a competent and elegant stack, we need add only two things: a button to take the user Home, and buttons to go forward and backward. All in the background.

Do the button for Home in the usual way. Choose a Home icon from the several available in HyperCard's icon library. Then add buttons for forward and back. The icons are in the library. We'll script what they do.

For the button to go to the next card, call up the script window, and you'll see that "on mouseUp" and "end mouseUp" are already there, with a blank line in between.

1 Add the line *go next card* in that blank line. In like fashion:

2 Add the line *go prev card* to the script for that button.

When finished, your stack should have background buttons something like Figure 7.19. Place the buttons as you wish, but remember the user's convenience, and

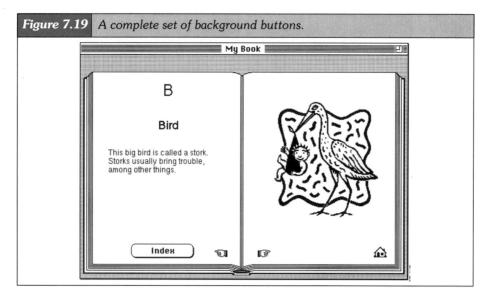

Figure 7.19 | *A complete set of background buttons.*

put the forward and back buttons close to each other. The **Home** button, by convention, goes in a corner.

Your stack is now looking pretty elegant, and the only thing left to do is, so to speak, pack it for shipping. As you've worked, the file has grown in size on disk, and some of the file space is actually free. HyperCard lets you get rid of the unused space by compacting a stack. Let's do this.

Check **Stack Info** under the Objects menu to see how much empty space there is in your stack. Then choose the **Compact Stack** option under the File menu.

ADVANCED SCRIPTING

When you created the DuperPaint stack, you got a nice painting program, except that each time you open it you have to tear off the tools and patterns palettes, and place them in the painting window, to look like SuperPaint.

Why not have HyperCard do that for you, each time you open DuperPaint? Here's how.

Open DuperPaint, and choose **Stack Info...** from the Objects menu, and click the **Script** button. Add this script:

```
on openStack
    show window "tools" at 0,10
    show window "patterns" at 0,155
    set visible of window "tools" to true
    set visible of window "patterns" to true
end openStack
on closeStack
    set visible of window "tools" to false
    set visible of window "patterns" to false
end closeStack
```

While there are commands here that are new to you, note that everything's in English. The coordinates, such as "0,10" for the Tools window, are horizontal and vertical measures of pixels, and the rest is how Hypertalk does things. A look at a few scripts makes this easy and intuitive.

And this script, all ten lines of it, has given you a relatively full-featured painting program, one that you can distribute to all of your friends who have HyperCard. They'll think you know what's going on with a computer. Of course, they're right.

CHECKLIST

Since HyperCard's such a creative tool, it's harder to provide a list of features familiarity with which describes competence with the program. A good stack, though, makes use of:

- a free-form paint environment,
- buttons, with icons and links,
- the card and background layers,
- fields and text formatting, and
- scripting, for elegance and much greater functionality.

HELPFUL HINTS

Apple's introduction of HyperCard brought a profound change to the Macintosh environment. Previously, there were two kinds of people in the Mac world: programmers and users. Programmers had highly specialized skills, and the rest of us could only use what they provided.

HyperCard and its easy-to-learn scripting made every Mac user a potential programmer. There's lots of power in this program, as you'll see by exploring a few stacks, and there are several thousand to choose from. Many are free, available from users' groups. What you can put in a stack is limited only by your imagination, and many users have created incredible, wonderful stacks dealing with everything in sight, with not much more practice than you've had here.

We especially recommend the huge collections of stacks offered by the Berkeley Macintosh User Group and the Boston Computer Society. See the Technical Notes in Appendix F for their addresses or for Apple's toll free number to get you in touch with a nearby users' group.

Every time you see a stack you like, you can call up the scripts that come with it. Check out button, field, card, and stack scripts. Copy them (if they are not copyrighted) into your own stacks. When you copy anything from one stack to another, the associated script comes along with it. Just copy a button, for example, just like you've copied text and graphics. The script is copied with it.

Here are some books you can get if you want to know more about HyperCard and its programming:

- *Understanding HyperCard* by Greg Harvey

- *The Complete HyperCard Handbook* by Danny Goodman

- *HyperCard Developer's Guide* by Danny Goodman

- *Hypertalk* by Lon Poole

We could easily say that it's hard to overestimate the value of HyperCard for everything from education to fun and games. The truth is, though, it's hard even to *realize* the value of this thing until you've seen a few stacks in areas of interest to you.

The exhilarating freedom that this brings is the sense that *you can do anything you want with this thing*. And why Apple says its computers, more than being tools for numbers or writing, really are tools for the mind.

Q & A

Q: *I can't open scripts or find the graphic menu.*

A: You need to set your user level in the Home stack before you can do anything in HyperCard except look at stacks. Go to the Preferences card, the last card in the Home stack.

Q: *I can't see much of anything on the Preferences card in the Home stack, where I would change the user level.*

A: You're working with a copy of HyperCard that ships with every new Mac. While on the preferences card, type **Command-M**, and you'll see a message box appear at the bottom of your screen. Type *magic* in this box, and press **Return**. You should now be able to access the User Level dialog.

Q: *I can't move graphic objects on a card.*

A: HyperCard uses the paint mode. You can select any area and move it or delete it, but not an object as such.

Q: *I want to search for some text in a stack, using HyperCard's Find command. I know it's there, but I can't find it.*

A: You are searching for text entered in the paint mode, rather than text in a field. The Find command can't find paint text because, after it's entered, it ceases to be real text. Enter text in fields if you want to work with it later.

Q: *I can't select a button or a field.*

A: Keep in mind which layer you're in—the card or background layer. What you want to select is in the other layer.

Q: *I copied a stack onto my hard disk and tried to run it. I keep getting messages that the program can't find or understand things.*

A: The scripts in that stack refer to the path to other stacks—which folder on which disk they are on. Your copy is on a disk with a different name, and the scripts can't find what they're supposed to. You'll need to open the script windows for the buttons that don't work, and change the references, or relink buttons.

SAMPLE EXERCISE

This is such a creative and free-form tool that a suggestion of any structure for an exercise strikes us as inappropriate. The best place to start for your first original stack is with something especially interesting to you. How would you express the magic and excitement of something you really enjoy, using the flexibility of this program? Animation, sounds, special visual effects can help, but the most important part of a good stack is its structure—how many choices you give the user to explore, whether it's in the context of a game or an interest. There's not much limit to what you can do.

CHAPTER 8

DESKTOP PUBLISHING

In this chapter you'll learn how to:

- place text and graphics in a page design program
- resize blocks of text, and resize and crop graphics
- wrap text around graphics
- work with master pages
- use word processing features of page layout programs
- distinguish between categories of fonts and their best applications
- fine-tune type and styles for truly professional results

Desktop publishing is one of the newest big industries around, and a major inno-vation of personal computers—what you'll do in an hour or two took profession-als two days before PC's. As well, their product was not as good as yours can be, since they did not have the immediate feedback and potential for change that you have here.

They worked largely by hand, on light tables. The exacting nature of the page design process was time-consuming and thus expensive. By contrast, the ease and speed with which you can make up a page by computer is a real asset to the creative process, in addition to saving bucks.

Computer page design also offers the invaluable asset of being able to make fast changes to a publication and judging relative effectiveness of different lay-outs. This makes practice in this area much easier.

An inviting page is an important tool to persuade people to read what you've written, or buy what you're advertising. Take some time with the next magazine you read, to judge the use and effectiveness of its page composition, and ask why advertising aimed at different markets makes use of different styles of layout.

This chapter may be one of the most useful for you, since whatever area of business, education or government you're in, people need to communicate ideas. Publications are often an effective way to do this, and a presentable brochure, newsletter, or journal is more inviting to read. Your good ideas will go further faster if they are well dressed.

GETTING STARTED

Start up PageMaker by double-clicking on its icon, and then choosing **New** from the File menu. First, you'll be asked to confirm or change the default page layout. Choose **Tall** orientation, click **OK**, and you'll get a representation of a blank page.

The **tool palette** appears in a small window at the top right. You can drag that window around like any other, or hide it to keep it out of your way as you work with different-sized views of your page.

You'll do a lot with the **Arrow tool**, and some with the **Cropping tool**. Depending on how you work, you might use the **Text tool** quite a bit. The other tools draw lines or shapes.

Figure 8.1 *PageMaker's initial window. The margins show as dotted lines and will guide text you place within them. You can, though, "bleed" pictures or text to the edge of the page, if your printer will print to the edge. The toolbox appears at the top right of the screen, but can be moved.*

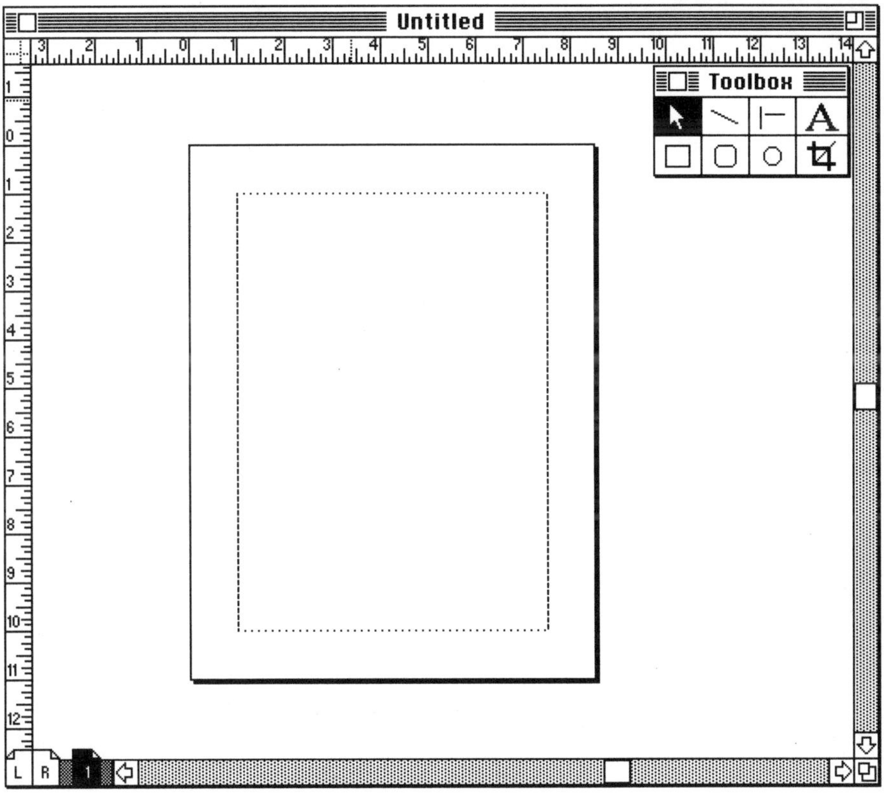

Figure 8.2 *PageMaker's toolbox.*

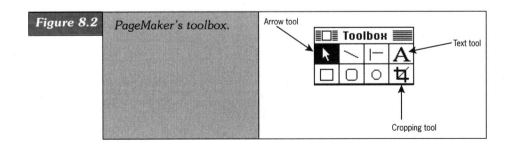

Page layout programs allow you different views of your page. PageMaker opens to *Fit in Window*, but the Page menu has options for views in several different sizes, up to four times the actual size. All are useful views; the higher magnifications help with accuracy.

The rectangle representing a blank page, with dotted lines for margins, is where we're going to place blocks containing either text or graphics, and lines or other generic graphics to separate or emphasize blocks.

Anything can be put anywhere on a page.

A word processing program allows mixing text and graphics, and PageMaker can also work moderately well for word processing. But you have the best of both worlds by creating and editing text in a dedicated word processor, and doing page makeup in a program designed for it.

Let's make up a rough, or dummy page, with some text and a picture. The emphasis at this point won't be on accuracy but, rather, fluidity.

First, make sure the **Guides** and **Snap to Guides** commands on the Options menu are on, and that the **Autoflow** command is off. A command has a check mark beside it if it's on.

Note the location, on either your hard disk or available floppies, of both text and graphics you'd like to place on your pages as practice. It's easy to make some, using SuperPaint and Word or comparable programs. Here's how:

- PageMaker imports Word documents directly, so you can write as usual in Word, and then place your writing in PageMaker for further work.

- PageMaker reads the file format (the program's own design for writing information to disk and reading it again) of several other word processing programs, but not all. It can, however, read a file made by any word processor if the file is saved as plain text (also called text only, or ASCII text). As we go, see if PageMaker will read your word processor's files as they are. If not, open one and, using the **Save As** command, save the file with a new name in the plain text format. PageMaker will then be able to use it.

- PageMaker can't read SuperPaint's own file format, but PageMaker can read standard graphics formats on the Mac called PICT, MacPaint (or just Paint, or MPNT), EPS, and TIFF. Open any SuperPaint file (or any other graphics program's file: most can write PICT or Paint files, and a few EPS or TIFF), and use the **Save As** command to make a copy in one of these formats. You'll have to give the copy a different name to avoid overwriting the original file.

1 Choose the **Place** command from the File menu. You'll get a standard open dialog box. Navigate to your text and graphics, and you'll find a list of both types that PageMaker can read.

2 Double-click on a text file (leave the radio button lit for **New Story**). You go back to your page, where you can see that the normal arrow cursor has been replaced by a design suggesting the top left corner of a page of type.

Figure 8.3	PageMaker's cursor after you double-click on a text file. You're ready to place that text.	

PageMaker does a lot of this—the shape of your cursor shows you what mode you are in. Had you selected a graphic to place, the icon would indicate not only that it's a graphic, but what format it is.

N O T E

3 Align the Place Text cursor with the top left corner of the margins, and click your mouse.

At this point, PageMaker *flows* the text into the margins, and your cursor returns to a normal arrow.

Figure 8.4	Text flowed into margins.

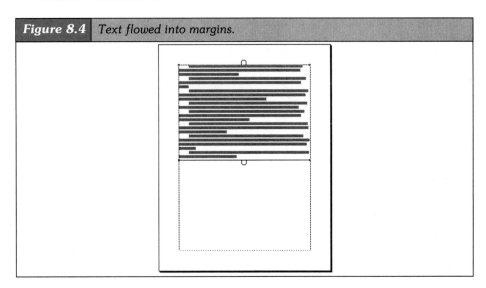

Your text is shown as gray lines (or *greeked*) simply because at this view it's too small to be drawn as text.

What you just did is get text from a word processing file. This isn't the same as opening a PageMaker file, which you would do using **Open** from the File menu.

N O T E

4 Choose **Actual Size** from the Page menu to see real text. Then go back to **Fit in Window**.

The chief difference at this point between what you have and a page in a word processor is the flexibility. You could move this text, all or part of it, freely around on the page.

5 Click in the middle of your text block, and *hold the mouse button down*. PageMaker takes a second, then your cursor changes to look like four arrows, pointing in different directions. You're *picking up* this text. Keeping the mouse button down:

6 Move the text block around. This is more useful when you have several smaller elements on the page, and want to rearrange them to see what looks best. Drop the block back within its margins.

Since this text is still selected, it has *windowshades* at the top and bottom. This is how you reshape, rather than just move, a block.

7 Click and hold in the handle of the bottom windowshade. Move it up the page about a third of the way.

Note that the handle now has a down arrow in it, as in Figure 8.6. PageMaker is telling you that there is now more of the story than fits in the area you've given it. This is useful for the editor who will continue the story on page 99.

The top windowshade can be moved as well, to make the text start at a different point on the page. Why not move the whole block? Well, you might have already fit the bottom of this story into ads below it, for example, but want to make more room at the top for a larger title.

Look at each end of each windowshade. They end in small black boxes, called *handles*

Figure 8.5 *The block of text has been picked up and moved down and to the left, to show flexibility in placement.*

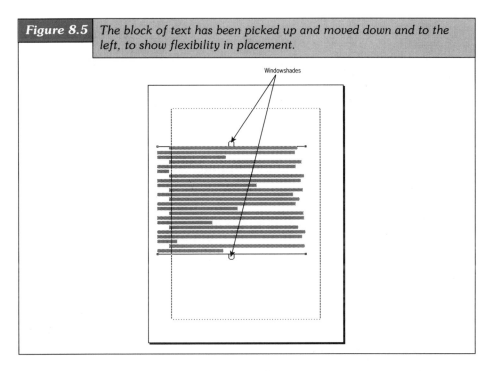

Figure 8.6 *Tools to resize or reshape this text block.*

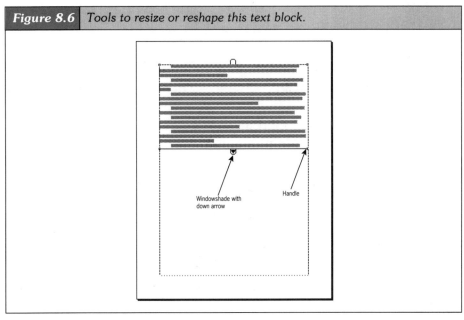

8. Click and hold on the lower-right handle. Your cursor changes again, this time to a diagonal arrow.

9. Move this around a little. The opposite corner of the block stays anchored, and you can otherwise resize and reposition to suit your needs.

10. Restore the original dimensions of your text. It's time for a graphic.

PLACING GRAPHICS

To place graphics in your layout:

1. Choose the **Place** command again, and this time choose a graphics file. The shape of the Place icon now indicates the format of your file. We'll explain this business of graphics file formats in a little bit.

2. Put your cursor somewhere off to the right of your page, in a part of the screen we call the *pasteboard*. What we want to do is look at the graphic first, modify it, and then place it.

3. Click the mouse, and watch your graphic take shape as in Figure 8.7. Scroll to bring it into full view, if necessary.

WORKING WITH ELEMENTS

At this point we can start to think about three treatments we'll make to our graphic: *resizing*, *cropping* and *placing*, and we don't want to think that these should necessarily be done in any set order. We're creative artists here, and it may take a little of this and a little of that to give us the effect we want.

But to learn, let's resize some first. Note the *handles*, three black dots at the top and three at the bottom of the graphic, equivalent to the text windowshades. (Scroll so that your graphic is in full view, if necessary.) Take your arrow cursor, and:

1. Click and hold on the bottom-right handle. Your cursor will change to diagonal arrows again.

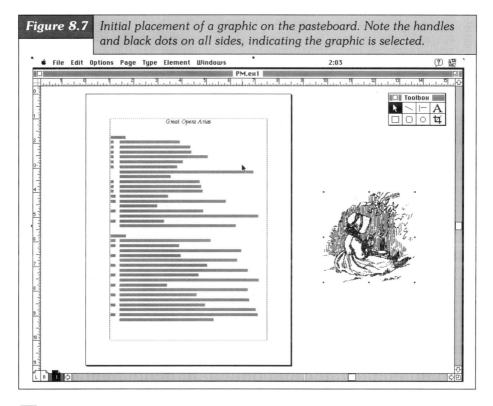

Figure 8.7 *Initial placement of a graphic on the pasteboard. Note the handles and black dots on all sides, indicating the graphic is selected.*

2 Drag the handle up and to the left, to make your graphic smaller. Let go of the mouse button.

It's smaller, all right, but I'll bet also a little skinnier or chunkier than before. Your drag was not proportional.

3 Choose **Undo Stretch** from the Edit menu and bingo, you're back where you started.

Let's resize it again, but this time:

4 Hold down the Shift key, and then click on the bottom-right handle and drag. Note that as you drag up or to the left, the boundaries of the graphic move in the other dimension proportionally as well.

This use of the **Shift** key is a Mac convention: most graphics programs or tools, SuperPaint included, do this.

Enough resizing. Bring your graphic back to its original size with the **Undo** command. If you've done something since the last resize, this won't work, since Undo undoes only the last action—at least in this program.

In Freehand, a drawing application, you can undo the last *hundred* actions, and Nisus, a word processor, lets you undo the most recent 32,767 actions. Overkill? I'd settle for ten, but I'd like more than one.

Your ability to think critically about software design, especially its user interface, will be a lot of value to you as you evaluate programs and ways to get things done.

What you can do if you can't Undo, and often the simplest move, is just erase and replace the graphic. With it selected, press Delete to erase, and place it again.

With it back at original size, come up to the toolbox and:

5 Select the **Cropping tool**. Then click once on your picture again to reselect it, and:

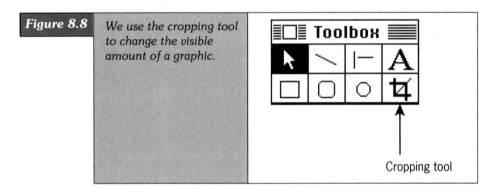

Figure 8.8 *We use the cropping tool to change the visible amount of a graphic.*

Cropping tool

6 Click and hold on the bottom right handle. Wait a moment for the cursor to change to diagonal arrows, and drag up and to the left. (If the cursor changes to a hand, you didn't quite click on a handle.)

When all you see is the top left few inches of the picture, release the mouse button.

We've cropped the graphic to the part that we want to use, and can now resize again. Choose the **Arrow tool**, and:

7 Resize it so that it's about two inches square. Now let's put it on the page.

8 Click to select it, and drag it onto the text, so it's somewhere around the right top. Quick and easy.

Except that the text runs right over it. Sometimes an effect like this is desired, perhaps if the graphic is large and has been done in a light shade of gray. Not quite what we want here, though. We want the text to *wrap around* the graphic. So:

9 Choose **Text Wrap** from the Element menu. You'll get a dialog box like Figure 8.9. Click on the middle icon in the Wrap option line. This should select that and the right icon in the Text flow line. So far so good. **OK** that dialog box.

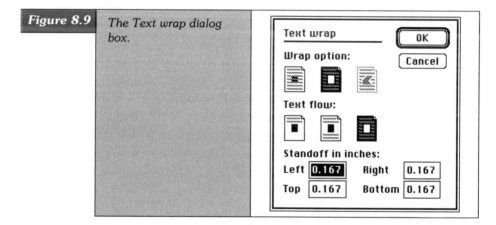

Figure 8.9 The Text wrap dialog box.

Text wrap

Wrap option:

Text flow:

Standoff in inches:

Left 0.167   Right 0.167

Top 0.167   Bottom 0.167

OK

Cancel

Your graphic now has space to call its own, and there are more lines and points (PageMaker indicators) around it than before. It's time for a closer look at all this, so:

Choose **Actual Size** from the Page menu. You should have something like Figure 8.10.

10 We could leave the text wrap as it is, but PageMaker allows us to customize it, or wrap it *around the graphic itself*. The new dotted line around it is the area that text can't enter, and that line goes from point to point. We can click on a point and move it, or make more points by clicking on the dotted line where we'd like to add a point.

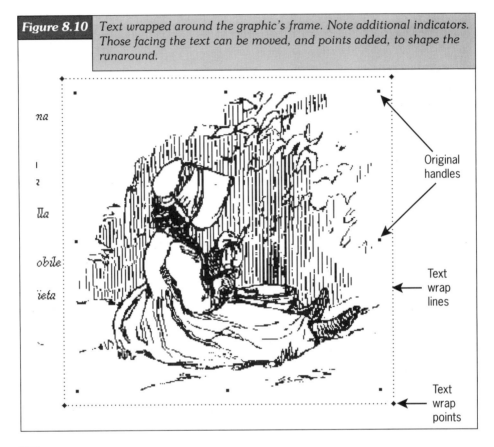

Figure 8.10 *Text wrapped around the graphic's frame. Note additional indicators. Those facing the text can be moved, and points added, to shape the runaround.*

Original handles

Text wrap lines

Text wrap points

11. Click and drag the text wrap points at the top and bottom left of the picture. Note how the text rewraps. Then:

12. Click on the dotted line two or three times to add additional points. Then reposition these.

See how you can make text follow the lines of a graphic. Used with some discretion, this is an elegant tool.

Hold it. The Art Director just walked in and looked at what you're doing. She says no, you've chosen the wrong part of your graphic. But its magnification and frame (area on the page) is perfect. What to do?

Here's the second use of the cropping tool. Select it, then click in the middle of the graphic, hold until your cursor changes into a hand, and drag the picture within its frame. Isn't that elegant? Crop and resize some more, until you have just what you want.

Conceptual point: PageMaker keeps the entire graphic you originally placed. Cropping changes only the size of the window through which you see the graphic.

N O T E

Save a couple of versions of this on your disk. You've saved the original several times already, right?

Another conceptual point, about quality of graphics formats: basically, Paint files can lose quality easily if you resize them in PageMaker, PICT files less so, and EPS files not at all.

Figure 8.11	*PageMaker cursors after you choose Place and double-click on a:*	Text file Paint file Pict file EPS file

As you remember from working with SuperPaint, the paint mode (making paint-format files) offers lots of versatility and detail, while the draw mode (making PICT files) is better suited to precision and high-resolution printing. EPS files, made by more specialized graphics programs such as Adobe Illustrator, offer yet greater precision.

The TIFF format is coming into more general use. Conceptually similar to Paint format, it offers much higher detail, especially in gray-scale and color.

There are thus two points to consider when making graphics to use in PageMaker: the kind of format determines how well you can paint or draw in differing styles; then, when placed in PageMaker, the format determines how well you can resize. Good luck with your artist.

THE STRUCTURED APPROACH

The other primary way to design pages is more common in a periodical publication, such as a newsletter. There the format is more standardized and logos, charts, and other graphics are more often found in separate boxes or columns. Let's do a newsletter something like the example at the end of this chapter: the *Computer Educator*.

To help with the positioning of columns and other elements, we'll use PageMaker's **column** feature, and also use **master pages**, templates for our newsletter that contain elements we'll want to repeat on every page. So, close your current file and:

1. Start a new document. In the initial dialog box, make this two pages and set all margins to 0.5 inch. Use **Tall** orientation. Click **OK**.

   Note that at the bottom left of your screen, there are icons for the master pages and actual pages, as in Figure 8.12. We want to go to the master pages to add, logically enough, master elements.

Figure 8.12	*Page icons. Page #1 is currently displayed. L and R represent the left and right master pages.*	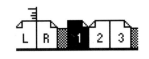

2. Click on the **master pages** icon. You should see a spread of two blank pages.

   Now take a look at the *Computer Educator*, to see what we're going to do. The first page has two wide columns at the right holding text, and a much narrower one at the left which is largely white space, but with a small graphic and caption.

   We made the design decision that the left column on the first page would be one fifth of the width of the page, and the two other columns would be twice as wide. So we want five columns on the right master page, for odd-numbered pages.

   For page two, we want evenly spaced columns, perhaps more typical for an inside page. So we'll give the left master page three even columns.

3 | Choose **Column Guides** from the Options menu, click **Set left and righ** **pages separately** and set the number of columns to three for left, five fo right. Leave the space between columns set at .167 inch. Your master page: spread should look like Figure 8.13.

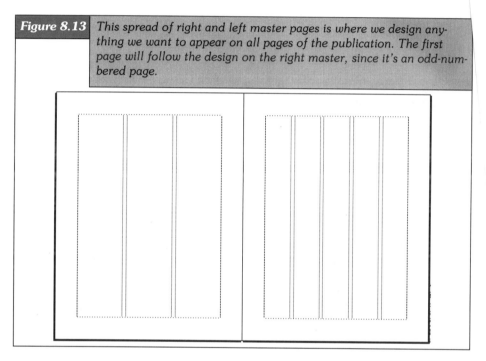

Figure 8.13 *This spread of right and left master pages is where we design anything we want to appear on all pages of the publication. The first page will follow the design on the right master, since it's an odd-numbered page.*

4 | Choose the **Vertical/Horizontal Line tool** and, from the **Element** menu, choose the line like the one at the top of the page in the example. Go to the master pages, and draw two lines, one along the top margin of each page. Then place the same type of line at the bottom. Once again, draw two separate lines.

5 | Now click on the page one icon, and we'll set up the masthead.

By clicking on the page one icon, you left the master page design and are now on individual pages. A *big* mistake beginners make is to forget to do this. They complete page one, then find they've done it all on a WARNING master page, so that pages three, five and seven will look just like page one. Not what the Art Director had in mind.

6 Choose the **Text tool**, click in the first column, and type whatever name your newsletter is going to have. Then choose **Select All** from the Edit menu, and make the text 28 point italic. (Use the **Other...** command on the Type Size menu to get 28 point, a standard size.)

Hmm. It seems to want to stay all in one column. No problem, just choose the **Arrow tool** and:

7 Grab a handle at the right end of the text block, either the top or bottom one, and resize the text block so that it covers five columns. This also puts all of the text on one line.

8 Put a box around the text. If you like, go to **Fill** from the Element menu and set an 80 percent fill for the box, and specify **Reverse** for the type style. The example was done this way.

9 Reposition the box and text so that the text is centered within the box.

This may be difficult at first, since you're now working with one element on top of another. PageMaker has two commands on the Element menu to fix this: **Bring to Front** and **Send to Back**. Select the box, and send it behind the text, so you can work with the text.

10 Put a line below the masthead, as in the example.

11 Type "THE" and size and position the word as you think best.

It's time to place the lead story. With the **Place** option:

12 Choose the lead story for your newsletter. Your cursor looks like the corner of a page again.

13 Put the cursor in the second column, under the bottom line of the masthead, and click.

The text flows into column two, and the down arrow in the handle of the bottom windowshade tells us there's more text. But what we wanted was text in a column that spans our page columns two and three. No problem. Using the Arrow tool:

14 Select the text, grab a right handle, and pull it over. Your page should look like Figure 8.14.

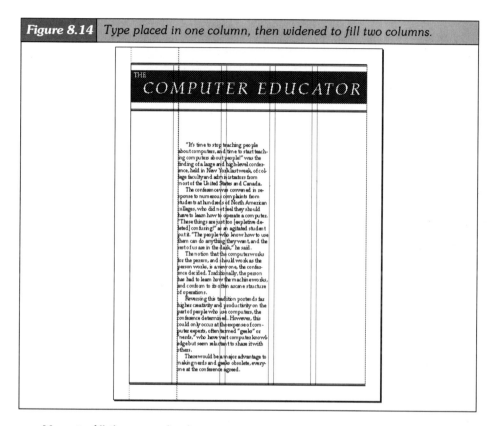

Figure 8.14 *Type placed in one column, then widened to fill two columns.*

Now, to fill the second column:

15 Click on the arrow in the bottom windowshade. You get your text-placing cursor back.

16 Click near the top of column four. You may want to choose the **Actual Size** view to help you align your cursor with the top of the first column of text. Or, after you place the text:

17 Click in the horizontal ruler at the top, and drag a *guide* down to the baseline of the first line of text in the first column. Vertically align the second column by this guide.

The text flows again, and fills up a narrow column again. But you know how to fix that. And once that's done, there's still text left to place. Go to page two, and put the rest into the left column.

Oops. We forgot a headline for our lead story. So let's do one. But instead of typing it in a column, like we did the masthead, and then fiddling with the width, just:

18 Choose the Text tool, and click off to the side of your page. To get some room, hold down the **Option** key, click on your page, and drag it to the left. Like a graphic, we can put text on the pasteboard to play with it. Type your headline, and make it Avant Garde and 28 point.

19 Make room for the head by selecting the first column of text. Grab the windowshade handle and move it down about an inch. We'll do fine alignment once the head is in place. Repeat this for the second column of text.

20 Align the tops of the text columns. Then go to page two, and note that the remaining text has grown because you reduced the size of the text area on page one. The whole story is still there.

21 Select your headline and move it into place. You're in charge of exact placement, since the Art Director, who loves to breathe down everyone's neck, just went to lunch. Leave room between elements, though.

Why? Take a look through a nearby magazine that seems to charge a lot for its advertising. At steeply expensive rates per page, why do advertisers leave so much *white space* between text and graphics?

Simply put, it increases the effectiveness of what text and graphics there are on the page. Try to find an example of the opposite, where the page looks crowded. Note how much less inviting it is.

This is less a matter of rules than of judgment born of practice. A keen eye for what you find appealing in page design is a big help in developing your own sense of how to make a page work. The experts recommend simplicity, an odd number of major elements on a page, not too many fonts, and an attention to composition, much as in painting, that leads the viewer's eye from one element to another.

22 Get a graphic and a caption for the left column on page one, and put lines above and below it.

Something like the example would be fine, or try whatever appeals to you. Creativity and variety are important parts of publication design.

Let's take a moment to look at a couple of Pagemaker's nicer features, to help with your work.

STORY VIEW

Spell checking, Find and Replace, and other word processing specialties, are available in PageMaker in *Story View* rather than Layout View.

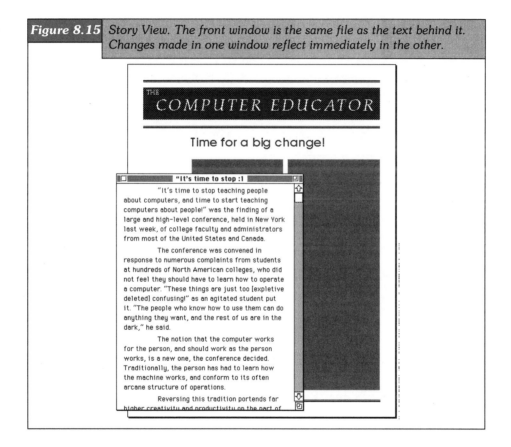

Figure 8.15 *Story View. The front window is the same file as the text behind it. Changes made in one window reflect immediately in the other.*

Story View is another window, in word processing style, of a text document on the made-up page. In Story View, the text is often easier to read and can be scrolled faster.

To see a file in this view, just click your text cursor in any text block, and choose **Edit Story** from the Edit menu. Choose **Edit Layout** to go back to your page.

Story View is an effective feature for text editing, and the increased clarity of its display makes its use preferable for accurate proofreading of text.

What confuses many users at first is the apparent notion that since this is another window, it's another document. It isn't, but just a way of looking more closely at whatever text your cursor was in when you chose this view.

CONTROL PALETTE

So far, all placement and sizing we've done has been by clicking, dragging, and eyeballing it. This is a fine way to work for much of what we do, but often more precision is desirable.

Pagemaker lets you size or move page elements by numerical measurement. After selecting an element on your page (try a graphic), choose **Control Palette** from the Windows menu, and you'll see:

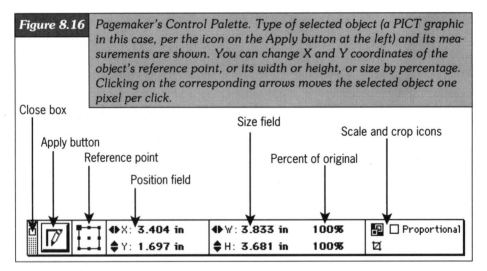

Figure 8.16 *Pagemaker's Control Palette. Type of selected object (a PICT graphic in this case, per the icon on the Apply button at the left) and its measurements are shown. You can change X and Y coordinates of the object's reference point, or its width or height, or size by percentage. Clicking on the corresponding arrows moves the selected object one pixel per click.*

Close box

Size field

Scale and crop icons

Apply button

Reference point

Percent of original

Position field

◀▶X: 3.404 in   ◀▶W: 3.833 in   100%   ☐ Proportional

◆Y: 1.697 in   ◆H: 3.681 in   100%

X and Y are the coordinates on the page for the object you selected. W and H are the size of the object, followed by the size as a percentage of the original, if the object is a graphic.

You can change any of these numbers by clicking in the number: a text cursor is displayed. Make what changes you want, and click on the **Apply** button, which also happens to show the format of the graphic you're working on.

You're well on your way. Let's end the step-by-step page makeup, to look at some fine points of design you'll want to keep in mind for professional-quality work.

FONTS AND FINE STUFF

One effective way to govern the look of a page is by choice of type styles. Typography plays a surprisingly large role in how words are received by the reader. You'll find many subtle instances in advertising. Want your text to appear clean and open, or rich and classy? It matters to the ad agency dropping a million or so on a campaign for a washing machine or a car.

What they're doing to you is an example of Marshall McLuhan's "The medium is the message." It's such a sensitive touch that many people never recognize it consciously. But in most areas of endeavor, your ability to organize effective presentation of the written word will become more important as you earn increasing responsibility.

Let's take a quick look at some kinds of fonts. There are three major types, shown in Figure 8.17. *Serif* is what we are used to in text: each letter has the major strokes that define its shape and, in addition, smaller strokes or 'caps' at the end of each major stroke. These serifs lead the eye from one letter to the next in a word, and actually make text easier to read.

Sans-serif, as you might expect, is the letter without these caps at the ends. Although not as readable in text, sans-serif presents a sense of directness of message through the simplicity of its style. Sans-serif fonts are often used for captions and headings, in contrast to serif body text.

The third kind of font is *cursive*, similar to handwriting. This can be effective in an advertising head or a sign, but is generally *much harder to read* in body text than either serif or sans-serif.

What these examples don't show you is the effect a font has in body text, where the *color of the block of text* is as important as the shapes of individual strokes.

A way to develop an *eye* for fonts is to scrutinize different kinds of publications. Why did they choose the fonts they did? Why did we?

Figure 8.17	Font sampler.

This typeface is Palatino, a traditional font.

News Gothic is a favorite in publishing.

Gill Sans is a favorite of the author.

Zapf Chancery is cursive, resembling fine calligraphy.

ΩΣΔ Symbol has Greek and math.

SIZES

The size of the type you use is an important part of making your publication inviting. Type height is measured in points, which are 1/72 of an inch. (Another unit of printing measure is the pica, 1/6 of an inch.) For most fonts, from 10 to 14 point is the most suitable size for body text. What you're reading right now is 10 point.

Another aspect of type size is the *x-height*, or the height of a lowercase letter. Souvenir, what you're reading, has a relatively large x-height.

Ten point Bodoni, with a small x-height, looks much smaller than 10 point Souvenir.

Keep track of what fonts you're using if you'll need to switch machines, perhaps in order to print. Mac users commonly get into trouble when they do work on one machine which has, say, the Avant Garde font installed. They then take their disk to another Mac which doesn't have Avant Garde. Surprise.

Best ways to avoid this are: do all your work on one computer, check to see that the other one has the fonts you're using, or carry a disk of them with you. Most Macintosh screen fonts are free, while the printer fonts used by a Laserwriter or higher-resolution printer are not. Most Laserwriters have several of the standard fonts built in, though.

Line spacing is worth considering too. Both tight and open spacing have their benefits. You're reading 10 point type on 13 point line spacing, offering a slightly less packed look than a dictionary, for example.

STYLES

Back when your grandparents used typewriters, the only ways to emphasize words were underlining and capitalizing whole words. Both are more difficult to read, and less effective emphasizers than italic. As well, all caps suggests that the writer is SHOUTING AT YOU. But too much body text in italic again becomes hard to read. Ditto for the outline and shadow styles the Mac offers you.

But used sparingly, outline type looks nice.

Too much variety in styles, and in fonts, detracts from the quality of presentation that fine typography otherwise promotes.

For example, look at what you just read: italic after outline. Too much variety too fast interrupts the flow of thought.

One elegant touch the Mac gives us is a nicer set of apostrophe and quotation marks than typewriter types get. What they get is:

"She's inside," he said.

while we can use what are variously called typographer's quotes, or smart or curly quotes, to get:

"She's inside," he said.

Most word processors and page layout programs offer this. If yours doesn't, stop by your users' group for Smartkeys, a free little gem that gives you smart quotes in any program.

Smartkeys also makes sure you put only one space after a period. What's this? Didn't your typing teacher tell you to use two? Yes, and the idea was that in the *monospaced* world of typewriters, where an i is equal to an m in width, two spaces were necessary to separate sentences legibly. This isn't true with a *proportional* font such as all you see here, and using only one space after punctuation obviates excess white space within the line of type, and so makes text more readable. Small stuff? Not really. Type can be beautiful, and worth making so.

CHECKLIST

In this chapter you've learned to design (or make up, or lay out) a page of text and graphics with complete flexibility of use of page elements. You can:

- place and size text,

- place, crop, and size graphics, and wrap text around them,

- place and use columns on a page,

- design the personality of a publication,

- work with PageMaker's word processing features, and

- judge typography for aesthetic impact and effective presentation.

As you've seen, page design programs like PageMaker tend to be big and full-featured. And, like other kinds of programs, each competitor in this area has a personality, and a set of strengths and weaknesses.

Programs similar to PageMaker include QuarkXPress, Ready,Set,Go!, Framemaker, and Ventura Publisher. Smaller variations include Taste and Publish It Easy. Each does most jobs, and there are reasons to prefer one to another for a specific application.

When comparing these products, it's often best to try them out with a specific project in mind. Take a disk of text and graphics, and a sketch of what you want to produce. Then see how well you and a program work together.

HELPFUL HINTS

Of what we've learned in this book, aesthetics counts the most in chapter two (graphics), and in page layout. There's quite a difference, though: illustration is just what you want it to be, while page design is full of conventions—which, like all conventions, are susceptible to overrule once you understand why they exist.

If you're interested in this area, you can't spend enough time looking at magazines: general format, major and minor features, and advertising. With everything you see, ask yourself why they did it that way. When you're looking at quality work, the answers can be telling.

Q & A

Q: *I want to place a text or graphic, but its name doesn't appear in PageMaker's Place dialog box.*

A: What you want to place is in a format that PageMaker can't read. Go back to your graphics or word processing program, and use the **Save As** option to save this file in a compatible format, as discussed in this chapter.

Q: *I want to spell-check some text, but the spelling command isn't active.*

A: You need to be in Story View (choose **Edit Story** from the Edit menu) to check spelling.

Q: *I can't select a graphic I've placed on a page.*

A: Another object is in front of it. Use the **Send to Back** command on the Element menu to put the frontmost object in back of the stack. You should now be able to access the graphic.

Q: *My text only wraps around a graphic as a rectangle, it doesn't follow the shape of the graphic itself.*

A: Choose **Text Wrap** from the Element menu, and change the wrap option.

Q: *It's difficult to size and then crop a graphic for the effect I want.*

A: This is part of the art of page design. Some people like to work with the graphic on the pasteboard; others like to put it on the page and then resize and crop it. Try each, and try resizing first, then cropping, and then the other way.

Q: *Every odd-numbered page in my document has the same objects on it.*

A: You've made a mistake everyone makes when starting out, of placing elements on master pages. Just cut and paste them off the masters onto the individual pages.

Q: *I'm on a numbered (not master) page and I can't select an element.*

A: The element is on a master page. There's no indication for this, except that you can't select it while on a numbered page.

SAMPLE EXERCISE

Finish up the *Computer Educator*, or something very much like it. Then save a new version of this file, and make some change to every element in it. Change all of the fonts, try some different sizes, place graphics at different points on the page. Print both versions, and judge which seems a more effective presentation of its content. Ask a friend to judge too, and ask her why she likes either one better. Then make a revised version. Pretend this is an advertisement that will cost a million dollars to run in a major magazine.

LAST THOUGHTS

This completes our tour of the Macintosh. If you're like many people, you've felt surprised to achieve competence on this computer in eight chapters. We have gone fast but, as you've seen, there's not much that's truly complicated and, greatly to the Mac user's advantage, many options and functions of different programs are similar in design and use.

You'll find this with programs competing with the ones we've chosen for this book, and you may prefer some aspects of the competition.

Since many preferences differ in this world of the *personal* computer, it's good to know that we can work with each other, each using a different word processor or database.

This is because competing products are largely file compatible—you can move data from one to the other without much trouble, although you don't always have the same flexibility with it once you've moved it. The page design programs, since their documents are more complex, don't talk to each other as well.

All of these programs have some features their competition lacks. All have some infuriating quirks—we get spoiled fast, don't we? All have some wonderful qualities, and all seem sometimes to have been coded on the moon. Look well before you buy.

As a final tip, may we suggest that you take an hour here and there over the next month or two to play with the programs you've learned, to stay in practice and to develop this splendid tool as an extension of, rather than an object of, your thought.

Time for a big change!

"It's time to stop teaching people about computers, and time to start teaching computers about people!" was the finding of a large and high-level conference, held in New York last week, of college faculty and administrators from most of the United States and Canada.

The conference was convened in response to numerous complaints from students at hundreds of North American colleges, who did not feel they should have to learn how to operate a computer. "These things are just too [expletive deleted] confusing!" as an agitated student put it. "The people who know how to use them can do anything they want, and the rest of us are in the dark," he said.

The notion that the computer works for the person, and should work as the person works, is a new one, the conference decided. Traditionally, the person has had to learn how the machine works, and conform to its often arcane structure of operations.

Reversing this tradition portends far higher creativity and productivity on the part of people who use computers, the conference determined. However, this could only occur at the expense of computer experts, often termed "geeks" or "nerds," who have vast computer knowledge but seem reluctant to share it with others.

There would be a big advantage to making nerds and geeks obsolete, everyone agreed.

"The sooner the rest of us can stop thinking about the @#$%^&* computer and start thinking about what we want to do, the better," they said.

There was a fair amount of opposition to these new ideas. Observers were generally of the opinion that the new idea showed promise but was fraught with difficulties. "It's often easier to teach people about computers than the other way around," one said. "Computers have known all along that they have the upper hand with things, and getting them to do what people want them to might be nearly impossible."

An attempt was made to contact John Rethorst, this manual's author, but to no avail. "I haven't seen him in years," an observer said. "Ever since the high-speed Macintosh Quadra came out." No one would comment, though, on persistent rumors that Rethorst had actually transformed himself into a Quadra on the football field at midnight some time ago.

Despite the variety of comments on the new proposal, most participating colleges have decided to go ahead and revise the curriculum. "This will give us valuable programming experience," a spokesperson said, "and leave our students with more time for the things that are really important in college, like parties. Computers may be better than we are in many or even most ways, but they just can't party at all."

This computer geek doesn't like the news.

APPENDIX A

VIRUS PROTECTION & OTHER SAFETY TIPS

What's a computer virus? It's a small program, written most likely by a computer programmer with a grudge, or by a well-intended person so young he doesn't realize the effects of his work.

The unique quality of this small program is that, analogous to a living virus, it can move from one computer to another by itself fairly easily, as long as there's something to move on—a floppy disk, for example, or telephone lines.

Once it's in your computer, again analogous to the living kind, it makes some changes to its liking, and most of these changes are not to the benefit of the host computer. Some more benign varieties just cause your Mac to beep more often, or for the cursor movement on the screen to be erratic.

Other viruses are malignant, and can be designed to erase your hard disk or cause other destruction. Whatever its effect on your machine, though, the virus is also written to infect other computers that come into contact with yours, again by means of a floppy or some other form of contact.

A new Macintosh virus appears about once a month. It is vital that you take necessary and sufficient steps to protect your computer and, especially, your data, from viruses. There are two means to do this:

- **prevent contact between your computer and others.** If you're writing the Great American Novel on an island in Puget Sound, you have an easier time of this than someone whose work requires frequent trading of floppies or access to computer networks over data or phone lines. Even if this method seems feasible, it is not foolproof (even floppy disks containing programs you buy, shrink-wrapped on the dealer's shelf, can contain a virus), so this second method has the strongest recommendation I can give it:

- **obtain and keep current, virus protection and eradication software.** The protection programs load into memory when you start up, and monitor all floppy disks you insert, or a range of other activity, to keep a virus from infecting your Mac in the first place.

  Should your Mac already be infected, the eradication type of software can find and erase the virus—hopefully before it has done too much damage. You should get this software on a locked floppy—you can see through the hole at the top right—and the floppy should stay locked, so that nothing, not even a virus, can be written to it.

Several anti-virus programs of both the protection and eradication types are available. Some are commercial; others are free. The free programs are as good as the commercial offerings, except that most of the commercial software comes with the publisher's support in the form of an 800 number or such for updates, to keep the anti-virus program current with the latest viruses. For the free programs, you have to go get a newer version—usually going no farther than your users' group or dealer.

Two of the best free programs are:

- **Disinfectant.** Written and frequently updated by John Norstad of Northwestern University (thanks, John!) This is both a protection and eradication program with extensive on-line help, to counter all known viruses. If you do not have access to a users' group, on-line services via a network or a modem, or a responsible dealer, you can obtain the latest version of Disinfectant by sending a stamped, self-addressed envelope and a blank 800K floppy to:

> **John Norstad**
> **Academic Computing and Network Services**
> **Northwestern University**
> **2129 Sheridan Road**
> **Evanston IL 60208**

■ **Gatekeeper.** This is a protection program only; its advantage relative to Disinfectant is that this will monitor your Mac's activity for the kind of activity that viruses tend to do, even if no known virus is detected (remember, there are new viruses all the time). Written by Chris Johnson of Austin TX (thanks, Chris!), Gatekeeper is available from on-line services, users' groups, and good dealers. If your dealer won't give you the most recent versions of these two anti-virus programs for the price of a blank disk, find another dealer.

COMMERCIAL PROGRAMS:

In current versions, these aren't better at what they do than the free programs, but your purchase price allows the publisher to offer telephone or fax support, often including a way that you can type in a string—a collection of numbers and letters—that tells the program how to look for a new virus, and erase it. This is simply faster than going and getting an updated version from your user's group.

Good commercial offerings include Central Point MacTools, SAM (Symantec Anti-Virus for Macintosh), and Virex.

OTHER SAFETY TIPS

Assuming you save regularly and often, and make backups of anything important, the largest source of danger to your data occurs in one of two ways: when something happens outside of your Mac, such as a power failure or your moving it when you shouldn't; and something inside the computer, as when it can accidentally misplace a file. Here's how to deal with both:

EXTERNAL INFLUENCES:

■ **fluctuations in voltage.** Get a surge suppressor. This $10 to $40 piece of hardware can eliminate a common nuisance—surges in power supply voltage that can fry your Mac's chips or your data. More expensive variations can actually offer a few moments' backup power—enough to save something to disk— should a total power outage occur.

- **moving a hard disk while it's running.** Like a record turntable, a hard disk has an arm which is often over the disk surface. Jostling the mechanism while it's running can cause the arm to collide with the disk, ruining that part of its surface. Other parts of the computer, monitors and such, can be moved while powered on. But since many Macs have hard disks built in, either make sure yours doesn't, or shut down before you move it even an inch.

- **static electricity.** If your work area has a carpet or whatever that tends to generate this, you may want to touch a finger to anything else before picking up a floppy, or going to work on your computer.

INTERNAL INFLUENCES:

In the course of reading from and writing to a disk, one of two errors may occur. The first is the corruption of, or an inaccuracy placed in, the disk directory. The directory is a small area on the disk that functions much like a telephone book: it tells the Mac where each file is located on the disk. If the directory becomes corrupted, or scrambled, your Mac won't be able to find a file and display its icon on the desktop, although the file is still there. The computer has just, literally, lost its address. Can you find it again? Yes, if you take the following precaution.

The second error is actually yours, not the machine's: you've simply made a mistake and put a file in the trash, and then emptied the trash. Is that file gone forever? Actually, the file itself isn't erased; the directory is just updated to show that it's gone. The actual file is still there. Can you restore it to normal use? Yes, if you take the following precaution.

PRECAUTION:

Get a file recovery/disk doctor program. Two good ones are Central Point MacTools, and Norton Utilities for Macintosh. Either of these includes a small extension that loads when you start up, and tracks the location on disk of anything you erase and also, periodically, makes a copy of the disk's directory. The program keeps this information in a separate place on the disk.

So, if the original directory becomes corrupted, the disk doctor program can restore it. And, should you want to "unerase" a file you threw away, the doctor can search your disk for recently deleted files, and restore their address in the directory—136 Maple Street is once again occupied, so to speak.

A catch here is that, should you want to unerase a file, you should do so soon after you erase it. Otherwise, when you save more data to disk, the Mac goes looking for free space on the disk on which to put it, notes that the directory says that 136 Maple Street is empty, and puts this new data there. At that point, the earlier data is physically overwritten, and the disk doctor can't help you.

SECOND PRECAUTION:

Be a backup fanatic. Make backups onto floppies of everything in sight, so that when (not if) your hard disk's directory becomes corrupted, you wait too long before unerasing a file, or there's a hardware failure, you'll have a second copy of everything you need.

There are numerous backup programs to help you do this. The simplest way is to use none of these: instead, just put a floppy in the drive when you're finished working with a document, and Save As onto the floppy. Don't erase anything, fill the floppy up, label it carefully and put it in a safe place.

If you can't be this methodical, backup programs include Central Point MacTools, Diskfit Pro, Redux and Fastback. Any of these, plus the cost of floppies, is a small price compared to losing work.

The advantage to backing up as compared to the disk doctor scheme is that your dog can actually eat your hard disk any time it feels like it, leaving the doctor with nothing to work with. A hardware failure is more than a software program can cope with, making it very nice to have copies of important data on other disks. The best recommendation is, use both the backup scheme and the disk doctor. Your data will, someday, thank you.

APPENDIX B

SHAREWARE

Now that we've looked at the major categories of commercially available programs for the Mac, and we know that data protection programs are here for us now and forever, is there anywhere left to go? You betcha!

Probably the most creative and, in sundry ways the most versatile utilities for the accomplished user—you—are not published and sold by behemoths like Microsoft or Claris, but are written by enthusiasts here and there and released as *shareware* or *freeware*, usually through users' groups. See the Technical Notes in Appendix F for what users' groups are about.

Freeware is just that. Shareware is a great concept: you get the program free and can try it out for a week or two. If you like it and want to use it, the author asks that you send her a check. The amount is usually a trifle, since you and the author both avoid the expense of advertising, packaging and commercial distribution. If you do send that check for these great utilities, you encourage their authors to produce more.

Here are some of my favorites:

- **Møire Idle** is a screensaver, something every Mac owner should have. Out of the box, the Mac's screen stays lit as long as it's on, and the continued bombardment of electrons can burn the screen phosphor in parts of the display—menus come to mind—that don't change with the hours. Screensavers like Møire wait until you haven't used your Mac for a time you set, say five minutes, and then change the screen display to something constantly changing, so no more burn-in. The nicer screensavers change the screen to an interesting display such as Møire's geometric patterns.

- **Darkside of the Mac**—a screensaver that's even better than Møire, I think, but for System 7 only.

- **SuperClock** puts the time on your menu bar, over at the right. Click on the display to see today's date, all in the font and size you choose. It has timer and alarm options too.

- **ButtonPad** is an improvement on the standard NotePad, by several orders of magnitude. Define up to sixteen note pads, and go to any one with a click. Text is saved automatically.

- **Flashwrite** is another fine tool for entering that quick thought we don't want to lose. It is on your screen in a flash, as it were, and gone just as fast, with your text saved as you write it.

- **Easy Envelopes**, an excellent utility for formatting and printing envelopes and, of even more value, an electronic rolodex for addresses or anything else you want. It has a very fast find function.

- **Smartkeys** makes sure you put only one space after a period or other punctuation, as the typesetting manuals say you should. It also offers smart quotes, substitution of dashes for double hyphens, and myriad other typing (ahem, typesetting) helpers.

- **Escapade** lets you stay on the keyboard while you work. Just press the first letter of any button in a dialog box, and it's chosen just as though you had clicked it with the mouse. **ButtonKey**, **YesNoCancel**, and **Commander Dialog** do this too. Most of these let you navigate around a dialog box using the command, tab and space keys as well. Who needs a mouse?

- **TypeIt4Me** is an excellent glossary. Are you tired of typing "reification" ten times a page? Why not tell this utility to enter that word automatically every time you type "r/."? And, if you tend to type "adn" every time you want to type "and," you can tell this program to correct it for you.

- **DT (for Desktop) Calculator** is "advertiseware" (free, but keep them in mind) from a Swedish software company. It is a very fast and accurate RPN (reverse Polish notation) calculator, with numerous scientific functions.

- **Convert** is also a fine calculator, with the added advantage that it converts units—metric to English, or anything else—while it's calculating.

- **Super Ruler** puts a ruler on your screen for any kind of graphics work. Move it around, change the units, vertical or horizontal orientation, the zero mark, and its length.

- **Artisto** lets you look at any Paint or PICT file without opening a graphics program, and then paste the graphic into whatever you're doing. A must for any kind of graphics/word processing or page layout work.

- **Calendar 1.7** is many times better than the standard Mac calendar DA. It lets you make notes for any day for hundreds of years into the future.

- **Calendar Reminder INIT** shows you whatever you've put into today's calendar file, when you start up your Mac. No more excuses.

- **Finances** is a very fast calculator for all kinds of money things. How long it will take to pay off a loan, how well your investments will do at this or that interest rate, and many more features. It is a substantial assistance to financial planning.

- **Magnify** shows you the area of the Mac screen you select—at eight times the magnification. Excellent for any kind of graphics work.

- **Helium** gives you options for those sometimes helpful, sometimes pesky System 7 balloon menus. Leave them off until you hold down a hot key that you choose, and there they are.

- **The Dvorak keyboard**, discussed in the word processing chapter, is available through **Electric Dvorak** or **Keyboard Switcher**, or (in System 7) from an Apple keyboard module. Typing is faster, easier and less painful in long sessions. Well worth the time it takes to learn it.

- **Mouse2** and **Pointing Device** make your mouse faster on the screen, and thus make your Mac easier to use. Indispensable for a large monitor, and nice for everyone.

- **Windows** adds a menu of that name to every application (including the Finder) that lacks one. Navigation through all of those windows becomes possible. How did we ever live without it?

- **BeHierarchic** (for System 7) adds submenus to your Apple menu, and all of those utilities, control panels, and such, are suddenly easier to find, and operation can be much faster.

Using the alias feature of System 7, for example, you can add an alias for your hard disk to the Apple Menu Items folder, and everything on that disk will now appear in the Apple menu, in hierarchical menus up to five levels deep. Viva organization!

APPENDIX C

MACINTOSH UTILITIES

Now that you can use a Mac and its major applications effectively, and have understood the vital information about viruses and troubleshooting (Appendix A), including the programs that offer this help, and have perused the information on Shareware (Appendix B)—great bargains that offer you increased flexibility and functionality—is there anything more to look at?

Yes, and if you'd like to consider this section, you can truly become a guru among Mac fanatics—a fabled *Power User*.

The utilities discussed here are commercial programs that let you do things faster and more easily than you might think possible. Apple doesn't include these features in the system software simply to encourage third-party development and competition. The results of that competition, which we'll look at now, are nothing less than breathtaking in their creativity and their improvements on the standard Mac interface.

QUICKEYS

How many times have you performed a sequence of steps, and wondered why you couldn't automate the series, for both speed and accuracy? When I wrote this book, I created all of the illustrations in the PICT format (see Chapter 8 for a discussion of file formats). I then had to change every one to the TIFF format for publication. All 175 of them. To do each required selecting the image, calling the menu command Save As, choosing TIFF in the resulting dialog box, typing the extension .*TIF* at the end of the name of each file, so both the Mac and I could tell them apart, and then saving and closing the file.

Using QuicKeys, I went through this sequence manually just once, not 175 times. QuicKeys recorded my steps and saved them as a macro file, much like Excel does, but a QuicKeys macro can be recorded for any program.

It then took me only one step per illustration, rather than the five that QuicKeys did. Accuracy benefits too, since humans don't do their best when performing repetitive actions.

QuicKeys can also translate any menu command into a keystroke—just choose the command and its keyboard equivalent, and you're set. This is most useful for keyboard-intensive workers like myself. Although some users are happy to leave the keyboard for the mouse each time they want to perform a command, other users develop a feel for the keyboard gestalt, and don't want to leave that mode of thought for the different interface of the mouse and menus. It may seem like a small point, but keyboard-equivalent utilities have been a good way for programmers to make money for a few years now.

Word and several other applications let you assign keyboard equivalents from within the program itself. Nice, but Quickeys lets you do it for any application— or for all of them at once.

Alternatives to this program include **Tempo**, **AutoMac** and **MacroMaker**. Tempo offers especially inviting complexity, such as a macro making a decision (called *branching*) depending on what's on the screen.

NOW UTILITIES

Now Utilities is for System 7 only. Rather than one focus, this is a collection of programs that make your Mac more powerful, fun, and easy to use in a number of ways.

Boomerang, the most important component, takes you back to the part of your disk where you were last, every time you open or save a document. You can assign keyboard equivalents to any file or folder, to open it right away. It has a fast Find function, for file names or—amazingly—the text within a file. And every Open and Save dialog box has a menu bar on top, with the last fifteen or so files and folders you've used. You can thus go to any of them immediately.

NowMenus lets you move your mouse over the menu bar, and the closest menu drops without your needing to click. Just a little smoother and more elegant. Move down to the command you want, and then click. You can also add a completely new menu or two or three, to display to the far left and right of the menu bar, and to pop-up anywhere on your screen, with the help of a hot key (command, control, or such) that you choose. You then choose the content of these new menus—the last twenty documents you've opened, or the most recent applications, or files or folders you want to reside there permanently. You can also define worksets—groups of applications or documents that you want to open all at once.

This program also makes your Apple menu hierarchical, and any choice that requires further choices—the Control Panel, for example—now shows those choices as a submenu, making their access much faster.

This feature, which the shareware utility **BeHierarchic** gives you as well, gets incredibly nice when used in conjunction with *aliases*, a System 7 nicety. Put an alias of your hard disk in the Apple Menu Items folder in your System Folder, and the contents of your disk is then available on the Apple menu, up to five levels deep in hierarchical menus. No more double-clicking. Make an alias of your Clipboard file in the System Folder, and put that in the Apple Menu Items folder. You can then access the Clipboard from within any program, whether it has an option to show the Clipboard or not.

NowSave lets you save the active file automatically, at whatever number of minutes, keystrokes, or idle time you set. Several other utilities, commercial and shareware, also offer this. Here's why not to utilize it: I was using it, working on a long document, and went to format it. I typed **Command-A** to select the whole file, and then wanted to format it with **Command-B**. I mistyped, and pressed only the letter B. My entire document was then replaced with the single letter B.

This is normally not a problem, because you have two ways to recover. The first is **Command-Z**, *Undo*, to replace the letter B with your document. But Undo has to be the *first action* you do. If I had typed a C after the B, the Undo command would then undo the entry of the C, and that's it.

The second recourse is to close the document without saving it. You might lose a few minutes of earlier work (but only a few minutes, since you save so often), but you won't lose the whole document.

But it was just at that moment that NowSave, saving the active file every ten minutes, stepped in to save it. I watched this with some interest, and then carefully chose the Undo command. Very carefully.

So automatic saving of the active file may not always be the best route to take. Well-designed applications such as WordPerfect or Finale (a fine music program) make backup files as you work—every ten minutes or so, and the automatic saving of these separate backup files doesn't affect the status of the file you're working on. Erase your active file accidentally? The backup is there, and within ten minutes of current.

NowSave does have a saving grace, called **Key Capture**, a feature also offered by the program **Last Resort**. This does a separate save of every keystroke you make to a text file in the System Folder. If you lose everything else, you can recover all you've typed by opening this text file. This is a great idea, and the chore of sorting through the raw data of your keystrokes is small compared to re-creating your ideas.

Other components of Now Utilities: **AlarmsClock** is an advanced rendition of the freeware SuperClock, with precise control over the reminders you give your Mac to give you. **WYSIWYG Menus** show you all of your fonts as they'll appear in your document, and lets you group fonts in whatever families you choose. **Startup Manager** gives you control over which extensions (called INITs in System 6) and control panels (CDEVs in System 6) load, and in what order. The advantage here is that not all extensions and control panels are compatible with each other, or you might not need all you have for the upcoming work session. Unneeded ones just take up memory, so why not turn them off? The freeware programs **INIT-Cdev** and **Extension Manager** do this too.

ADOBE TYPE MANAGER

Adobe Type Manager is highly useful for any page layout work, or any graphics work that includes text, and is nothing less than a miracle for anyone with PostScript fonts and a non-PostScript printer. This utility uses the precise outlines of PostScript printer fonts to improve typefaces vastly as they show on the screen, and print text at the resolution of your printer, even if it doesn't have PostScript.

Truetype fonts do the same thing, but there are fewer available. If you're able to live with Truetype, it's a simpler option. Mac fanatics argue about PostScript versus Truetype, but they both produce great results on the screen and on any printer. And both coexist quite peaceably in your Mac, and even in the same document—as long as you don't use a PostScript font and a Truetype font that have the same name. But you'd have to be a real Mac fanatic to do that.

ON LOCATION

On Location makes its own index of all of the files on your disk, and also indexes the text in the types of files you specify. It can then find and open a file that has the name or contains the text you're looking for, and it does it very fast. This is a nice tool for users with large hard disks. Other utilities can find the same data but take much longer, since they have to look through each file instead of through their own index.

SUPERLASERSPOOL

SuperLaserSpool takes documents you're sending to any printer, and spools—saves—them to disk, and then feeds the data to the printer, returning use of your Mac to you faster than otherwise. Apple's print utilities, included with system software, do this as well but more slowly, and don't support every printer, including the Imagewriter.

SUITCASE

Suitcase gives you control over use of fonts, desk accessories, Fkeys, and sounds. For System 6 users, Suitcase is almost a requirement, since the Mac system won't allow more than fifteen DAs to load. In System 7, you can load as many DA's (or anything else) onto your Apple menu as you want, but management of fonts,

Fkeys, and sounds is still easier and more effective with Suitcase. **Master Juggler**, a competing utility, offers this same versatility.

DICTIONARIES AND THESAURI

Many publishers offer these. *The American Heritage Electronic Dictionary/ Roget's Thesaurus* is one choice, although its interface isn't interactive with your word processor—you have to copy and paste words to and from this utility, unless you get QuicKeys to do that for you. **Word Finder Plus** is a nice thesaurus, and there are several others. Each has the advantage of being more complete than what most word processing programs include. In any case, you'll find that an on-line thesaurus is vastly easier to use than the paper variety and, since vocabulary is fundamental to expression, this tool pays for itself in quality of your writing very quickly.

APPENDIX D

HARDWARE

So now that you know all about how Macintosh programs work, which Mac should you buy?

It's a big question, and the main considerations are: stationary or portable; speed of processing, and, if stationary, size of the screen. Speed is not just a luxury for some work—if you're doing complex design or illustration, a slower Mac is simply unusable. Conversely, if you're writing the Great American Novel, keep in mind that word processing doesn't take much in terms of computing power. Screen size is a necessity for some graphic design and most page layout, and is only a luxury for most anything else.

Another consideration is size of the beast overall. Why buy something that takes up all of the real estate on your desk if a compact Mac does all you want and leaves you part of your desk as well?

A note on portability: Having a battery inside, and a travel case outside, is valuable for many. Think of all of the work you'll get done on the plane (unless you really read novels on the plane). Portability costs something, but for many users it's worth it.

Here's what's available, with a discussion of each option. Which ones will you need, and which are unnecessary expenses? Let's look at what each model offers: how fast, how big, how much memory and storage space—and, how expensive.

Speaking of expense, you can often find better deals on hardware and software through mail order. The tradeoff is that your local dealer should be better able to help with your questions about setting up hardware and installing software. Dealerships vary with quality of after-sales service, so it's a good idea to check with someone who has bought from a particular dealer.

The more responsible mail-order (or should we say phone-order: call a toll-free number, use your credit card, and shipping can be overnight or close to it) companies also offer technical support. With either a local dealer or a phone-order company, though, check to see how long they've been in business. Recommendations from your friends at your users' group (see Appendix F for how to find a users' group) can be most helpful.

Among IBM-compatible computers, there's a much wider range of hardware available for the simple reason that anyone can make an IBM-compatible computer. Even the advanced user can, by buying a monitor here, a motherboard there, and putting it all together in her garage. Macintosh users have it easier: any Mac you buy is made by Apple Computer. The only exception is the Outbound line of portables, a viable alternative to Apple's Powerbook machines.

MACINTOSH MODELS

Among the Macintosh models available, there are two broad types: stationary and portable. Most Macs are of the stationary type, meant to live on your desk and not be moved too often. The portable Macs, also called Powerbooks (or, generically, *notebooks*) can serve about as well as the stationary Macs for many purposes, and can of course be taken with you, to get all of that work done on the plane.

Note that any Macintosh can run any Mac program, except that a few graphics programs require a computer with a color monitor.

Following is Table D.1, a comparison of the features of the different Macintosh models.

Table D.1	Comparison Table.

Model	Clock Speed (Mhz)	Memory capacity (MB)	Hard disk size (MB)	Expansion Slots	Color	Price[†]
Classic II	16	10	40-80	0	No	$1079-$1209
LC II	16	10	40-160	1	Yes	$1239-$1489
IIsi	20	17	40-160	1	Yes	$1749-$2139
IIci	25	32	80-230	4	Yes	$2539-$3089
IIvx	32	68	80-230	4	Yes	$2949-$3319
Quadra 700	25	20	80-400	2	Yes	$4219-$5849
Quadra 950	33	64	230-400	5	Yes	$6539-$8169
Powerbook 145	25	8	40-80	0	No	$2149-$2499
Powerbook 160	25	14	40-120	0	No	$2429-$3149
Powerbook 180	33	14	80-120	0	Yes*	$3869-$4229
Duo 210	25	24	80	0	No	$2249
Duo 230	33	24	80-120	0	No	$2609-$2969
Duo Dock	**	**	**	2	Yes	$1079***

[†] (depending on RAM and hard disk size)
* with an external monitor
** depending on Duo model
*** docking station only—requires a Duo to run

- **Clock speed in megahertz.** This is how fast the processor chip runs, and implies not only how fast the chip can calculate, but how quickly the computer can access data in RAM. While a useful benchmark, it is not the only influence on overall speed. Other factors are how much RAM is available per program, whether you're operating a color system in color mode (slower), and how large a disk cache you have set.

- **Memory capacity in megabytes.** This is RAM, not disk size. More RAM is highly useful for working faster with complex applications (such as graphics or page layout) or documents, or working with more than one application at a time (multitasking). But for word processing or databases, 2MB to 4MB of RAM is all you'll need.

- **Hard disk size.** Data storage needs vary widely according to use. If you're planning to work with databases very much, you'll want plenty of storage space for your files. Ditto if you're in graphics, or if you like a variety of programs. Excel, for example, takes up 7MB on a disk if you load all of its optional features, and Word takes 5MB. If you load only the essentials, Excel uses 2MB and Word uses 1MB. If you plan to do largely word processing or fairly straightforward spreadsheet use, and don't need to keep a library of data on disk, you should find a 40MB disk plenty of room.

One caveat: many Mac models are available without a hard disk built in—only a floppy drive. This configuration is useful if you already have a hard disk or want to buy one separately (to carry with you from machine to machine, for example, or to lock up at night instead of having to lock up the whole computer), or are able to depend on a network for its hard disk. The floppy-only configuration is offered not because you can use a Mac anywhere close to its capacity without a hard disk—you can't—but so you can add your own.

Another caveat: you can buy a larger hard disk at any time. The upgrade can be internal, replacing what's already there, or external, adding to capacity and offering a safety plus as well: if one disk crashes, the data on the other should be untouched.

- **Color.** The greatest thing since sliced bagels, for the first two weeks. Then reality sets in, and you wonder what you need the feature for. For some graphics or page layout work, of course. For spreadsheets, yes, both for charts and to make a worksheet easier to read. But for word processing? Databases? Think about this, since color costs money and slows your computer down. I know a few people who bought color Macs and then turned the color off, just for the increase in video speed.

  As with hard disks, you can get a color computer with a black-and-white monitor, and always upgrade to a color monitor later. Or you can get a larger monitor. And you can keep the one you have and use both at once.

- **Expansion slots** are necessary to link your Mac to some (not all) networks, to run IBM-compatible programs at a reasonable quickness, to increase speed for number- or memory-intensive computing, more colors, a second monitor, or for several esoteric configurations. Most users won't ever need a slot, but consider carefully how you might wish to customize or upgrade your computer in the future.

In the end, the decision as to how much computer you need is not an easy one. Many beginning users underestimate how valuable a Mac will turn out to be. An equal number buy impressive color and speed and end up not utilizing it. The best advice I can give is, after studying these options, to observe someone in your field with your work habits who's up on the Mac, calculate how little of an investment you can get away with, and then add 25 percent to it.

Here, as in so many instances, seeking out and joining a users' group—either a local one or one of the two biggies—is a great idea. They have special-interest groups for beginning users, or for those who want to talk about hardware options. See Appendix F to get in touch with a users' group. I have tried hard to see that the hardware information here is accurate at present, but nothing in this field stays in one place very long. Dealers also don't always seem to have current or complete information. Shop around, compare the prices in ads in MacWorld and MacUser magazines, become a nuisance to your friends with Macs, and join that users' group.

STATIONARY MODELS

- **Classic II/Performa 200.** The two model designations for the same hardware exist because of the two retail channels: the Classic II is sold through traditional computer dealerships, while the Performa line is offered through retail outlets such as Sears. This is the only remaining "compact Mac," the small box that sits on your desk and you still have part of your desk left. It's as fast as many of the larger models, but doesn't offer color. Larger monitors are available as add-ons, should you later opt for serious graphics or page layout work. Otherwise, this gives you access to Macintosh computing for the lowest price.

- **LC II/Performa 400.** This model offers color and the ability to expand memory or other capabilities through slots at the back, where you can insert cards made by Apple or other manufacturers (also called *third-party* vendors). There are many more options with this model than with the Classic II, either when you buy it or should you choose to upgrade performance later on.

- **IIsi.** This comes with a little more memory and is a little faster than the LC II.

- **IIci.** Again, it is a little faster than the model below it. This one also has more space for expansion. It also comes with a math co-processor as standard (this can be added to the less expensive machines) for greater speed in some applications, such as spreadsheets or high-end graphics.

- **IIvx/Performa 600.** Here, the IIvx is faster than the Performa, but you can add a card to the latter to make up the difference. Again, it is a little faster than the model below it. More importantly, this model offers the option of a built-in

CD-ROM drive, allowing you to access enormous amounts of data on a wide range of subjects by buying relatively inexpensive data CD's—entire encyclopedias, Shakespeare's works, and more.

- **Quadra 700.** The Quadra machines are Apple's workstations—meant as dedicated design computers, in a thoroughly professional environment. This is much faster than the less expensive models, and offers far greater capability.

- **Quadra 950.** The top of the line. The fastest Mac, with the most expansion capability, and the most memory. Complex graphic rendering or CAD design works best with this machine.

PORTABLES

- **Powerbook 145.** It is fairly fast, but doesn't include a connector for an external monitor—something many users would like, when they're back at home or office.

- **Powerbook 160.** This model adds gray-scale to its built-in monitor, external color capability, and a connector for an external monitor.

- **Powerbook 180.** This model has a better built-in display, although at a premium price. Check both this and the 160 to see if the 180's crisper monitor is worth it.

- **Powerbook Duo 210.** This model is meant for primary use hooked up to Duo Dock hardware in your office, and for occasional trips. It's smaller and lighter than the regular Powerbooks, but less flexible when it's on its own. It likes, but doesn't require, the Duo Dock, below.

- **Powerbook Duo 230.** As above, but a little faster.

- **Duo Dock.** Bring your Duo home to its docking station, where color capability and two expansion slots await it. This is a fine solution for those whose work requires a portable Mac, yet who also need more comprehensive capabilities at home base.

APPENDIX E

SYSTEM 7

When you use the Mac, you're making use of the hardware—chips, disks and things—and the program you've chosen, such as FileMaker or Excel.

There's a third component in the scheme, largely transparent to you, called the *System Software*, that acts in two ways:

- It's a library of resources for every program you use. When FileMaker or Excel needs to draw a dialog box or get a font, it goes to the System for it. This allows every program to be smaller than it would have to be if it stored its own font and other information, and it encourages every program to have a look and feel similar to the others you'll use.

- It translates between the program you're using (also called the application) and all of those chips. Again, if every application had to do this for itself, it would have to be much larger and more complex in design.

The current System Software comes free with your Mac, and is already installed on the hard disk if you bought one with your computer. All set up and ready to go.

Apple keeps making improvements in the System, though, and periodically releases a new version of it. The most recent is version 7. System 7 is noteworthy because it includes many changes from System 6 but, because System 6 is simpler and requires less RAM, many users who started with System 6 have chosen to stay with it.

If you have just bought or are about to buy a Mac, System 7 comes with it. Don't worry, be happy. If you have System 6 or earlier, though, you may wish to consider an upgrade to System 7. This Appendix describes the differences, and what's involved in the switch.

The first consideration is cost. System 7 (and *every* earlier version) has been free from dealers, if you bring the disks. Or, you could buy the disks plus a manual for $50. The most recent release, version 7.1, now costs $79 by mail order, although users' groups may be able to offer a better price.

The other cost is upgrading your hardware to the 2MB of RAM that System 7 needs. Earlier versions would run themselves and at least one application with 1MB, and all Macintosh models came with 1MB as standard equipment. Any Mac can be upgraded to 2MB or more of RAM. Depending on your model, this could cost as little as $50 per Megabyte.

IS AN UPGRADE TO SYSTEM 7 WORTH IT?

Let's look at the advantages of System 7. Most of these depend on having a recent version of the applications you want to use: If you're doing fine with copies of Word and Excel dating from 1987, written well before System 7 was announced, you'll find that System 7 offers only a few improvements. Current versions of applications, though, make extensive use of 7's offerings.

NEW FEATURES

These features are new to System 7:

■ **Balloon help.** These are interactive, real-time help messages for menus, windows, and dialog boxes. Choose **Show Balloons** from the Balloon Help menu to turn the balloons on, and then drag your mouse over anything on the screen you'd like a description of. See Chapters 1 and 5 for a detailed explanation of this.

- **Application menu.** If you have more than one program running at once, you can switch from one to any other more quickly this way than you could with earlier systems. Just click on the small icon of the active program, visible at the right of the menu bar, to see a menu of all open programs.

  Working with multiple open programs was available with System 6, if you used a system addition called Multifinder. With System 7, Multifinder is built-in, and a little easier to use.

- **Automatic organization of the System Folder.** This folder contains all of the information your Mac needs to run. In previous system versions, any number of things that you added to the folder stayed at the same level, allowing a list of up to hundreds of dictionaries, or small programs that loaded at startup—such as many of the shareware items discussed in appendix B—or basic control panels and such that gives you greater control over your working environment. System 7 organizes these things so they're easier to find and work with.

- **More control and ease of working with fonts and desk accessories.** In system versions earlier than 7, you needed to use a special program to install a font or DA. With System 7, you can just drag these items into your system folder, and they'll be put in the right place, automatically.

- **More DA's, and a flexible Apple menu.** With earlier systems, you were limited to fifteen DAs, and DAs were all you could put in the Apple menu, at the left of the menu bar. With System 7, you can install as many DAs as you like, and also anything else, in the Apple menu. The applications you use most, for example.

- **Aliases.** An *alias* is an icon that duplicates the icon of any file or folder. You can make an alias of anything and put it anywhere you like. In the Apple menu, for example, so you can open it without digging through several folders. Or, you can put an alias for "Quarterly Report" in the Update folder, while leaving the original in the Reports folder. Opening the alias opens the original.

  This is a nice feature for use on a separate Mac, but becomes really powerful when your computer is networked to others, and you want to access easily other files or folders over the network.

- **Sharing.** If you're on a network, you and others can make files or folders available to others on the network. You can limit the access—see only, for example, or make changes—that others have to any folder on your disk.

- **Better control over the Finder.** As it ships, the Finder displays all text in 9 point Geneva. You can change this to anything you want. You can also choose icon sizes, and whether these line up straight or are staggered in Finder windows. You can display folder sizes (although this slows operation down a bit), and choose how much data (modification date, for example, or version) is displayed in a list view of a window.

  An especially nice feature of System 7's Finder is that it shows you contents of folders within folders, in an outline view. Lists of the contents of subfolders are shown indented from the lists of the main folders in any window.

  You can also manage the Finder from the keyboard. Press any letter to select the item in the active window whose name starts with that letter. Press **Tab** to move to the next icon, alphabetically. Your **Arrow** keys move from any icon to any other, in the direction you choose. The built-in Finder Shortcuts file, available from the Balloon Help menu, illustrates all of these.

- **The Trash doesn't empty automatically.** In earlier versions it did at certain times, and users reported that they lost files accidentally. In System 7, what you put in the Trash isn't actually erased until you choose to do so.

- **Labels.** With a color Mac, you can assign colors to icons, sort by color, and give different colors labels with names you can change. This is helpful with organization and ease of work.

- **The Find Command.** Although the ability to find any file on any disk was available in earlier system versions, it was limited compared to this. In System 7, you can search disks for all or part of a name, or by size, creation date, or several other criteria. The Finder doesn't just tell you where it is, it takes you right to it, and you can open, move, or copy it immediately.

- **Virtual memory.** This is powerful stuff. Say you have 2MB of RAM and could use more, and you have 20MB free on your hard disk. You can turn some disk space into RAM, and then work with more programs at once. This is the cheapest way to acquire more RAM, and could well pay for your initial investment in System 7.

- **Publish and subscribe.** This is an even more powerful feature of System 7, and is shown in detail in Chapter 5. What it does is let you place all or part of any file in any other file—a graphic in a page layout document, for example— and when you or anyone else updates the graphic, the page layout document updates too. This is a great tool for keeping all parts of your work current, and is even better when there's a shared effort.

- **Inter-application communication.** Not only can you specify that one document updates another, as with publish and subscribe, but you can direct one application to open another, obtain information, and bring it into the controlling application. You've noticed some conceptual similarity between Excel and FileMaker, for example, although each is much better than the other in some ways. How about if you tell Excel to open FileMaker and a datafile, get something out of it, and import it into Excel for manipulation in ways a spreadsheet can do best? It's all here.

In general, current versions of applications offer these features under System 7, and do everything else under earlier system versions. As time goes on, though, more and more applications will need System 7 to run at all, because their developers want to make use of System 7 for the functions it offers them, and that earlier systems don't. Although every program this book covers runs under System 6 as well as 7, future releases of applications may not. You may need to upgrade your system version to upgrade an application version.

The other side of the coin is, do you need to upgrade anything? We looked at SuperPaint version 3, which does more than version 2. Did you need it to do more than version 2? If you're a professional graphic artist, you'll probably appreciate the advances. But, since it does more, it takes up more room on your disk, takes up more RAM, and runs more slowly, just because it's doing more. Same with everything else, and System 7 too.

It's something like buying a car, and then next year's models come out. Sleeker and spiffier to be sure, but not necessarily any better at all for the kind or quality of work you do. Your humble author is going to finish this book and then go back to getting a Ph.D. in moral philosophy and education, and a 1984 Macintosh with Microsoft Word version 1 would be fine for the task. So don't be swayed by the latest and greatest, but look critically at what any upgrade would do for you. Joining a users' group and their ongoing conversations on myriad topics is, here as elsewhere, most useful.

APPENDIX F

TECHNICAL NOTES

What would this book be without a tech note?

It was produced on a Macintosh IIsi with 17 megabytes physical RAM. Hard disks were an 80MB internal and a 44 megabyte Syquest Cartridge Drive, barely adequate, and an Apple 21-inch monchrome monitor.

The body text is set in Souvenir, 10 point on 13 point leading. Subheads are Serif Gothic 16 point bold; captions are Souvenir 9 point.

The text was written in WordPerfect Mac, an elegant and capable word processor. Conversion and editing was performed in Microsoft Word 5.1. Pages were laid out and separated in QuarkXpress 3.11. Our operating System is 7.1, which with thirty-plus extensions and control panels loaded, didn't crash much more than once a day. Graphic work was accomplished in Photoshop and Aldus Freehand, and screens were captured using Flashit, a nice piece of shareware.

Virus protection, a most important issue, was accomplished with John Norstad's wonderful program Disinfectant and Chris Johnson's fine Gatekeeper. Although the commercial alternatives may be as good, we are grateful that what we've used is provided free to the Macintosh community. These programs, and many other fine resources, are available on electronic bulletin boards or from most users' groups. Two good groups are:

Berkeley Macintosh User Group
1442-A Walnut St. #62
Berkeley, CA 94709
415-849-9114

Boston Computer Society
One Center Plaza
Boston, MA 02108
617-367-8080

or call 800-538-9696 for the name of the users' group nearest you.

Glossary

Words in bold type are cross-referenced.

active a menu **command**, or a **button**, or **scroll bar**, that can do something. If the item is not active, its function is not available right now.

active window the **window** in front of any others on the screen, and which has a **title bar** in it.

alignment the relationship between text and its margins: **left-aligned** text is flush at the left margin but not at the right; **centered** text puts an equal amount of space at each end of each line; **justified** text is flush with both left and right margins, an effect achieved by putting extra space between words or letters within the line.

Apple Menu the **menu** at the far left of the screen. Also called the **Desk Accessory** menu.

Apple Menu item   anything showing in the **Apple Menu**. These often control operation of the Mac or of printing.

application   a **program** which you work with directly—to write or draw with, for example.

arrow   a small **icon** on the screen showing the position of your **mouse**. Also called the arrow **cursor**.

ASCII   a standard **format** for moving text between **programs**, or between computers. It stands for American Standard Code for Information Interchange.

background   in HyperCard, a layer containing text or graphics shared by more than one card.

back up   to make a second **copy** of a **file**.

balloon help   a Mac feature that gives you short explanations of what's on the screen, contained in cartoon-like dialog balloons.

bitmap   a collection of dots that form letters, numerals, or graphics. Such a collection makes up all images on the screen, and the output of some printers. See **dot-matrix**.

block   in page layout, any amount of text as an **element**.

body text   in page design, text other than captions or headlines.

boot   to start a computer.

button   **1.** a representation of a small rectangle on the Mac screen, with a word or a few words in it. Often the way to give the Mac a **command**.

2. the physical button on top of the **mouse**.

card   in HyperCard, a screen containing text, sound or graphics, and **buttons** to **link** any of these to text, sound or graphics on any other card or **stack**.

cell   a box in a **worksheet**, where you enter a number or a **formula**.

check box   in a **dialog box**, a choice represented by a name with a small box to its left. **Clicking** your **mouse** in the box (or, in most programs, on the name as well) puts an X in the box, indicating that the option is activated.

chooser an **Apple Menu** item (also called a **Desk Accessory**) that lets you choose which printer to use.

click pressing the **button** on top of the mouse, especially when the screen **cursor** is on top of something you want to **select** or **open**.

clipboard a special part of **RAM** that holds data you've cut or copied, so that you can paste it. Like all RAM, it disappears when you turn the Mac off. See **cut**, **copy**, and **paste**.

close a Mac **command** that removes the active **document** from the screen. If you have made changes to the active document since you last saved it, the Mac asks you if you want to save these changes.

close box an **icon** at the top left of a window. When you click in it, you close that window. Equivalent in use to the **close** command on the **file menu**.

codes what used to be involved in learning computers. Since replaced by **icons** and plain English.

column
1. in a **spreadsheet**, a vertical block of cells, one cell thick.
2. in word processing or page design, a **block** of text separated vertically from other elements on a page.

Command an instruction you give the Mac. Commands are listed on **menus**, or represented by **icons** in a **palette**.

Command key a key on the Mac keyboard identified by an apple or a cloverleaf **icon**. Pressing this key and holding it while pressing another key is a common way to give the Mac instructions.

composition in desktop publishing, the aesthetic expression achieved by the balance and coordination of **elements** on a page.

control panel an **Apple Menu item** that offers options about the Mac's operation.

copy	**1.** to read data from one disk and write it to another, or (less often) from one part of one disk to another part of that same disk.
	2. a Mac command that takes any data you've selected, and places it in a special part of **RAM** so that you can then **paste** the data elsewhere.
cropping	changing the amount of a graphic that we can see on a page, without changing the size of the graphic itself.
cursive	a **font** that resembles handwriting or calligraphy.
cursor, Arrow	the **icon** on the screen that moves as you move your **mouse**. Also simply called **arrow**.
cursor, Text	an I-beam shaped **icon** used to work with text. Wherever you click it is where the text you next type is displayed.
cut	a Mac command that places data you've selected on the **clipboard**, a special part of **RAM**, so that you can then **paste** the data elsewhere. The **cut** command removes the original **selection** from your **document**.
DA	see Desk Accessory.
database	**1.** an organized set of data of any type: a telephone book, a recipe file, a library card catalog.
	2. a **program** that creates and uses this data.
datafile	see database, definition 1.
decimal tab	a **tab** stop that lines numbers up so the decimal point in each is aligned vertically with those above and below.
desk accessory	a small program listed in the **Apple Menu**.
desktop	the contents of a Mac's screen, seen as a metaphor for a physical desktop. **Folders**, **disks**, and their **windows** are visible and movable.
dialog box	a rectangle on the screen containing items such as names of files, and asking you for input such as what to name a new file, or where to put it. Often contains

check boxes and **radio buttons**, giving you choices about **formatting** or other aspects of the **program**.

dimmed
said of a **button**, **check box**, or **radio button** when its text is **grayed-out** and its function currently not available.

directory
see **folder**.

disk drive
the mechanism that reads data from, and writes data to, a disk. **Hard drive** is sometimes used synonymously with **hard disk**.

disk
a piece of plastic, much like a record, that holds data—either **programs** or **documents**.

display type
type of a larger or contrasting size or style, used to complement or offset body text.

document
anything you've made using the Mac. Letters, drawings, or **worksheets** are all documents.

dot-matrix
a type of computer printer that presses ends of wires against an ink ribbon to print small dots on paper. The dots form letters or numerals, or graphical lines or shapes.

double-click
to press the **button** on top of the **mouse** twice, quickly.

double-sided
referring to a **floppy disk**, one that can hold data on both sides. The most common floppy disk today.

dpi
dots per inch, a measure of **resolution** on the Mac screen or printed output.

drag
to **click** the **mouse button** on an **icon** and, holding the button down, to move the mouse so that the icon moves with it.

eject
a command to push a floppy **disk** out of the **disk drive**.

element
in desktop publishing, any single piece—a **block** of text or a graphic—on a page. Also called **object**.

EPS
encapsulated postscript, a graphics file **format**. Also written as **EPSF**.

erase
: **1.** to delete a file from a **disk**, by dragging its **icon** into the **trash**.
: **2.** to **format** an entire **disk**.

field
: in a **database**, one kind of information. In HyperCard, a place on a card designed to hold text.

file
: anything that has an **icon**. Either a **program** or a **document**.

file format
: a **program's** design for reading and writing its information from and to a **document**.

fill
: in graphics or desktop publishing, the degree of darkening of an area, expressed as a percentage.

find
: a command that lets you search for a string of text.

Finder
: the **program** that runs when you first turn on the Mac. It lets you **copy** or organize **files**, run **programs**, or open **documents**.

floppy disk
: a piece of plastic, much like a record, that holds data—either **programs** or **files**, and is small enough to carry around.

folder
: a graphical representation of what's on a part of a **disk**, used to organize data on a **disk**. You can put nearly as many folders on a disk as you'd like.

font
: a particular design and style of letters. Also called **typeface** or **typestyle**.

footer
: a line or few lines at the bottom of the page in a word processing **document** that stay the same on every page.

format
: **1.** to **erase** a **disk**, and make it ready to put data on.
: **2.** the way a **program** reads and writes data on a disk.
: **3.** the way text is presented, such as size and style of letters, and margins and spacing.

formula
: in a **worksheet**, this contains references to other cells, and instructions for instance to add or subtract the value of one cell from another.

fun	what Macintosh users have with their computers.
graphical interface	the idea that a computer should show you what's going on by symbols, or **icons**, rather than codes. See **interface**.
grayed-out	when text in a **menu** or **dialog box** appears in a light gray, or dimmed, instead of black. This means that the command or function is not currently available.
greeked	in desktop publishing, a representation of text at a small size by gray bars or by miscellaneous letters of the Greek alphabet.
guide	in page design **programs**, a thin straight line that you can 'pull out' of the vertical or **horizontal ruler** to place next to text or graphic objects for alignment.
Hand tool	in Pagemaker, the tool used to move the page around on the screen.
handle	in Pagemaker, an **icon** that controls alignment of a **block** of text.
hard disk	a metal disk, much like a record, that holds data—either **programs** or **files**, and that is built into the computer or into a cabinet plugged into the computer.
header	a line or few lines at the top of the page in a word processing **document** that stay the same on every page.
highlight	see **select**.
hypertalk	the HyperCard **program's** implementation of hypertext.
hypertext	a concept that any word or text, or graphic, can be related to any other by idea rather than by proximity on a page or in a book.
icon	a picture that has a meaning. On the Mac, an icon may represent a **program**, **document**, **disk,** or **command**.
Imagewriter	a Mac printer of the **dot-matrix** type.
initialize	to **erase**, or **format**, a disk.

insertion point   the blinking vertical bar that shows you where the text you type is displayed. You can move the insertion point by clicking with your text **cursor** at any point on the screen.

interface   the structured relationship you have with a computer; the language and the systems of recognition you use to operate the computer.

jargon   difficult and technical language that was once required to talk about computers. Now replaced by plain English.

justified text   see **alignment**.

keyboard equivalent   a keystroke, perhaps with the **Command** key, that replaces choosing a command from the **menu**.

landscape   see **orientation**.

Laserwriter   a Mac printer that forms an optical image of a page, and then uses technology similar to a photocopier to print the image on paper.

layout   **1.** in a **database**, the positions on a page of each field, and of other text and graphics.

   2. In page design, the placement of text and graphics on a page.

left-aligned text   see **alignment**.

left tab   the most common kind of tab, which puts text to its right.

learning   growth of the whole person. Has little to do with gaining skills.

linking   **1.** a dynamic relationship between **documents**, so that data in one document updates another document.

   2. In HyperCard, a relationship between two or more cards so that one card can reference another, or so you can go from one card to another.

load   to start a **program**.

macro   a set of instructions you record, saved as a set, so that you can give the computer all of the instructions at once, just by issuing one command.

marquee	a shimmering dotted line around all or part of a bitmap graphic, or HyperCard **button** or **field**. Used to indicate that the item is **selected**.
master page	in desktop publishing, a representation of a page on which you place **elements** that you want to appear on every page. Similar to the **background** in HyperCard.
masthead	the title of a publication, perhaps with issue number or other indexing information, and date and place of publication.
memory	**1.** see **RAM**. **2.** inaccurately used to refer to data on disk.
menu	a list of commands in a **program**, accessible from the **menu bar**.
menu bar	words at the top of the Mac screen, showing lists of what commands are available.
mode	in a database, a paradigm that lets you work with one of these: **fields**, **layouts**, or **records**.
mouse	the thing you use to move an **arrow**-shaped pointer around the screen. It has a **button** on top that you use to click on **icons**.
multifinder	in System 6, a feature that allows you to run more than one **program** at once. Automatic in System 7.
multitasking	using two or more **programs** at once, in conjunction with each other.
New	a command on the File menu that starts a new document.
object	in page design, anything—text or graphics—that can be put on a page. Also called an **element**.
on-line help	descriptions of **program** commands and functions, available on-screen by choosing the help command.
Open	a command on the File **menu** that opens an existing **document** from a **disk**.

operating system	the basic software that drives the Mac. Transparent to the user, unlike the operating systems for some other computers, which require the user's involvement.
orientation	placing a page in vertical (or portrait, or tall), or horizontal (or landscape, or wide) view.
paint	**1.** one kind of graphics **format**.
	2. a **program** that works in this format.
palette	a set of **icons** at the side of a window that represent tools to **format** text or paint a picture.
paste	a command that takes data, such as text, that you've already **cut** or **copied** from elsewhere, and inserts it at the **cursor** position.
pica	a printer's measure, equal to one sixth of in inch.
PICT	a graphics **file format**.
pixel	one dot on the Mac screen.
placing	in page design, the act of putting a **block** of text or a graphic at a certain place on a page.
point	a printer's measure. One point is 1/72 of an inch.
pop-up	a **palette** or **menu** that expands when you click on it.
PostScript	a page-description language developed by Adobe Systems, allowing high precision and **resolution** in printed output.
portrait	see **orientation**.
print	to direct the data in your active window to a printer.
program	a set of instructions to the Macintosh to do something. Using a program, you can paint a picture or write a paper.
programming	a highly technical activity to make Macintosh applications that are then easy for the rest of us to use.
publish and subscribe	a means of dynamic linking between two **documents**, from the same or different **programs**.

radio button

in a **dialog box**, a **program command** shown by its name with a small circle to its left. Clicking your **mouse** in that circle darkens it and activates that choice.

ragged

text that is not even along one or both margins. See **alignment**.

RAM

stands for **random access memory**: data contained on microchips in the Mac, which represents the working area of the computer. The contents of your active **window** are in RAM. All data in RAM is lost when you turn the computer off.

random access memory

see **RAM**.

record

in a database, one specific entry. For example, in an address book, information on one person is a record.

resize box

the **icon** at the bottom right of a window in the Finder. You click and drag in this to change the size of the **window**.

resolution

the fineness of the dots making up an image on the screen or on paper. See **dot-matrix** and **dpi**.

right-aligned text

see **alignment**.

right tab

a **tab** that places text immediately to its left.

rule

in desktop publishing, a line between **elements**, or leading from one element to another.

ruler

in a word processing or page design **program**, a graphic, non-printing ruler along the top or left of the screen, helping with alignment. A ruler can include **icons** for tabs and margins.

runaround

placement of text so that it follows the edges of a graphic.

sans-serif

a type style in which each letter does not have small strokes at the end of most major strokes. The illustration and heading **fonts** of this book are sans-serif.

Save

the command that puts a copy of the data in **RAM** onto a **disk**.

Save As   the command to save a new copy of a **document**, with a different name.

script
1. in a database; see **macro**.
2. In HyperCard, a set of instructions to the **program** such as to show animation, go to another card, or access any feature of the program for you.

scroll   moving your view of a Mac **window** up or down, or right or left, using scroll bars.

scroll bar   the vertical bar at the right side of a **window**, or the horizontal bar at the bottom, that lets you move around within the window.

select   the choice of an **icon**, some text, or a graphic made by **clicking** on it with the **arrow**. The choice then reverses color from black on white to white on black, to show it's selected. Also called **highlight**.

selection   anything—an **icon**, object or text—that has been chosen by the user, usually with the mouse.

serif   a **type-style** in which each letter has small strokes at the end of most major strokes. The main text **font** of this book is serif.

shift-click   to hold down the Shift key and click the **mouse button**. Used to select a range of data.

single-sided   referring to a **floppy disk**, one that can hold data on only one side. Less common today than double-sided disks.

spread   in desktop publishing, two facing pages viewed at once. Important to look at as a whole, to judge composition.

spreadsheet   an **application** that lets you work with quantitative data, and make charts from it.

stack   in HyperCard, a set of cards in one file, relating to a common idea or association of ideas.

string   any amount of letters and numbers. Your name, including the space between first and last, is a string. So is "12345xyz."

Stylewriter a Mac printer of the dot-matrix type.

subscribe see **publish** and **subscribe**.

system a **program** on a disk that the Mac needs to run, but that you don't use directly.

tab a means of aligning lines of text with each other. See **decimal tab**, **left tab**, and **right tab**.

text wrap in desktop publishing, arranging text so that it flows around the borders of a graphic.

title bar the top part of a **window**, with horizontal lines running across it, and the **close box** and **zoom box** at either end.

tool bar a **palette** of **icons**, each of which represents a **command**.

trash an **icon** on the Mac screen. Drag an icon of a **file** over the trash icon, and choose **Empty Trash** from the Special **menu** to **erase** the file. Drag an icon of a disk over the trash icon to eject the **disk** from the Mac.

typeface see **font**.

typestyle see **font**.

typography the art of choosing different **fonts** and styles for effective communication.

undo a Mac **command** that undoes the last step you made. If your last action was typing, this command erases what you typed.

virus in computer terminology, a program written to be invisible to the user, which moves by itself from one computer to another, and which disrupts the normal functioning of the computer or causes more serious damage, such as **erasing** data. See the Technical Notes in Appendix F for important information on virus prevention and eradication.

white space	in a publication, areas on a page without text or graphics. Critical to composition.
window	a rectangular area on the Mac's screen, shown as a box with four sides. In an **application**, a window shows you the text or graphics currently in **RAM**. In the **Finder**, a window shows you what's in a **folder** or a **disk**.
windowshade	in Pagemaker, **icons** that control vertical alignment of a block of text.
word processor	1. a computer **application** that lets you write, and include graphics. 2. a small computer with a word processing **program** built in. Usually much less capable than definition 1.
word-wrap	a feature of a word processing **program** that obviates use of the Return key at the end of a line: a new line starts automatically.
worksheet	a **document** produced by a **spreadsheet application**.
zoom box	an **icon** at the top right of a **window**. When you **click** in it, you change the size of the window.

Index